Elizabeth Barrett Browning

Studies in Eighteenth and Nineteenth-Century Literature

General Editor
Andrew Sanders, Professor of English, University of Durham

Studies in Eighteenth and Nineteenth-Century Literature is an exciting series of lively, original and authoritative critical studies aimed at the student and general reader. Each book takes as its subject an author, genre or a single text. Some titles guide students through the perplexing cross-current of critical debate by offering fresh and forthright reappraisals of their subject. Others offer new and timely studies which are of importance and value to the student. The series avoids critical identity or tight ideological approach, allowing the authors to explore the subject in their own way, taking account of recent changes in critical perspective.

Published titles

Forms of Speech in Victorian Fiction
Raymond Chapman

Henry Fielding: Authorship and Authority
Ian A. Bell

Utopian Imagination and Eighteenth-Century Fiction
Christine Rees

Robert Browning
John Woolford and Daniel Karlin

Wilde Style: The Plays and Prose of Oscar Wilde
Neil Sammells

Elizabeth Barrett Browning

Simon Avery and Rebecca Stott

Longman

An imprint of **Pearson Education**

London • New York • Toronto • Sydney • Tokyo • Singapore • Hong Kong • Cape Town
Madrid • Paris • Amsterdam • Munich • Milan

PEARSON EDUCATION LIMITED

Head Office:
Edinburgh Gate
Harlow CM20 2JE
Tel: +44 (0)1279 623623
Fax: +44 (0)1279 431059

London Office:
128 Long Acre
London WC2E 9AN
Tel: +44 (0)20 7447 2000
Fax: +44 (0)20 7447 2170
Website: www.history-minds.com

First published in Great Britain in 2003

© Pearson Education Limited 2003

The rights of Simon Avery and Rebecca Stott to be identified as Authors
of this Work have been asserted by them in accordance with the Copyright,
Designs and Patents Act 1988.

ISBN 0 582 40470 3

British Library Cataloguing in Publication Data
A CIP catalogue record for this book can be obtained from the British Library

Library of Congress Cataloging in Publication Data
A CIP catalog record for this book can be obtained from the Library of Congress

10 9 8 7 6 5 4 3 2 1

Typeset in 11/13pt Minion by Graphicraft Limited, Hong Kong
Printed in Malaysia

The Publishers' policy is to use paper manufactured from sustainable forests.

CONTENTS

A Note on Names   vii

Texts Used   viii

Acknowledgements   x

  Introduction: A Poet Lost and Regained   1
  Simon Avery

1 Constructing the Poet Laureate of Hope End:
   Elizabeth Barrett's Early Life   23
   Simon Avery

2 Audacious Beginnings: Elizabeth Barrett's Early Writings   43
   Simon Avery

3 The Culture of the Soul: Elizabeth Barrett
   Browning's Poetics   65
   Rebecca Stott

4 The Voice of a Decade: Elizabeth Barrett's Political
   Writings of the 1840s   86
   Simon Avery

5 Genre: A Chapter on Form   113
   Rebecca Stott

6 'How Do I Love Thee?': Love and Marriage   134
   Rebecca Stott

7 ''Twixt Church and Palace of a Florence Street':
   Elizabeth Barrett Browning and Italy   156
   Simon Avery

8 'Where Angels Fear to Tread': *Aurora Leigh*   181
   Rebecca Stott

Chronology   210

Abbreviations   239

Bibliography   240

Index   246

A NOTE ON NAMES

Any writer on Elizabeth Barrett Browning has to decide what name to use when referring to her. Christened Elizabeth Barrett Moulton-Barrett, the full name she never used in print, she published her first works under the initials E.B.B., expanded this to Elizabeth B. Barrett with the publication of *The Seraphim, and Other Poems* in 1838, and then, following her marriage to Robert in 1846, signed herself Elizabeth Barrett Browning. Some studies of the poet have chosen to refer to her as Elizabeth Barrett Browning regardless of whether or not she was married at the time, while at least one has referred to her predominantly as Mrs Browning throughout (Hayter, 1962). In this study, however, we have chosen to use Barrett when discussing her pre-1846 works and Barrett Browning when discussing her post-1846 works. Sometimes this leads to a slippage between the two names in a single chapter, as in the chapter on the 1840s when Elizabeth Barrett publishes *Poems* in 1844 and Elizabeth Barrett Browning publishes the expanded *Poems* of 1850, or in the wider-ranging chapters on the development of her poetics or her use of different genres. Nevertheless, we feel this is necessary in order to keep consistency. As Dorothy Mermin has argued, this is a poet who clearly recognises the importance of names and naming in her poetry and the imposed or self-elected identities which this signifies (Mermin, 1989: 37–8). It seems only right, therefore, to be exact when referring to the poet herself.

TEXTS USED

At the time of writing there is no complete edition of Elizabeth Barrett Browning's works in print except the Wordsworth *Works of Elizabeth Barrett Browning*, edited by Karen Hill, which has no notes or scholarly apparatus and places the poems published in *The Seraphim, and Other Poems* (1838), *Poems* (1844) and *Poems* (1850) together so that it is difficult to trace the correct order of publication. *Aurora Leigh* is available in complete version in Cora Kaplan's 1978 Women's Press edition or, more recently and with extensive notes, annotations and background documents, in Margaret Reynolds' edition published by Norton. A number of selected editions of Barrett Browning's works edited by Malcolm Hicks (Carcanet, 1983), John Bolton and Julia Bolton Holloway (Penguin, 1995) and Colin Graham (Everyman, 1996) are currently available, as well as selections in recent anthologies of Victorian women's poetry edited by Angela Leighton and Margaret Reynolds (Blackwell, 1995), Isobel Armstrong and Joseph Bristow (Oxford, 1996) and Virginia Blain (Longman, 2001).

Throughout this study we have used as our base texts Reynolds' edition of *Aurora Leigh* and the comprehensive, although now out of print, *Complete Works of Elizabeth Barrett Browning*, edited by Charlotte Porter and Helen A. Clarke (New York: Thomas Y. Cromwell, 1900, reprinted 1973). We have therefore followed the punctuation and layout of individual poems as they are established in these editions. However, for each quotation we have given line numbers so that the extracts can be easily traced in other editions.

Writers on Elizabeth Barrett Browning are extremely fortunate in having a huge number of letters to work from which are both insightful in themselves and important as contextual material for the study of the poetry. As Henry Chorley wrote of them in the nineteenth century:

> Her letters ought to be published. In power, in versatility, liveliness and finesse;
> in perfect originality of glance, and vigour of grasp at every topic of the hour;
> in their enthusiastic preferences, prejudices and inconsistencies, I have never

met with any, written by man or woman, more brilliant, spontaneous and characteristic.

(Quoted in Hayter, 1962: 205)

This mammoth publication project is currently being undertaken by Wedgestone Press under the editorship of Philip Kelley, Ronald Hudson and Scott Lewis. To date, fourteen volumes of *The Brownings' Correspondence* (covering both Elizabeth Barrett and Robert Browning's correspondence) have been published, totalling 2,716 separate letters – and this is only up until December 1847. Like all Barrett Browning scholars, we are greatly indebted to this ongoing work and have taken most of the quotations from Barrett's letters during this period from this edition. Citations within the text (e.g. *BC* 2:238) refer to volume and page number. Sources for the post-1847 letters include the letters to Mary Russell Mitford, edited by Meredith B. Raymond and Mary Rose, and the letters to Mrs David Ogilvy, edited by Peter N. Hayden and Philip Kelley. Abbreviations used for these editions, as well as for all other frequently cited source texts, are listed before the bibliography.

When quoting from Barrett's letters we have had to be extremely careful with punctuation. Overall, *The Brownings' Correspondence* replicates Barrett's spelling and punctuation as it appears in the manuscripts, even where words are incorrectly spelt or the punctuation seems rather erratic. We have followed *The Brownings' Correspondence* directly when quoting from it. The only difficulty arises through Barrett's tendency to use two dots as a punctuation mark which indicate a pause something akin to a dash, as in the following letter to Hugh Stuart Boyd:

What a letter! The worst of me is, that whenever I begin, there is no getting to the end of me. Forgive me . . because it is the same for my friendship for you.

(*BC* 8:85)

Again, following *The Brownings' Correspondence*, we have replicated this original piece of punctuation wherever it appears. However, as these dots might be confused with the dots used to mark where we omit part of a sentence when quoting, we have subsequently put our own ellipsis dots in square brackets [. . .].

Finally, a note about the publication of *Aurora Leigh*. Studies of Elizabeth Barrett Browning's work sometimes cite 1856 as the publication date of *Aurora Leigh* and sometimes 1857. The poem was originally published in November 1856, with 1857 on the title page, and a second impression appeared in January 1857 and a third in March. Throughout this study we have cited 1856 as the original publication date.

ACKNOWLEDGEMENTS

There are many people who have helped with the writing of this book in one form or another and we would like to acknowledge them here.

Simon Avery would like to thank Rebecca Stott for her enthusiasm, assistance, patience and advice throughout this project, and both former colleagues in the English Department of Anglia Polytechnic University and present colleagues in the Department of Humanities, University of Hertfordshire, for their support. He would also like to express his thanks to Sam Copnell, Vicky Griffin, Anita Pacheco and Anna Snaith, who have helped him to the end of the writing process with their encouragement and good humour; to his parents, Nina and Mike Avery, for their love and support and for introducing him to the pleasures of reading many years ago; and to Ben, who has lived with this book daily for many months and without whose endless encouragement, patience, proof-reading and help in so many ways, the manuscript would probably not have been completed. He would like to dedicate his part of the book with love to his grandmother, May Billam, who died while it was being written.

Rebecca Stott would like to thank Simon Avery for several years of on-going conversation about nineteenth-century intellectual history and about the wisdom, innovation and beauty of Elizabeth Barrett Browning's poetry. The process of writing the book has been a mutual intellectual adventure. She also thanks him for his unflagging attention to detail in editing the various drafts and for not losing patience with the punctuation problems the poems present. She would also like to thank her colleagues at Anglia Polytechnic University for their support and to her family for tolerating her disappearance into Barrett Browning's poetry for most waking hours in the spring of 2002.

The publishers are grateful to the University of North Carolina Press for permission to reproduce an extract from *Elizabeth Barrett Browning, Woman and Artist* by Helen M. Cooper. Copyright © 1988 by the University of North Carolina Press.

INTRODUCTION: A POET LOST AND REGAINED

SIMON AVERY

SEARCHING FOR ELIZABETH BARRETT BROWNING

London, 29 June 2001. One hundred and forty years since the death of Elizabeth Barrett Browning, I am walking in the rain down Weymouth Street, N1, in an attempt to trace what remains of one of the nineteenth century's most famous poets in a city she called home for a significant period of her life. I reach what must be a contender for one of the most famous addresses in British literary history: Wimpole Street. Imposing five-storey houses stand on either side of the road, many with balconies or hanging baskets, giving an air of opulence in keeping with the area surrounding Harley Street and Portland Place. The original 50 Wimpole Street, the home of the Barretts from 1838, was taken down in 1912 but the building which is now in its place has a small brown circular plaque placed between the first- and second-floor windows. On it, barely large enough to read without straining, is recorded 'Elizabeth Barrett Browning/ Poetess/ Afterwards wife of Robert Browning/ Lived here 1838–1846', the phrasing almost suggesting that Barrett gave up poetry when she married. And carved into the wall, just below ground level, is a simpler wording: 'Elizabeth Barrett Browning/ 1806–1861/ Poet/ Lived in a house on this site.' Neither commemoration would attract the attention of casual passers-by, although perhaps a visitor to the heart hospital of which 50 Wimpole Street now forms a part might moment-arily pause to consider the building's former use. An odd but somehow fitting conflation of ringlets and illness passes through my mind as I walk back down the road.

Getting off the underground at Charing Cross Station, I make my way across Trafalgar Square and through the revolving doors of the National Portrait Gallery. Up four flights of stairs, jostled by crowds of tourists, I reach the Victorian galleries on the second floor. Turning left past the forbidding collection of large black busts of great nineteenth-century politicians and thinkers perched high up on the wall (Charles Darwin, John Henry Newman, Charles Stuart Parnell, T.H. Huxley, George Cruickshank even, but no woman of course), I find myself in an oddly quiet room of portraits of Victorian artists and writers – Jenny Lind, the Brontë sisters, Charles Dickens, Alfred Tennyson, Charles Kingsley, Thomas Macauley. And then, in two frames hung at angles so that they face one another, Michele Gordigiani's famous 1858 oil paintings of Robert Browning and Elizabeth Barrett Browning. Gordigiani's Barrett Browning is one of the most striking images of the poet, painted sitting in a high-backed chair, her dark eyes staring directly out of the canvas in a manner which is challenging, even confrontational. The accompanying gallery label, however, notes that while she was highly regarded in her own day, 'her reputation now rests chiefly on *Sonnets from the Portuguese* (1850), and the long narrative poem, *Aurora Leigh* (1857 [*sic*])'. Certainly, she seems from this to have nothing like the status of her husband who is defined by his label as 'one of the great poets of the nineteenth century, pre-eminent for his intellectuality'.

What these remnants of Barrett Browning's existence in London suggest is that she is now, at best, remembered for a fraction of her works or for her position in relation to her husband. Yet in her own day, Elizabeth Barrett Browning was one of the most highly regarded poets throughout Britain, Europe and America. So how did this change occur? What factors influenced and engendered her astonishing decline in literary stature? In the following sections I will explore how Barrett Browning has been consecutively applauded, marginalised, ousted from the literary canon, and then slowly recovered by modern critical theory, a narrative which starkly reveals not only the changing reception of this particular poet and her work, but the changing priorities and fashions of literary history and criticism more widely.

THE POET IN HER LIFETIME

Throughout much of her lifetime, Elizabeth Barrett Browning was considered a shocking poet, a risk-taker, an innovator, a rebel, an iconoclast even. Almost entirely self-educated, she committed herself to the task of becoming one of the most successful poets of her generation from an exceptionally early age. Subsequently pursuing her art with a vigour which is often startling for its intensity, her first major poem, *The Battle of Marathon*, was in print by the time she was just fourteen. Twenty-five years later, following the publication of four further volumes including the widely praised two-volume *Poems* of 1844, she possessed a growing international reputation throughout America and Europe and was considered one of the leading writers of the nineteenth

century. Working within a surprisingly wide range of established literary genres
– epic, lyric, verse drama, religious meditation, sonnet, ballad and dramatic
monologue – and often concurrently reconfiguring these for new purposes,
she was always an experimenter, constantly pushing at the boundaries of
received ideas concerning the purpose and form of poetic writing. As she was
to maintain in the Preface to her 1844 collection, while there might be faults
in her poems, she was nevertheless always completely dedicated to her art:

> Poetry has been as serious a thing to me as life itself; and life has been a very
> serious thing: there has been no playing at skittles for me in either. I never
> mistook pleasure for the final cause of poetry; nor leisure, for the hour of the
> poet. I have done my work, so far, as work [. . .] and as work I offer it to the
> public . . .

> (*CW* 2:148–9)

Fundamental to this work was Barrett's sense that she was something of a
literary pioneer, carving a way forward through unmarked territory, particularly given her gender. For as she wrote to her friend Henry Chorley in a now
famous letter of 1845, she clearly considered herself displaced from any
female poetic tradition:

> England has had many learned women, not merely readers but writers of the
> learned languages, in Elizabeth's time and afterwards,—women of deeper
> acquirements than are common now in the greater diffusion of letters: and yet
> where were the poetesses? The divine breath which seemed to come and go, &,
> ere it went, filled the land with that crowd of true poets whom we call the old
> dramatists, . . why did it never pass even in the lyrical form over the lips of a
> woman? How strange! And can we deny that it was so? I look everywhere for
> Grandmothers & see none. It is not in the filial spirit I am deficient, I do assure
> you—witness my reverent love of the grandfathers!—

> (*BC* 10:14)

Of course today, with the tremendous amount of recent recovery work of
women poets from Aphra Behn to Barrett's own late-Romantic and Victorian contemporaries, we clearly *can* 'deny that it was so' and from Barrett's
other correspondence we can see that she was in fact very well aware of the
work of a whole range of other women poets. Rather, in employing this
genealogical model which effectively makes her into a literary orphan, Barrett
seems to be attempting to clear a space for herself as a new type of woman
poet and to be defining herself *against* the traditions of women's poetry
established by her direct predecessors and contemporaries such as Felicia

Hemans (1793–1835), Letitia Elizabeth Landon (known as 'L.E.L.', 1802–38), and Eliza Cook (1817–89). Each of these poets was extremely popular in the nineteenth century, setting levels of sales for poetry which were rarely matched, and yet as critics such as Norma Clarke (1990), Angela Leighton (1992) and Glennis Stephenson (1995) have demonstrated, each of them also left a legacy of disabling and inhibiting assumptions about the role of the woman poet which was subsequently difficult to dislodge. In particular, this legacy related to the traditionally 'feminine' subjects on which they wrote and which the critical establishment quickly reinforced as the female poet's 'proper sphere': love (especially unrequited or lost love), death and grieving, domesticity and the importance of the family unit, nature and pious religion – that is, poetry principally of the emotions and affections which was considered to uphold essentialist gender stereotypes and the wider status quo. Much of Landon's poetry, for example, focuses on betrayed heroines and 'hearts forsaken' (*The Improvisatrice*, 1824, in Landon, 1997: 61), while Cook's verse plays into a model of excessively sentimental feminine poetry as in 'The Old Arm-Chair' (1837) which opens:

> I love it, I love it; and who shall dare
> To chide me for loving that old Arm-chair?
> I've treasured it long as a sainted prize;
> I've bedewed it with tears, and embalmed it with sighs.

(ll.1–4)

And while critics such as Tricia Lootens (1996*b*) are beginning to show that Hemans' work might actually undercut dominant nineteenth-century ideologies in subtle ways, for many of her contemporaries Hemans embodied an overriding conservatism which is felt in poems such as 'Homes of England', 'Casabianca' (her most famous poem which opens 'The boy stood on the burning deck'), and even in the energetic 'Corinne at the Capitol' (1828). Hemans was inspired to write this particular poem after reading Madame Germaine de Staël's 1807 novel about Corinne the acclaimed woman poet and artist, a book which, she said, 'seem[s] to give me back my own thoughts and feelings, my whole inner being' (Moers, 1977: 177). And yet after detailing Corinne's wisdom, power and independence for five vigorously written stanzas, Hemans' agenda turns and she concludes the poem – seemingly without any irony – with a reassertion of the superior joys of housewifery:

> Radiant daughter of the sun!
> Now thy living wreath is won.

Crown'd of Rome!—Oh! art thou not
Happy in that glorious lot?—
Happier, happier, far than thou,
With the laurel on thy brow,
She that makes the humblest hearth
Lovely but to one on earth!

(ll.41–8)

Unlike Elizabeth Barrett, both Hemans and Landon had families to support by their writings and were therefore forced, at least partly, to try to accommodate popular tastes. Notwithstanding this, however, Barrett was often highly critical of their works both in her private correspondence with Mary Russell Mitford and in the two public poems she wrote to commemorate her predecessors: 'Felicia Hemans' and 'L.E.L.'s Last Question'. In her poem on the death of Hemans, for example, Barrett celebrates the life of the 'bay-crowned' poet as she ascends into heaven but also suggests that her work possesses an irredeemable thinness: '*softly* in our ears her silver song was ringing' (ll.1; 31, my italics). And in a letter to Mitford in November 1842, she argued that while Hemans certainly had 'genius' and a 'high moral tone', she nevertheless 'always does seem to me a lady rather than a woman [....] She is polished all over to one smoothness & one level' (*BC* 6:165).

Barrett's condemnation of Landon, however, was often more extreme, for while she clearly admired Landon's 'vividness & [...] naturalness,' she repeatedly emphasised her lack of energy and variety. In the Mitford correspondence, therefore, she describes her as 'toujours *tourterelle*' ('always a turtle dove') and 'a bird of a few notes' (*BC* 3:159), a view which she then articulated publicly in 'L.E.L.'s Last Question'. Published in *The Athenaeum* in January 1839, Barrett expresses in this poem an unreserved criticism of Landon as the poet of one overriding emotion: 'Love learnèd she had sung of love and love,—/ . . . / All sounds of life assumed one tune of love' (ll.15; 21). As she would unequivocally write to Mitford, '[m]y idea in connection with her poetry is, that she is capable of something *above* it' (*BC* 3:194).

Barrett's view of herself as an innovative poet therefore developed in large part from a reaction to the seemingly narrow, undemanding, conservative and 'feminine' subjects which she saw in the work of her immediate female literary forebears. Landon might not be capable of producing 'something *above*' what she had already written, but Barrett was always sure that she herself would be. Indeed, while she might often take similar subject matters – for example, the trope of the betrayed heroine – she almost invariably develops them in new directions, giving them a new power and contemporary resonance (see Chapter Five). And as we will demonstrate throughout this study, Barrett consistently moved uncompromisingly into subject areas which were traditionally associated with male poets, particularly in her debates around politics and power structures. This is not, of course, to say that she was the first woman poet to work in this area; indeed, as Anne K. Mellor has demonstrated, there was a strong tradition of women producing political poetry in the Romantic period, including Charlotte Smith, Hannah More, Lucy Aitken and Anna Letitia Barbauld (Mellor, 1999: 81–98). But Barrett was possibly the only woman poet to continue dealing *overtly* with the wider political sphere during the transition from the Romantic period to the Victorian period. Indeed, her political engagement was often the main factor which distinguished her poetry from that of her early to mid-Victorian contemporaries such as the Brontë sisters, Jean Ingelow and Christina Rossetti. As Rossetti would write in 1870, a few years after Barrett Browning's death and the publication of her own highly successful *Goblin Market and Other Poems*, 'It is not in me, and therefore it will never come out of me, to turn to politics or philanthropy with Mrs Browning: such many-sidedness I leave to a greater than I' (Rossetti, 1997: 348).

From her earliest writings onwards, Barrett spoke out assertively, refusing to be silenced by the dictates of the literary establishment and refusing to be confined to traditional models of feminine decorum. Often aligning herself with the second-generation male Romantics Byron and Shelley (see Stone, 1995: 49–93), she spent much of her career calling for liberty, both physical and psychological, from systems of oppression and violence, as well as championing the downtrodden and the marginalised, whether they were women, the working classes, children, slaves or whole countries such as Greece and Italy which were attempting to achieve independence. Seeking to represent contemporary life unflinchingly, as she put it in her magnum opus *Aurora Leigh* (1856, 5:213), she often sharply critiqued the ways in which society operates and thereby developed into a formidable literary presence. From the explorations of aspects of democracy and tyranny in *The Battle of Marathon* (1820) and *An Essay on Mind* (1826), through the exposé of the ills of capitalism, slavery and sexual oppression in *Poems* (1844; 1850) and *Aurora Leigh* (1856), to the repeated interrogations of European politics in *Casa Guidi Windows* (1851), *Poems Before Congress* (1860) and the posthumous *Last Poems* (1862), Barrett Browning was never worried about courting controversy and often seemed to relish in it. At the same time, she also produced some of the most accomplished and original religious, nature and love poetry of the nineteenth century, including *The Seraphim* (1838), a mediation on the crucifixion and the nature of grace, and the powerful, if often misread, *Sonnets from the Portuguese* (1850).

Given Barrett Browning's position as a woman poet breaking new ground, then, it is not surprising that her reception history during her lifetime was often highly ambivalent. From the earliest reviews of her long philosophical *An Essay on Mind* onwards, she was repeatedly constructed as something of an over-reacher, a woman pushing into male terrain in ways which more conservative critics found somewhat unnerving. Consequently, a wide range of reviewers referred to Barrett Browning's works using metaphors of wildness, instability and uncontrollability, as in the following 1842 review of *The Seraphim, and Other Poems* in *The North American Review*:

> Flaunting and unprofitable weeds shoot up side by side with flowers. . . . The steadiness of her flight bears no proportion to the vigor of her wing. Her great defect is a certain lawless extravagance, which delights in the wild, the mystic, the wonderful; which blends into the same group the most discordant images, and hurries her into a dim cloud-land far remote from human sympathies, and where the eye aches in attempting to follow her. There is a profusion of dazzling and glittering phraseology, as if a multitude of brave words had been hurled into the air and fallen confusedly upon the page. The firm earth seems to roll away from under our feet, and we are tossed upon a restless sea of fantastic imagery till the brain reels. In her wish to avoid what is prosaic, tame, and commonplace, she passes into the opposite extreme, and mistaking reverse of wrong for right, accumulates image upon image, and lavishes with too profuse a hand her poetical vocabulary, gilding refined gold, and painting the lily.

> (*BC* 6:376)

Such condemnation was to continue throughout Barrett's lifetime and indeed beyond it, but it was always equally matched by a substantial body of criticism which insisted upon the vigour, power and energy of her work. This was particularly so following the publication of *Poems* in 1844 (expanded and reprinted in 1850), the collection which marked a major shift in her critical status. *The Monthly Review*, for example, found the poems full of 'independent effort' and 'original power' (in Donaldson, 1993: 24), while *Eclectic Review* spoke of them as possessing 'masculine vigour of intellect, and grave mastership of the language' (Donaldson, 1993: 48). Indeed, many felt Barrett Browning's stature to be so great by mid-century that when Wordsworth died in 1850, she was seriously proposed by *The Athenaeum* as a potential candidate for the newly vacated post of Poet Laureate. It would be, the reviewer argued,

> an honourable testimonial to the individual, a fitting recognition of the remarkable place which the women of England have taken in the literature of the day, and a graceful compliment to the Sovereign herself. . . . There is no living poet of either sex who can prefer a higher claim.

> (*Athenaeum*, April 1850)

As the machinations of the literary establishment would have it, of course, the post was given to a man, Alfred Tennyson, whose long elegy to Arthur Hallam, *In Memoriam*, had been published that year.

Six years later, however, Barrett Browning's incendiary bombshell of a poem, *Aurora Leigh*, was published, the work which remains central to assessments of her achievement and her influence as a nineteenth-century poet. This radical and iconoclastic nine-book epic which tells the narrative of a woman determined at all costs to become a successful poet, also tackles head-on many of the major issues of the period (including aspects of the condition of England, utilitarianism, philanthropy, the 'woman question', prostitution, education, the role of religion, and life in the new urban environments), employing language which is often startling and shocking for its violence or use of images derived from the female body. Indeed, as the feminist Frances Power Cobbe wrote in 1860, *Aurora Leigh* has the relation to the world of conventional poetry that 'a chiselled steel corset does to a silk bodice with lace trimmings' (quoted in Stone, 1995: 175). It was, Barrett Browning wrote in the dedication to the Brownings' close friend and champion John Kenyon, the work into which 'my highest convictions upon Life and Art have entered' ('Dedication' in Reynolds, 1996: 4). These convictions, however, were to meet with some of the greatest condemnation she was ever to receive as well as some of the greatest applause. The *Dublin University Review*, for example, utilising an essentialist model of femininity, considered Barrett Browning's work 'coarse in expression and unfeminine in thought' (quoted in Kaplan, 1978: 13), while *The National Review* wrote that the poem's liberties were 'repulsive' (in Donaldson, 1993: 70). In a similar vein, W.E. Aytoun, writing in *Blackwood's Edinburgh Magazine*, argued that the poem had something 'very hideous or revolting . . . around it, and produces a sensation of loathing, from which we do not immediately recover' (in Reynolds, 1996: 416). In contrast, however, Ruskin praised *Aurora Leigh* as 'the greatest poem in the language, surpassed only by Shakespeare', and George Eliot, reflecting upon Barrett Browning's work in the *Westminster Review* in January 1857, called it 'the greatest poem' by 'a woman of genius' (in Dennis, 1996: 129). With *Aurora Leigh*, then, Barrett Browning's name was clearly established as a poet of great power and originality, and by the time of her death in 1861 she had firmly secured her place as a leading woman writer of the day.

In an essay written in the *fin-de-siècle* entitled 'English Poetesses', the playwright and social commentator Oscar Wilde argued that Barrett Browning's style and subject matter – the 'wonder of the prophet' in her work, her refusal to 'sandpaper her muse', and her overall 'force and fervour' – had been an important influence on many subsequent writers and a major catalyst for the further rise to prominence of the professional woman poet in the second half of the nineteenth century (Wilde, 1908: 110). Certainly, it is clear that Barrett Browning became an enabling model of success for many subsequent women poets, thus effectively transforming herself into that literary mother or 'grandmother' which she had lamented the absence of in her 1845 letter to Henry Chorley. One way of measuring Barrett Browning's stature as this literary mother is to examine the celebratory verses which other women poets wrote for her, a practice which was common in the nineteenth century as women attempted to establish both a supportive literary sisterhood and a self-conscious poetic tradition. Dora Greenwell, for example, author of important essays on 'Our Single Women' (1868) and a range of other social issues, wrote two poems for her predecessor a decade apart, the first entitled 'To Elizabeth Barrett Browning, in 1851' (the year of the publication of *Casa Guidi Windows*) and the second 'To Elizabeth Barrett Browning, in 1861' (the year of her death). Both of them are full of celebratory rhetoric as Greenwell explores the power of Barrett Browning's works:

> I lose myself within thy mind—from room
> > To goodly room thou leadest me, and still
> > Dost show me of thy glory more, until
> My soul, like Sheba's Queen, faints, overcome . . .

('To Elizabeth Barrett Browning, in 1851', ll.1–4)

Similarly, in 1852 the women's rights activist Bessie Rayner Parkes paid tribute to the 'subtle depths' (l.3) of Barrett Browning's work and advocated her as a model of female success for others to follow:

> . . . how I rejoiced that you were great,
> And all my heart exulted in your fame;
> A woman's fame, and *yours*!

(ll.19–21)

The novelist, essayist and poet Dinah Mulock Craik took her praise even further in her poem 'To Elizabeth Barrett Browning on Her Later Sonnets. 1856' where she addresses her foremother as both 'Sister!' and 'Comforter!' (ll.3; 6) before powerfully constructing her as nothing less than a Christ figure healing the sick: 'many a time thy soul's white feet/ Stole on the silent darkness where I lay,/ . . . / And I rose up and walked in strength complete' (ll.6–7; 10). Indeed, fashioning herself as a sinner to Barrett Browning's Christ, Craik proceeds to record how she 'Clung to thy garments when my soul was faint,—/ Touching thee, all unseen amid the throng' (ll.17–18).

Perhaps the most powerful poetic tributes to Barrett Browning by another woman poet, however, were those written by her transatlantic literary daughter, Emily Dickinson, whose own poems, as Betsy Erkkila demonstrates in her study *Wicked Sisters*, were greatly influenced by Barrett Browning's works and particularly *Aurora Leigh* (Erkkila, 1992: 68–79). Dickinson wrote three poems celebrating Barrett Browning: 'Her—"last Poems"', 'I went to thank her—', and 'I think I was enchanted'. In the first of these, Dickinson associates Barrett Browning's death with the death of poetry itself:

Her – 'last Poems' –
Poets – ended –
Silver – perished – with her Tongue –

                                                                    (ll.1–3)

Indeed, as Dickinson reveals in the most powerful of her tributes, 'I think I was enchanted', it was her discovery of Barrett Browning which subsequently enabled her own poetic development into America's greatest nineteenth-century woman poet. On first reading 'that Foreign Lady' (l.3), Dickinson recalls, she was so affected by the power of the work that she configures the poet as a witch who is capable of transforming nature's 'meanest Tunes' (l.12) into 'Titanic Opera' (l.16) and who creates a 'Conversion of the Mind' (l.22) in her disciple through her 'Tomes of solid Witchcraft' (l.29). Such an image evidently drew upon both Romney's fears of Aurora's poetry in Book Two of *Aurora Leigh* ('I saw at once the thing had witchcraft in't,/ Whereof the reading calls up dangerous spirits', *AL* 2:78–9) and points to the transgressive potential which Dickinson and other women poets found in Barrett Browning's work.

So Barrett Browning the witch; Barrett Browning the writer of Titanic operas; Barrett Browning the poet of great power, force and vigour. Such was the legacy that both inspired admiration and instilled fear in her readers. What occurs next in the poet's reception history, however, takes the constructions of Barrett Browning in completely different directions.

MODERNISM, MARGINALISATION AND MYTHOLOGISATION

With the onset of the modernist period, conventionally dated as c.1880–1930, a general backlash against Victorian poetry occurred as part of a wider reaction against everything which the Victorian age was perceived to represent. Interestingly – and ironically for our narrative – the only Victorian poet to be widely admired in the period was *Robert* Browning, whose experiments with the form of the dramatic monologue and focus on psychological complexity and the relativity of truth in works such as 'My Last Duchess', 'Fra Lippo Lippi', 'Andrea del Sarto' and the extensive *The Ring and the Book*, meant that he was seen by many as one of the fathers of poetic modernism. His wife, who had been far more widely read and admired in her lifetime, now became little more than a footnote to her husband's success, reconfigured into *Mrs Robert* Browning, so that by 1931 Virginia Woolf could humorously but astutely write in her essay on *Aurora Leigh*:

> fate has not been kind to Mrs Browning as a writer. Nobody reads her, nobody discusses her, nobody troubles to put her in her place. . . . In short, the only place in the mansion of literature that is assigned to her is downstairs in the servants' quarters, where, in company with Mrs Hemans, Eliza Cook, Jean Ingelow, Alexander Smith, Edwin Arnold, and Robert Mongomery, she bangs the crockery about and eats vast handfuls of peas on the point of her knife.

> (Woolf, 1979: 134)

The internationally renowned poet who was once considered for the laureateship and who was celebrated as a national hero by the Italians for her part in the *Risorgimento* (see Chapter Seven) was therefore pushed to the margins of literary history, a process compounded by the machinations of early twentieth-century literary canon formation which, under the auspices of scholars such as F.R. Leavis who removed all women but Jane Austen and George Eliot from his 'Great Tradition' (Leavis, 1948: 1), virtually erased Victorian women poets from view altogether.

Yet as Barrett Browning the formidable poet was ushered out in the first few decades of the twentieth century, Barrett Browning the mythic romantic heroine was ushered in. Robert Browning had attempted to protect his wife's memory by refusing to authorise any biography during his lifetime, but in 1899, ten years after his death, the Brownings' son Penini finally allowed the correspondence from his parents' courtship of 1845–6 to be published. The Victorians had, of course, already been fascinated by the elopement of these two leading poets, and evidence such as the courtship letters only fuelled this fascination further during the modernist period. The once powerful Barrett Browning was subsequently reconstructed as the frail chaise-longue-bound invalid most famously imaged in Rudolph Bessier's highly popular 1931 play *The Barretts of Wimpole Street*. Wasting away under the tyrannical jealousy of her ogre-like father, Elizabeth is depicted as suffering victim until the noble knight/lover/poet Robert sweeps in to save her, whisking both her and the ever loyal spaniel Flush away to freedom, health and new life in Italy.

Like many mythic constructions, there are some elements of truth in this narrative (see Chapter One), but Bessier's play grossly exaggerated the facts. As a consequence, Barrett Browning the writer of combative and demanding works which were often condemned for their polemical politics in the nineteenth century (Dante Gabriel Rossetti warned his sister Christina about following Barrett Browning's style of 'falsetto muscularity', for example (Marsh, 1994: 429)) was effectively eradicated and replaced by Barrett Browning the writer of that (in)famous first line from Sonnet 43 of *Sonnets from the Portuguese*: 'How do I love thee? Let me count the ways.' Endlessly mediated through Valentine cards and romantic comedies on stage and screen throughout the twentieth century, these ten words quickly became something of a metonym for Barrett Browning's complete *oeuvre* and still remain her most famous to date, keeping the poet both firmly rooted within the romantic framework and subordinated to her husband.

Indeed, this nexus of mythologised images has been notoriously hard to dismantle, since, as Marjorie Stone argues, 'the legend of Elizabeth Barrett Browning's romantic rescue does not reflect a cultural paradigm that is merely Victorian' (Stone, 1995: 3). In the wake of *The Barretts of Wimpole Street*, a number of other pseudo-biographical plays produced over the next two decades similarly emphasised the romantic Barrett. In 1940, Marjorie Carleton published *The Barretts: A Comedy in Three Acts*, for example, and in 1958 Betty Quin published *Romantic Journey: A Play About Elizabeth Barrett Browning*, which ends with Elizabeth's bathetic declaration to her maid Wilson, ' "Mrs Robert Browning!" I never thought three words could make such poetry!' (Quin, 1958: 21). Furthermore, in 1934, *The Barretts of Wimpole Street* was made into a highly successful film starring Norma Shearer and Fredric March, and even as late as 1970 that pink queen of popular romance, Barbara Cartland, took up the story in her piece 'The Perfect Romance of Elizabeth and Robert Browning', published in the short-lived magazine *Famous Loves*. Defining her subjects as 'A fragile beauty, slowly dying, and a poet with a zest for living' (Cartland, 1970: 7), Cartland portrays Barrett throughout as an invalided neurotic constantly on the verge of hysteria, who requires Robert, 'the best example we know of a middle-aged Romeo' (7), to bring her flowers and teach her to walk again. Black and white illustrations which depict both Barrett and Flush looking up lovingly into Robert's eyes with much the same expression only serve to reinforce the conservative power politics of the relationship as Cartland sees them. Indeed, Cartland's stance on Barrett's works is quite clear when she asserts: 'Elizabeth Barrett was certainly an individual far above the common herd; but she was not a genius. It is as a woman, not as a famous poet, that she is immortal' (7).

The result of these representations, of course, is that the successful poet is reduced to fading maiden, defined solely in terms of her relations with men – her father or her husband – and lacking any kind of independence or agency. We might paraphrase her most famous line: 'How shall we misrepresent thee? Let me count the ways.' As I will show, however, from the mid-twentieth century onwards these misrepresentations have themselves started to be readjusted.

CRITICAL RECOVERY: RE-READING ELIZABETH BARRETT BROWNING

During the first six decades of the twentieth century, concurrent with the reinforcement of Elizabeth Barrett Browning as a mythical – or at best, biographical – subject, little scholarly attention was paid to her works. She had no presence in the criticism emerging from movements such as New Criticism or Structuralism, for example, and while a number of the major Victorian poets started to receive renewed attention as the century moved on, Barrett Browning and her poetic sisters were still left occupying Woolf's basement. Indeed, even as late as 1982, Richard A. Levine in his study *The Victorian Experience: The Poets*, could include essays on Tennyson, Robert Browning, Clough, Arnold, D.G. Rossetti, Meredith, Swinburne, Hopkins and Hardy, but none on even the major women poets such as Barrett Browning or Christina Rossetti, thereby suggesting that writing poetry was not considered a viable 'experience' for Victorian women. And the publication of Barrett Browning's poetry itself fared little better. Indeed, with the exception of *Sonnets from the Portuguese*, her works were frequently omitted from anthologies or included only grudgingly and with qualifications or disclaimers. In Trilling and Bloom's popular anthology *Victorian Prose and Poetry* (1973), for example, Barrett is relegated to the 'Other Victorians' section with Emily Brontë, Edward Lear and Lewis Carroll where she is represented solely by her late poem 'A Musical Instrument' which, according to the editors, is her best lyric and far outstrips anything from *Aurora Leigh* which is deemed 'very bad' (1973: 689).

The first full-length critical study of Barrett Browning in the twentieth century, written by Alethea Hayter, was published in 1962 and despite its rather conservative-sounding title, *Mrs Browning: A Poet's Work and Its Setting*, it still includes some very compelling and astute analysis. Nevertheless, it was not until the mid- to late 1970s that substantial changes in the perception of Barrett Browning's work started to occur when, with the rise of feminist critical practices in the academy, nineteenth-century women's writing began to be re-read and re-evaluated in exciting and challenging ways.

CRITICAL APPROACHES OF THE 1970s

Much of the new feminist critical work which emerged in the 1970s initially focused on women's prose writings. As Angela Leighton has noted, for example, Elaine Showalter's ground-breaking *A Literature of Their Own* (1977) is principally concerned with the *novel* of their own (Leighton, 1992: 1). However, other early feminist explorations such as Ellen Moers' *Literary Women* (1977) and Sandra M. Gilbert and Susan Gubar's seminal study *The Madwoman in the Attic: Women Writers and the Nineteenth-Century Literary Imagination* (1979) began to pay attention to at least some works by the 'Big Three' women poets of the period: Elizabeth Barrett Browning, Emily Brontë and Christina Rossetti. In Barrett Browning's case, this renewed interest was furthered by the republication of *Aurora Leigh* in 1978 after the poem had been out of print for over seventy years. Edited by Cora Kaplan and published by the Women's Press, Barrett Browning's most important work, like Christina Rossetti's *Goblin Market*, subsequently began to be recovered as something of a lost feminist classic.

Kaplan's substantial introduction to her edition remains one of the most important and influential essays on *Aurora Leigh* to date. Writing from a Marxist-feminist perspective, Kaplan is particularly concerned both with what she sees to be the class prejudices embodied in the poem (the representations of Marian and the working-class 'mob', for instance) and with the feminist exploration of women's empowerment which the poem delineates, including Barrett's overt use of imagery drawn from the female body. More widely, Kaplan establishes a critical framework for the poem which sets it in dialogue with a range of other contemporary literary texts, including Germaine de Staël's *Corinne*, Charlotte Brontë's *Jane Eyre*, Elizabeth Gaskell's *Ruth* and Charles Kingsley's *Alton Locke*. As Tess Cosslett has argued, such an emphasis on *Aurora Leigh*'s intertextuality, its 'energetic "patchwork" nature', suggests that Kaplan's analysis 'reflects a reaction against New Critical ideas of organic form' (Cosslett, 1996: 69).

Unsurprisingly, given its focus on the development of a woman poet and its numerous other female-centred issues, *Aurora Leigh* has remained central to the feminist revival of interest in Barrett Browning, including the discussion of the poet in Gilbert and Gubar's section on women's poetry entitled 'Strength in Agony' (a phrase taken from Barrett's sonnet 'To George Sand: A Recognition') in *The Madwoman in the Attic*. Like Ellen Moers'

Literary Women, *The Madwoman in the Attic* is a psychoanalytic feminist study which aims to establish a specific tradition of female writing which is characterised as much by the problems of women *daring* to write ('the anxiety of authorship') as the more general and gender-unspecific problems of *what* to write ('the anxiety of influence'). As with much 1970s feminist criticism, the fundamental focus throughout Gilbert and Gubar's work is on the physical and psychological violence perpetuated on women by patriarchy, and women's literary responses through repressed anger or the exploration of self-sacrifice. In 'Strength in Agony', Gilbert and Gubar specifically argue that nineteenth-century women poets substituted an 'aesthetic of renunciation', a poetic expression of suffering and self-abnegation, in place of the 'self-assertion lyric [male] poetry traditionally demands' (1979: 564), and their paradigm for this model of female creativity is Christina Rossetti, proclaimed as the greatest woman poet 'of renunciation as necessity's highest and noblest virtue' (564). Barrett Browning, they suggest, follows much the same line although she 'ultimately substituted a more familiar Victorian aesthetic of service for the younger woman's somewhat idiosyncratic aesthetic of pain' (1979: 575). In particular, Gilbert and Gubar find problems in Aurora Leigh's final marriage to Romney, although they are willing to allow for a more open reading in suggesting that the closure 'conceals (but does not obliterate) Aurora Leigh's revolutionary impulses' (579).

Gilbert and Gubar's work is often confrontational and overstated – as might be expected from this early stage of feminist recovery work – and as Toril Moi has argued, there are distinct problems with the essentialist model of femininity they promote whereby *all* women experience violence from a monolithic patriarchy and all react with anger (see Moi, 1985: 57–69). Nevertheless, their study helped to foster a range of psychoanalytic and formalist readings of Barrett Browning's work which have been enlightening in a variety of ways. Sandra Gilbert's own essay 'From *Patria* to *Matria*' (1984), for example, deploys the same critical approach as *The Madwoman in the Attic*, exploring Barrett Browning's poetic representations of Italy as mother, sister and muse in order to link the struggles for Italian unification to Barrett Browning's own struggles for self-identity. And slightly later, but similarly drawing upon a predominantly psychoanalytic approach, Angela Leighton's study *Elizabeth Barrett Browning* (1986) explores the poet's use of various members of her family as her muses and figures of inspiration. As Leighton suggests:

> While Wordsworth celebrates a notional presence of nature [as inspiration/ muse], a nurturing consciousness or pervading spirit of things, [Barrett Browning] generally connects such forces with the intimately loved figures of her real family and above all with the figure of her father. It is he who haunts

her poetic consciousness and against whom she wages the longest struggle for self-expression.

(Leighton, 1986: 13)

While Leighton's text was important in giving the attention of a full-length study to Barrett Browning, significantly situated with the Harvester *Key Women Writers* series, its thesis is often rather reductive in that it fails to take account of wider social and political contexts outside the immediate family. These issues, however, would start to be addressed in the next major shift in critical approach towards Barrett Browning's work.

CRITICAL APPROACHES OF THE 1980s

As Cheryl Walker has mapped out in an essay on the critical history of Emily Dickinson's poetry, by the mid-1980s there was a shift in focus in feminist criticism away from an overt emphasis on women poets as victims to an exploration of women poets as literary foremothers and positive role models whose poetry, under the influence of French psychoanalytic criticism, can be read as articulating pleasure (*jouissance*). As Walker writes, 'The triumph of female art here becomes not its ability to capture women's experience but its capacity to de-stabilise the entrenched and often de-humanising assumptions of masculine thought' (Walker, 1999: 38).

Indeed, by the end of the 1980s, three new full-length studies of Barrett Browning had appeared which address the issues which Walker outlines here. In *Elizabeth Barrett Browning: Woman and Artist* (1988), Helen Cooper examines the evolution of Barrett Browning's woman-centred poetics, offering readings of her works from *The Seraphim* to *Aurora Leigh* which are primarily concerned with the poet's self-empowerment and her struggle to find a voice. Similarly from a feminist perspective but with a narrower focus, Glennis Stephenson's *Elizabeth Barrett Browning and the Poetry of Love* (1989) demonstrates how Barrett Browning's love poems from the early ballads to *Last Poems* are far more intricate and ideologically slippery than those critics who had been overwhelmed by the myth of Barrett as romantic heroine have suggested. And Dorothy Mermin's major study of 1989, *Elizabeth Barrett Browning: The Origins of a New Poetry*, with its in-depth analyses of works from the poet's complete *oeuvre*, champions Barrett Browning as 'nothing less than the first Victorian poet and first major woman poet in England' (1989: *x*). A highly influential study and one of the best in the field, Mermin's work sees Barrett Browning as 'the first woman to establish herself in the main English tradition (the one that forms the literary consciousness of other poets and educated readers of poetry)' (1–2) and firmly places her back on the map of nineteenth-century literary Britain, re-establishing her as 'the great . . . mother of both [poetic] daughters and sons' (2).

However, not all studies of the late 1980s were quite so celebratory. Deirdre David's 1987 *Intellectual Women and Victorian Patriarchy: Harriet Martineau, Elizabeth Barrett Browning, George Eliot*, for example, picks up on the ambivalences of Kaplan's Marxist-feminist introduction to *Aurora Leigh* and through a wider study of Barrett Browning's poetry which draws upon Antonio Gramsci's theories of the social function of the intellectual, David constructs a more conservative and essentially anti-feminist Barrett Browning who in large part complies with the hegemony of a male-dominated middle-class culture. According to David, Barrett Browning's relationship with patriarchy is at best that of 'both saboteur and collaborator' (David, 1987: *x*). Her thesis is important in exploring the complex relationships between Barrett Browning and dominant social ideologies, and in many ways this study can be seen to prefigure some of the central preoccupations of 1990s feminism where, as Walker notes, a new emphasis was placed on the relations between gender and the determinants of class, race and sexuality (Walker, 1999: 38–43).

CRITICAL APPROACHES OF THE 1990s

The critical reappraisal of Barrett Browning's work in the 1990s was influenced in a variety of ways by the reappraisal of writings by a range of other, often less well-known Victorian women poets. This 'second wave' of critical attention to nineteenth-century women's poetry was initiated in large part by the publication in 1992 of Angela Leighton's study *Victorian Women Poets: Writing Against the Heart*. In this book Leighton traces a tradition of eight women poets (Hemans, Landon, Barrett Browning, Christina Rossetti, Augusta Webster, 'Michael Field', Alice Meynell, Charlotte Mew) who increasingly fought against the conservative view of women's poetry being predominantly concerned with a 'highly moralised . . . sensibility' associated with the heart (Leighton, 1992: 3). Combining attention to biographical and historical context with close textual analysis, Leighton's arguments concerning Barrett Browning are arguably more complex in this book than in her earlier psychoanalytical discussion (1986) since she situates Barrett Browning within this emerging tradition of nineteenth-century women's poetry, highlighting continuities and developments in subject matter, imagery and politics with the other poets she chooses to consider. In particular, she argues that it is Barrett Browning 'who first brings to the somewhat frozen postures of women's poetry in the early nineteenth century a sense of a reality beyond the claims of the heart' (Leighton, 1992: 80) and therefore establishes her as an innovative figure in Victorian women's writing.

This process of establishing a tradition of nineteenth-century women's poetry was subsequently augmented in the mid-1990s by the publication of two major anthologies: *Victorian Women Poets: An Anthology*, edited by Leighton herself with Margaret Reynolds; and *Nineteenth-Century Women Poets*, edited by Isobel Armstrong and Joseph Bristow. These anthologies include works by many women poets who had sometimes been forgotten for nearly a century, including Mathilde Blind, Mary Coleridge, Dora Greenwell, Jean Ingelow, Amy Levy, Constance Naden, Adelaide Proctor, Mary A.F. Robinson and Elizabeth Siddal. Their recovery has given a renewed sense of the diversity of approaches, styles and subject matters tackled by women in the nineteenth century and has also furthered the critical project of establishing the sense of a nineteenth-century poetic 'sisterhood'. And yet such a project is not without ideological problems. For in establishing an alternative tradition, some feminist critics run the risk of 'ghettoising' women poets as a separate group outside the main canon as it already exists rather than accepting them into a new wider and more inclusive canon. Similarly, if taken to an extreme, the argument that a common language or identity can be traced throughout women's poetry, particularly in terms of imagery used, could fall again into an essentialist model of gender. Indeed, as Jan Montefiore points out, there are even more fundamental problems concerning the idealisation of women's poetry since 'it has to be admitted that sometimes the "buried treasure" does turn out to be just old iron' (Montefiore, 1994: 65), a view which Germaine Greer endorses in her study *Slip-Shod Sibyls: Recognition, Rejection and the Woman Poet* when she writes, 'The dilemma of the student of poetry who is also passionately interested in women is that she has to find value in a mass of work that she knows to be inferior' (Greer, 1995: xi). Certainly, it seems arguable that while much of the recovered women's poetry is extremely accomplished, engaging and provocative, a good proportion of it also serves to demonstrate why, in comparison, Barrett Browning's work was considered so powerful and original.

Studies of Barrett Browning produced during the mid- to late 1990s have tended to combine feminist and new historicist approaches and to explore her poems in relation to a wider range of cultural discourses, both literary and social. Marjorie Stone's important study *Elizabeth Barrett Browning* (1995), for example, situates Barrett Browning's writings in relation to the inherited discourses and traditions of Romanticism, arguing that Barrett Browning cannot be fitted into the general models of female Romanticism as outlined by Anne K. Mellor in *Romanticism and Gender* (Stone, 1995: 52).

For Stone, Barrett Browning is particularly important because she reveals the continuities between Romantic and Victorian poetry. Stone therefore explores, for example, the means by which Barrett Browning engaged with the Romantic ballad form, reconstructing it in new, often gender-specific ways which would then influence the ballad writing of the Pre-Raphaelites, and examines how *Aurora Leigh* engages with the Victorian traditions of sage discourse, with that genre's

> representation of a prophetic speaker, its pronounced biblical allusions and typological patterning, its polemical sermonising on the times, its argumentative intertextuality, its exploitation of metaphor and definition as strategies of persuasion, its quest for a sustaining 'Life Philosophy', and its vision of a new social and spiritual order.

> (1995: 138)

As might be expected, however, Barrett Browning subtly subverts the generic conventions which she inherits and Stone demonstrates how *Aurora Leigh* functions as a more female-orientated version of sage writing.

Also working from a new historicist approach, Linda M. Lewis in her study *Elizabeth Barrett Browning's Spiritual Progress: Face to Face with God* (1998) explores the poet's work in relation to some of the nineteenth-century's dominant and resistant religious discourses and thereby seeks to readjust what she regards as a serious omission in Barrett Browning criticism to date. Lewis explores the ways in which Barrett Browning revises both biblical and classical myths, and details in particular her engagement with such issues as transcendental mysticism, Christian misogyny, grace, death and resurrection. Recent work on Barrett Browning, then, as with much current literary criticism generally, seeks to resituate the writer back into historical contexts and to interrogate the interrelations between literary discourses and wider social and political developments. What is subsequently becoming evident from this criticism is a very real sense of the sheer complexity of Barrett Browning's writing and thinking, a complexity which continues to develop as we map out, in Elaine Showalter's words, 'the forces that intersect an individual woman writer's cultural field' (Showalter, 1982: 32).

THIS STUDY

The practice of literary criticism is, on many levels, one of dialogue, as critics build up, reshape or challenge readings advocated by other critics. In this study we have sought to enter into dialogue with a range of views on Barrett

Browning and to enter into the lively debates which are currently being generated by the renewed interest in her work. As critics, we are both particularly interested in Barrett Browning's relations to, and participation in, nineteenth-century intellectual history, her engagement with key social and political debates of the period, and her examination of the power relations and struggles which comprise society and the individual's place within society. We have therefore tried to explore the ways in which Barrett Browning's writings relate to wider historical contexts and at the same time to consider the aesthetic and formal qualities of these writings since, as Jan Montefiore points out, 'No other kind of writing holds its own words up to the light as poetry does' (Montefiore, 1994: 6).

Our study takes a broadly chronological view of Barrett Browning's career as a poet, although the chapters on genre and poetics are more wide-ranging in the periods they consider. We have tried to balance the attention paid to those poems which our research suggests are currently most studied and discussed (for example, *Aurora Leigh*, 'The Runaway Slave at Pilgrim's Point', *Sonnets from the Portuguese*) and those which are less well known but often equally interesting and challenging, such as *A Drama of Exile*, 'Lady Geraldine's Courtship' and *Casa Guidi Windows*. We have also taken care to include discussion of Barrett's early writings with the hope of both demonstrating how her aesthetics and politics developed and stimulating further discussion on these more neglected works.

The study opens with a biographical account of Elizabeth Barrett's childhood and youth spent at the family home of Hope End, paying particular attention to her increasing challenge to inherited models of femininity and her developing political consciousness. This is not, of course, a complete biographical survey but an initial mapping out of some of the ideas which influence Barrett's subsequent writings. (A more detailed biographical survey can be found in the chronology.) In Chapter Two we explore how some of these ideas are reflected in selected works taken from Barrett's three initial volumes – *The Battle of Marathon* (1820), *An Essay on Mind, and Other Poems* (1826) and *Prometheus Bound, and Miscellaneous Poems* (1833) – and consider how Barrett emerged into a public poet.

In Chapter Three, 'The Culture of the Soul: Elizabeth Barrett Browning's Poetics', we examine how Barrett Browning saw the role of the poet in an age when this issue was being hotly debated in literary circles. Drawing upon evidence from across her career, we demonstrate how she became committed to the idea of the poet as a public figure at the centre of culture, not afraid to take on controversial political and social issues. In the following chapter, 'The Voice of a Decade', we build upon these arguments through a detailed examination of the political poetry Barrett wrote in the 1840s, the decade when her national and international standing was firmly established.

Considering such areas as the role of women in politics, debates about leadership, the 'Condition of England' question and slavery, we argue how Barrett Browning was a highly controversial writer who rigorously questioned structures of established power and authority.

Chapter Five on genre examines how Barrett Browning constantly flouted generic expectations and conventions in her writings. We pay consideration to her use and reconfiguration of epic, sonnet, ballad and dramatic monologue, and explore the means by which the poet often forged new connections between genre and gender. In Chapter Six, 'How Do I Love Thee?', we then further deconstruct the myth of Barrett as romantic heroine by examining the intricacies of her writings on relationships and the institution of marriage. We explore the influence of Swedenborgian thinking in relation to the arguments of *Aurora Leigh* and selected works from *Sonnets from the Portuguese*, and consider the emphasis on betrayal in love and the harsh material realities of marriage in a range of Barrett Browning's other writings. We thereby demonstrate how the poet viewed love within the context of a wider range of socio-economic structures and discourses.

In Chapter Seven, "Twixt Church and Palace of a Florence Street', we return once more to Barrett Browning's political thinking and consider her writings on the importance of Italian unification. The Brownings made Italy their home from the time of their marriage in 1846 until Barrett Browning's death in 1861, and during this period Barrett Browning was obsessed with exploring the intricacies of Italian politics and championing the cause of unification. This chapter explores her often highly ambiguous thinking about Italy as it is mediated principally through *Casa Guidi Windows* (1851) and selected works from *Poems Before Congress* (1860).

In the final chapter of this study, we return to *Aurora Leigh* in detail and consider a range of issues raised by this complex and highly original work. Barrett Browning clearly expected – and indeed, seems to have wanted – the poem to give offence to many readers and we explore how she created a dissenting poem which challenged conventional ideas on a range of issues, including marriage, duty, social reform and the Condition of England.

When they were living in Italy, Elizabeth Barrett and Robert Browning exchanged manuscripts of their recent work and each commented on the writing of the other, editing it and making suggestions for possible revisions. Our collaborative project has been similarly conversational and we have adopted a similar process. Principally, however, Simon Avery has authored the chapters on Barrett's biography, the early works, the 1840s and Italian politics, as well as the introduction and chronology; and Rebecca Stott has written the chapters on the role of the poet, genre, love and marriage, and *Aurora Leigh*. This division of labour has inevitably resulted in overlapping discussions of texts but we felt it important to return to central poems from different perspectives and consequently we have entered into dialogue with one another's work in ways which highlight and complicate the multiplicity of interpretative possibilities. What we therefore hope emerges from this study overall is renewed evidence of Elizabeth Barrett Browning's engagement with contemporary debates, a wider understanding of her many challenges to accepted thinking, and a greater sense of the originality and sheer power of much of her startling work.

1

CONSTRUCTING THE POET LAUREATE OF HOPE END: ELIZABETH BARRETT'S EARLY LIFE

SIMON AVERY

WRITING HISTORIES

In 1853, Elizabeth Barrett Browning wrote to her friend Isa Blagden that she had 'the greatest horror' of becoming the subject of biographical speculation, of being 'caught, stuck through with a pin, and beautifully preserved, with other butterflies and beetles' (quoted in Hayter, 1962: 110–1). Since her death, however, Barrett Browning has been 'stuck through with a pin' and 'preserved' by biographers on many occasions and continues to be so. Indeed, over the past fifteen years alone her life has been scripted and rescripted in a number of strikingly different ways. The most detailed study to date remains Margaret Forster's *Elizabeth Barrett Browning*, published by Chatto and Windus in 1988, which drew upon newly published letters and other biographical materials in order to challenge and deconstruct many of the standard images which had accrued around Barrett Browning through the processes of mythologisation. Forster presents a far more active and intellectual woman than the myths had previously allowed for, and yet throughout the study there is little detailed consideration of Barrett Browning's actual writings or her development as a poet. Consequently, Barrett Browning's life is separated from her art in a manner similar to, although not to the same degree as, Elizabeth Gaskell's mid-nineteenthcentury biography of Charlotte Brontë.

In the 1990s, however, two new biographical studies were published which give more attention to the poetry than does Forster's work. Barbara Dennis's *Elizabeth Barrett Browning: The Hope End Years* (Seren, 1996) focuses predominantly on Barrett's early life at the family home in Herefordshire as part of a series of books which commemorate writers and artists of that region. Although Dennis sometimes tends to conflate Barrett too easily with her major protagonist Aurora Leigh, her study is insightful in its exploration of Barrett's youth and how Barrett's experiences during this period influenced her writings. Dennis also reveals much about Barrett's early literary influences by drawing upon the evidence of the poet's extensive reading which is documented in her unpublished notebook of 1822–24. In contrast, Julia Markus' *Dared and Done* (Bloomsbury, 1995) takes a wider focus in examining the Brownings' courtship and married life, again drawing upon new research in order to suggest that at times the relationship between the two poets might not have been as ideal as it is usually considered to be. Markus gives close attention to the poetry of both the Brownings, thereby demonstrating how their professional as well as personal lives intersected, and also offers some intriguing, if sometimes tentative, arguments concerning Barrett Browning's family background (see the discussion of slavery below).

We can clearly relate the different emphases and agendas in these biographies to the theoretical considerations of history which have emerged in the 1980s and 1990s from the work of New Historicist critics such as Jerome McGann and Marjorie Levinson (see Levinson *et al.,* 1989). As New Historicism has demonstrated, history – and here we can include biography or 'life-history' – never exists objectively, complete and uncontested, but is rather mediated through particular perspectives and choices. That is, individual historians consciously select specific pieces of evidence while discarding others in order to construct a version of history which is, overtly or not, a biased narrative. Therefore history comes to be made up of competing versions which reconstruct the same events or period from different perspectives, and as a consequence it is crucial that readers of histories are aware of the particular agendas, biases and assumptions of the historian who has selected and arranged that narrative.

It is intriguing to realise, then, that the twenty-year-old Elizabeth Barrett had already highlighted precisely these points over 160 years before New Historicist critics formally theorised them, for in her long philosophical poem *An Essay on Mind* (1826) she advised:

> . . . in th' historian's bosom look,
> And weigh his feelings ere you trust his book;
> His private friendships, private wrongs, descry,
> Where tend his passions, where his interests lie—
> And while his proper faults your mind engage,
> Discern the ruling foibles of his age.

(ll.314–19)

In the spirit of this quotation, therefore, I will begin by declaring my own 'passions' and where my own 'interests lie'. In writing this short version of Elizabeth Barrett's early life, I am particularly concerned with constructing a narrative which explores the poet's resistance to received ideas of socially acceptable feminine behaviour as they were embodied in what Michel Foucault terms 'dominant ideologies'. Drawing extensively on the volumes of *The Brownings' Correspondence* which continue to be published by Wedgestone Press, as well as other biographical source materials, I foreground Barrett's developing proto-feminist and political thinking, and interpret it in ways which I believe will be useful for our analyses of her writings in subsequent chapters of this study. What should emerge from this exploration, therefore, is a construction of Elizabeth Barrett as a challenging and original thinker who contested received ideas and socially endorsed gender expectations from an early stage in her life.

FAMILY AND GENDER POLITICS AT HOPE END

As Margaret Forster and Barbara Dennis have emphasised, it is important to acknowledge that Elizabeth Barrett was brought up not in the urban environments with which she is so often associated – Wimpole Street in London or Casa Guidi in Florence – but in rural Herefordshire amidst the Malvern Hills which she described in her diary as a 'sublime sight' and 'such a sea of land' (*D* 6). Born in 1806, the same year as John Stuart Mill, another figure who would become associated with liberal ideas, Elizabeth was the eldest of the twelve children of Edward Barrett Moulton-Barrett and Mary Graham-Clarke (one child, Mary, died aged four in 1814), and in 1809 she moved with her parents to what would become the family home for the next twenty-three years, Hope End near Ledbury in Herefordshire, a house which cost her father the inordinate sum of £27,000. With its name meaning 'closed valley' in archaic English (Forster, 1988: 9), the original house of Hope End was pulled down by Barrett's father soon after the family's arrival there and subsequently rebuilt as an imposing mansion in the Regency Indian-Gothic style, a fashion most famously seen in Brighton Pavilion. Set within 375 acres of parkland with a deer park, icehouse and grotto, the house itself possessed twenty bedrooms, vaulted ceilings, stained-glass windows, domes and minarets, giving it an air of opulence which Barrett's mother said was reminiscent of the Arabian Nights Tales (Forster, 1988: 11). Significantly, the poet who would expend much of her creative energy drawing attention to the plight of the deprived in society, herself grew up in extremely privileged surroundings.

Hope End therefore offered a seemingly idyllic home for the Barrett children and certainly at this stage in Elizabeth Barrett's life, her relations with her family were supportive and secure. As I claimed in the introduction, the persistent myths surrounding Barrett would have us believe that her father was *always* the grotesque parody of Victorian patriarchal authoritarianism which Bessier depicted in *The Barretts of Wimpole Street*. As Forster and Dennis have shown, however, this account is somewhat misconceived, for during the Hope End period Edward Barrett was deeply loved and respected by his children. Indeed, Barrett's early poems written to celebrate the birthdays of family members constantly address her father with 'the simple language of the heart' and 'th'enduring strains of filial love' (*BC* 1:125) and construct him as a benevolent protector from 'that world, where vices roam' (*BC* 1:19). Furthermore, as Mermin points out, Barrett clearly considered her father to be a fundamental catalyst in her literary development (Mermin, 1989: 15–16), viewing him as the man who 'sowed the very bottom of my mind' (*BC* 1:11) and who helped to formalise her future vocation. As Barrett herself wrote in 1820:

> In my sixth year [Kelley & Hudson suggest Barrett meant her ninth year] for some lines on virtue which I had pen[n]ed with great care I received from Papa a ten shilling note enclosed in a letter which was addrest to *the Poet Laureat* [sic] *of Hope End*; I mention this because I received much more pleasure from the word *Poet* than from the ten shilling note [. . .] '*Poet laureat of Hope End*' was too great a tittle [*sic*] to lose—

> (*BC* 1:350)

Certainly, Edward Barrett's support for his daughter's literary endeavours is evident in his paying for the printing of her first major poem, *The Battle of Marathon*, which was dedicated by the poet 'To him, to whom "I owe the most", and whose admonitions have guided my youthful muse, even from her earliest infancy' (*CW* 1:1). This and the numerous other expressions of love between father and children in the correspondence suggest that the assumptions concerning Edward's tyrannical behaviour need modifying and readjusting somewhat when considering these early years.

Rather, during her youth it was Barrett's relationship with her *mother* which was more problematic. Again, there is no denying the great love Barrett had for Mary, who is revered in the early poems as 'So supremely distinguished in the anals [*sic*] of our little lives' (*BC* 1:58) and whose untimely death in 1828 is recorded in Barrett's correspondence in terms of utter anguish: 'I never can forget what I have lost. Her voice is still sounding in my ears—her image is in my heart' (*BC* 2:176). And yet there is also no denying that Mary represented a model of middle-class womanhood against which Barrett increasingly defined herself, for despite her evident intelligence, her mother spent much of her life almost continually pregnant and taking care of the family – pressures which eventually compounded to break her health. Indeed, in a letter to Robert in 1846, Barrett made a rare direct reference to her mother which highlights the psychological damage engendered by her restricted life. She was, Barrett wrote,

> of a nature harrowed up into furrows by the pressure of circumstances [. . . .] A sweet, gentle nature, which the thunder a little turned from its sweetness—as when it turns milk—One of those women who can never resist,—but, in submitting & bowing on themselves, make a mark, a plait, within, . . a sign of suffering. Too womanly she was—it was her only fault—

(BC 13:305–6)

Beneath the rhetoric of love and loss here is a barely veiled critique of a system which beats wives and mothers into submission (see the discussion of marriage in Chapter Six). Mary is compared to a ploughed field, an image which signals her main function as bearer of new life, but a field which has been 'harrowed' by a harrowing frame, suggesting processes of dominance and violation. (This contrasts sharply with Barrett's earlier use of the image of her father as furrower, 'sowing the very bottom of my mind' with creativity.) And in the second image pattern, Mary is again depicted as vulnerable, subject to a signifier of sublime power, thunder, which results in 'a sign of suffering' within. Nevertheless, there is also a significant slippage here in the allocation of blame for Mary's fate, for at the close of the quotation Barrett suggests that her mother complicitly surrendered to the condition of being '[t]oo womanly' and thereby upheld the system which would eventually annihilate her. From an early age, Barrett herself determined never to give in to such complicity.

Barrett's initial resistance to conventional modes of feminine behaviour is clearly articulated in two extant autobiographical prose pieces written around the time of puberty: 'My Own Character', which was started in 1818 when Barrett was twelve but then quickly aborted, and the more expansive and exploratory 'Glimpses into My Own Life and Literary Character', written in stages over 1820–1 (both reprinted in <i>BC</i> 1). In these documents Barrett repeatedly emphasises her passionate, hot-tempered and impatient nature, her 'violent disposition' and her extraordinary will-to-power as she asserts her authority over her siblings and 'spurns that subserviency of opinion which is generally considered necessary to feminine softness' (<i>BC</i> 1:349; 355). Moreover, in a later, thinly disguised autobiographical piece about the wilful 'Beth', written, according to Kelley and Hudson, for her niece in the early 1840s (<i>BC</i> 1:360), Barrett went further in the articulation of her hatred of conventional women, arguing that she 'could not abide their littlenesses called delicacies, their pretty headaches, & soft mincing voices, their nerves & affectations' (1:361). Condemnation indeed.

It is hardly surprising, then, that Barrett rebelled against anything which smacked of conventional middle-class femininity. Her diary is full of references to robust physical activity on the hills surrounding her home in a clear belying of the stereotype of the ailing and invalided girl ('I cantered up the road & up the hill, without holding the pummel. The poney [*sic*] carried me swiftly'; 'I got off the horse, & ran around [. . .] in my allegro style', *D* 38), and her letters also record her annoyance with the 'glittering kaleidoscope of Fashion' (*BC* 1:109) and the 'stupid Evening[s]' of social visiting (*BC* 2:81) which she increasingly left to her sisters Henrietta and Arabella. Indeed, as Barrett later told her close friend Mary Russell Mitford, at the age of ten she rather 'leant towards being poor Lord Byron's PAGE' (*MRM* 2:7), thereby recoiling from the feminine stereotypes around her through a fantasy of cross-dressing which oddly would have both empowered her (as a boy rather than a girl) and made her subservient to one of the most notorious sexual libertines of the age. The ambiguous nature of power differentials in relationships and the possibilities which cross-dressing provided for subverting the status quo would become key ideas in many of Barrett's later writings, while, as we will see in the next chapter, Byron himself was to be one of the major influences on her early thinking about both poetry and politics.

The major influence on Barrett's developing proto-feminist consciousness at this stage, however, was Mary Wollstonecraft, the Jacobin mother of feminism whose work Barrett read with eagerness and enthusiasm. As she wrote to Mitford in 1844:

> I used to read Mary Wolstonecraft [*sic*],— (the 'Rights of woman',) . . when I was twelve years old, & 'quite agreed with her.' Her eloquence & her doctrine were equally dear to me at that time, when I was inconsolable for not being born a man. Ah—if I had thought that I sh^d have lived all my life without leaving my petticoats, both in the actual & metaphorical sense, how, at ten years old, I sh^d have frowned myself to scorn!

> (*MRM* 3:40)

While we can question the perspective of Barrett's statement here – by 1844 there is no doubt that she had escaped her *psychological* petticoats at least – the quote clearly points to the importance which Wollstonecraft's key work, *A Vindication of the Rights of Woman*, had in the young girl's philosophy. By the time Barrett was reading *Vindication*, a quarter of a century had passed since its original publication. Nevertheless, the text's radical and subversive views on the gender socialisation of middle-class women, who are portrayed throughout the work as physically and intellectually enfeebled, still shocked a conservative establishment which viewed Wollstonecraft, in Horace Walpole's famous image, as a 'hyena in petticoats' (Todd, 2000: 168) – itself an interesting precursor of Barrett's own petticoated image. Wollstonecraft suggested that reform for women needed to be part of a wider reform of society as a whole, and particularly as part of a dismantling of authoritarian power systems which she saw as being grounded in artificial criteria such as inherited wealth or in arbitrary status such as the aristocracy, the army or the church. Such arguments therefore meant that she was often associated with the same anarchic energy which had galvanised the French Reign of Terror and British Luddism, but for the young Barrett, Wollstonecraft offered new ideas concerning the possible negotiation of received gender norms which she eagerly embraced. Fundamental to these ideas was the liberating potential of education.

'WADING MANFULLY': CHALLENGING INTELLECTUAL EXPECTATIONS

Following Wollstonecraft, Elizabeth Barrett was acutely aware of the limitations of socially approved middle-class feminine education, the so-called 'accomplishments' system which she was to satirise with great disdain in Book One of *Aurora Leigh*. Here Aurora, having recently arrived in England from Italy, is forced by her aunt to engage in a variety of fatuous pursuits – including spinning glass, stuffing birds, modelling flowers in wax, and repeating 'the royal genealogies/ Of Oviedo' or 'the internal laws/ Of the Burmese Empire' (*AL* 1:425; 407–9) – all of which are meant to make her more 'womanly' and a 'model to the universe' (443; 446). Indeed, as Barrett recorded in 'Glimpses', she soon realised that in order to be taken seriously as a scholar and a poet she would have to cross-dress psychologically and 'manfully [. . .] wade thro the waves of learning stopping my ears against the enchanted voice of the Syren' (*BC* 1:355). Through the image of the siren here, associated in Greek mythology with both the *femme fatale* and the cult of the dead, Barrett clearly suggested how she must resist traditional models of femininity if she was to develop intellectually. And wade 'manfully' in learning she certainly did, reading liberally and eclectically in a wide range of challenging writings by British, European and American novelists, poets, historians and philosophers, including the works of Dante, Milton, Shakespeare, Pope, Voltaire, Kant, Berkely, Spinoza, Wordsworth, Scott, Austen and de Staël, thereby allowing her mind, she suggested in an apt exploratory image, to 'roll itself out, as the chart of a [. . .] voyager' (*D* 93).

This intellectual voyaging also involved an early commitment to the study of languages. In line with accepted pedagogical theory concerning the 'proper sphere' of female knowledge, Barrett began by studying French but rather than limiting herself, as Aurora Leigh's aunt dictates, to the 'classic French' which was considered acceptable for a young woman to pursue (*AL* 1:399), she was later to use her understanding of the language to read avidly all those contemporary French novelists – Balzac, Hugo, Sand, Stendhal, Eugène Sue – whose works were considered scandalous and morally corrupt by the conservative cultural establishment and which were therefore deemed unfit for female readership – 'naughty romances' which should not be given to 'miscellaneous readers', as she described them to Mitford (*MRM* 3:16). Certainly, Barrett would often speak of reading such texts in terms of transgression and even sexual encounter. In 1845, for example, after having read Stendhal's *Le Rouge et Le Noir*, she told Mitford that it was 'a book for you to read at all risks—you must certainly read it for the power's sake. It has ridden me like an incubus for several days' (*MRM* 3:100). In comparing her experience of reading to being sexually violated by an incubus, a mythical male demon who attacked women while they were asleep, it is little wonder that Barrett often shocked Mitford with her frank expression.

From the age of eleven, however, Barrett made a more radical challenge to prescribed female education by commencing the study of Latin and Greek. As many historians and critics have shown, the learning of the classics was arguably the biggest single discriminating factor in the education of the two genders (see, for example, Showalter, 1977: 42–4). While Latin and Greek were staple fare for young men at public school and university and remained the languages of power in public affairs, the intellectual rigour which the grammar required and the perceived moral dubiousness of many of the ancient texts meant that they were considered unsuitable for women. Therefore a young woman who embarked on a course of classical study, as Barrett, Emily Brontë and Mary Ann Evans (the young George Eliot) all did, was often considered to be committing an act of cultural transgression which overtly challenged the established relations between knowledge and gender.

As the eldest daughter of the family, however, Barrett appears to have been actively *encouraged* by her father to study alongside her brother Edward (known as Bro) under Daniel McSwiney, a Catholic classics scholar and by all accounts something of a dandy figure who came to Hope End over the course of three years from 1817 to 1820 to act as tutor. Like Aurora's father, therefore, Edward Barrett senior sought to 'wrap his . . . daughter in [a] large/ Man's doublet' of learning (*AL* 1:727–8) and there is no doubt that his educational foresight, something which is often overlooked in biographical studies of Barrett Browning, was fundamental in the development of the poet.

Barrett's relationship with her brother Bro during this period was little short of complete adoration. 'If ever I loved any human being,' she wrote in 1821 in an essay entitled 'Bro's Character and Mine compared', 'I love this dear Brother . . the Partner of my pleasures of my literary toils. My attachment to him is literally devoted!' (*BC* 1:354). However, where intellectual matters were concerned, Barrett possessed an overriding competitive streak which revealed itself in the need to prove herself Bro's superior in spite of – or more likely, because of – her gender. 'I am not content till I excel,' she wrote, 'but Bro is satisfied with mediocrity—! He possesses too much humility to soar and therefore generally stoops lower than is necessary' (*BC* 1:357). For Barrett herself, such mediocrity never seemed a possibility and consequently she applied herself to her classical studies with an understanding which was often quicker and more accurate than that of her brother and which clearly impressed McSwiney. Even when Bro was sent to public school at Charterhouse, following the standard nineteenth-century model where only the male offspring were afforded formal opportunities for education, and McSwiney consequently stopped coming to Hope End, Barrett refused to be beaten by the system and persisted with staggering determination in her private studies.

This determination was to pay great dividends several years later when, after the publication in 1826 of *An Essay on Mind*, a poem rich in classical allusion and erudite learning (see Chapter Two), Barrett was contacted independently by two highly renowned classical scholars, Uvedale Price and Hugh Stuart Boyd, who were to enable her to develop her intellectual abilities further. Price was already eighty years old when he first contacted Barrett, well respected not only for his knowledge of ancient languages but also for his musicianship and thinking on landscape gardening (his study in favour of natural beauty in landscape gardening, *An Essay on the Picturesque*, had appeared in 1793, for example, and led to a friendship with Wordsworth). Within weeks of writing to the young poet, however, Price had developed such confidence in Barrett's intellectual powers that he asked her to read the proofs for his forthcoming *Essay on the Modern Pronunciation of the Greek and Latin Languages*, a task she rose to with skill and perception and not a small degree of over-confidence. Barrett's annotations to Price's manuscript frequently read as a battle of minds as the young girl sharply disagrees with the elderly scholar's reasoning, replying to his assertion that disyllabic spondees do not exist in English, for example, with the answer that they can be felt in Milton's poetry by 'any unlearned reciter who has feeling and a correct ear' (*BC* 1:258–9). Despite such disagreements on the technicalities of metre, however, their epistolary relationship was to continue for many years, with Barrett admiring Price as 'a new Nestor' who had revived the study of classical poetry (*BC* 2:42), and drawing upon his extensive knowledge in order to extend her own intellectual horizons.

However, it was rather the relationship with the blind scholar Hugh Stuart Boyd, a man who was both internationally revered for his classical knowledge and a notable poet in his own right, which would be more important for Barrett's development since he offered her a depth of intellectual engagement to which she had never before had access. Barrett and Boyd corresponded for a year – sometimes twice a day – before they eventually met, discussing the wide range of classical writings which Barrett was reading, including works by Theocritus, Nonnus, Hesiod, Homer, Sophocles, Euripides and Plato. She later regularly visited Boyd, acting as both his reader and amanuensis, and eagerly adopted a role not dissimilar to that of Milton's daughter to her blind mentor. Under his tutelage Barrett fully committed herself to the study of the language and culture of ancient Greece – she never had the same affinity to Latin, writing to her uncle Samuel as early as 1816, for example, that 'I do not like [Latin] at all, I think it twice as difficult as French, but I suppose like many stupid things, it is very useful' (BC 1:27) – and consequently developed an interest which, as the next chapter will demonstrate, would also foster her long-term concern with *contemporary* Greek affairs.

Recently, a number of critics have speculated about a deeper, perhaps even sexual attraction on Barrett's behalf for '[t]his God-loved man' as she called him ('Hugh Stuart Boyd: His Blindness', l.2) (see, for example, Dennis, 1996: 82–4; Forster, 1988: 56–9). Certainly her 1831–2 diary reveals what appears to be little short of a complete obsession with Boyd as entry after entry speculates on his real feelings for her and articulates her fears that she means no more to him than his other female readers. Indeed, many of the entries see her almost fashioning herself as a spurned lover and demonstrate her jealousy of Boyd's immediate family, critiquing Mrs Boyd, for example, as '[e]mpty minded, & without real *sensibility*—which extends to the tastes as well as to the feelings—frivolous and flippant. What a woman to be Mr Boyd's wife!' (D 48). As she wrote in August 1831, 'I am ashamed of writing down my own feelings & the causes of them' (D 84).

Whatever the truth of the relationship – and we can only speculate on it tentatively – it *is* certainly evident that Boyd offered Barrett the opportunity to study a wider range of classical writers and thinkers than most men would study at public school or university (as Bro noted, his exams at Charterhouse consisted solely of 'Homer parsing and construing [. . .] Ovid repetition [. . .] and Greek vocabulary', BC 1:166). Moreover, Boyd gave her an entrance into worlds of knowledge from which, as a young woman, she would normally be excluded. As she would write to her mentor in 1828, 'The eyes of your memory [. . .] are both microscopic & telescopic—& will see further than any eyes physical or intellectual, that I know anything about' (BC 2:147).

After both Barrett and Boyd had left Herefordshire, their relationship changed, but Barrett would always regard her teacher highly – it was to his house, for example, that she returned on the afternoon of her secret marriage to Robert in September 1846 – and in her commemorative sonnets to him written after his death in 1848, she remembered him as 'Steadfast friend,/ Who never didst my heart or life misknow,/ Nor either's faults too keenly apprehend' ('Hugh Stuart Boyd: His Death, 1848', ll.10–12). Certainly, through their studies together Boyd helped to fuel in Barrett that dissenting spirit towards established ideas which would also emerge in other areas of her early life.

THE POLITICS OF OPPOSITION

The study of classics was not the only traditionally male area of intellectual endeavour which the young Barrett sought to enter, since from an early age she was also deeply committed to politics and political thought, a commitment which, given the wide-ranging evidence, has received surprisingly little attention in studies of Barrett's youth. Barrett was born into a political world characterised by immense upheaval in the midst of the European wars against 'Little Boney', as France's imperial leader Napoleon was parodied in the British press, and one of her earliest extant notes, written when she was just six years old, asks her mother to convey to her father the latest information which she has gleaned from Bro on the war's progress: 'tell dear Papa the Rusians has beat the french killd 18.000 men & taken 14,000 prisoners' (sic, BC 1:9). Although the report is inaccurate – it was actually the Russians who were defeated at Smolensk – the note reveals an early attempt by Barrett to act as a mediator of political knowledge, a role she would continue to cultivate throughout her life. The note also reveals the central part which the Barrett men played in the development of Barrett's political thinking; indeed, throughout Barrett's youth and early womanhood, her father seems to have been particularly keen that his eldest daughter should be party to the political discussions in the house. Certainly, as she wrote to her father at the age of eight when he was away from home, she missed his tales of political events which she relied upon to break up the tedious monotony of existence in the household:

> Hope End in spite of the romantic prospects which environ it in spite of the beauty of beholding Nature wrapt in her bridal robe which we have at present IS dull and IS lonely[;] the sun rolls over our heads—no Papa is here to greet us with his hospitable smile—The moon shakes off her yoke—No whig to enliven our fire side hours with history of the election—.

(BC 1:45)

What is particularly interesting about this letter is the way in which the young Barrett depicts her father at the side of the hearth, that locus which, in established nineteenth-century gender ideologies, constituted the traditional domain of the dutiful middle-class wife. Barrett therefore already appears eager that political narratives rather than domestic concerns should take centre-stage in her drawing room, as they would in her aesthetic theories later on in her life. In *Aurora Leigh*, for example, she would write of her firm belief that her age possessed a substantial amount of 'heroic heat,/ Betwixt the mirrors of its drawing-rooms' (*AL* 5:205–6), a belief which quite possibly had its origins in the political debates she engaged in with her father and brother during these early years.

As this letter also makes explicit, Edward Barrett's political allegiance lay specifically with the Whigs, the party of opposition which he staunchly supported throughout his life. He campaigned vigorously for local Whig candidates such as Robert Price, son of Uvedale Price, for example, and regularly travelled to London to attend debates on national and international policy in the House of Commons. He was also elected High Sheriff of Herefordshire in 1812 and again in 1814 (one of Barrett's early poems addresses him as 'Mr Sheriff', *BC* 1:14), and was sworn in as Freeman and Guildmerchant of the City of Hereford in 1819. Such an enthusiasm for active political engagement was not confined to Barrett's father alone, however, but was shared by other men of the family. Edward's brother, Samuel Moulton-Barrett, for example, the uncle to whom Barrett Browning seems to have been particularly close, became Member of Parliament for Richmond in Yorkshire in 1820, a constituency he served for eight years, and Bro himself became a prominent speaker in the local debates preceding the passing of the 1832 Reform Act, a major Whig victory which, among its other terms, extended the franchise to the middle classes in a first step towards universal suffrage.

The Whig party to which Edward Barrett and his family subscribed had at the heart of its philosophy a fundamental concern with the legal, civil and religious rights of the individual, rights for which Barrett, like Wollstonecraft before her, would spend most of her life fighting. In particular, the Whigs sought to protect their code of civil rights from the actions of over-ambitious monarchs and statesmen and therefore, in direct opposition to the Tories' support for royal authority, they constantly pushed for a reduction in the political interest of the crown. This concern certainly comes through in Barrett's writings from the earliest works onwards. Already in 1815, for example, when only nine years old, she appears to have been considering the ambivalent nature of the monarchy when she wrote:

A King is a Man, the same as a Beggar; but their education is changed by
Fortune's gifts—we bow the knee before him, because we are bound by the
Word of God, saying, Fear God and honour the King.

(*HUP* 1:84)

Although on first reading this could appear to endorse something akin to the
divine right of kings (indeed, Edward Barrett scrawled underneath it 'the
rank sentiment of a Tory'), Barrett might already be drawing attention to
the problems of authoritarian power systems in her argument that we are
'bound' and oppressed by both religious and monarchical structures. Moreover, she suggests that the differences between classes are founded solely
upon materialism and processes of socialisation. Such an articulation of the
fragility and tyranny of authority, fundamental to both Whig philosophy and
Wollstonecraft's attack on the divine right of kings in *A Vindication of the
Rights of Woman*, would become a trope to which Barrett would repeatedly
return throughout her work.

Barrett's early commitment to Whig ideals is also evident in a letter of
outraged disgust she wrote when aged eleven to Herefordshire's Tory Lord
Lieutenant when the Habeas Corpus, the fundamental legal right of all individuals to a trial before imprisonment, was temporarily suspended in 1817.
And three years later, she scripted a short dramatic piece in support of
another key Whig cause, the persecuted Queen Caroline. In 1792 Caroline of
Brunswick had married the then Prince Regent who was, by many accounts,
a manipulative and licentious man. The couple separated in 1796, a few
months after the birth of their daughter Charlotte, and Caroline eventually
went to live on the Continent, from whence reports of indiscretions filtered
through to Britain, although suggestions of adultery were later deemed to
be false. Following the death of their daughter, however, and the Regent's
accession to the throne, the new King George IV sought to divorce Caroline
and have her excluded from the coronation. The very public scandal which
ensued only served to reinforce the low esteem with which much of the
populous held the monarchy in the wake of George III's propensity for
governing through political favourites, his madness, and his son's colourful
history, and subsequently most of the country came out on Caroline's side.
Of course, for the Whig Party this was a marvellous opportunity to reinforce
the idea of monarchical tyranny, and for Barrett herself the case was only
strengthened by the gender issues at stake. Consequently, in her unpublished
dramatic scene written in blank verse, she depicted a strongly emotional
farewell between Caroline and her daughter on the former's departure from
England in 1817. Writing when the divorce crisis was at its height in 1820,

Barrett constructs Caroline as at once a powerful proto-feminist figure, a dedicated mother and a strong moral guardian:

> CAROLINE: . . . not th'envenomed shaft of persecution,
>   Not the pestilential breath of malice,
>   Not the wiles of hate or of guile,
>   The foul abuse of wilful perjury,
>   Can rob this poor breast of that blessed calm,
>   Conscience. . . .
>
>   Yes, they may rend my heart with bitter pangs,
>   Torture my flesh and agonize my nerves,
>   Tear every sinew—I can mount superior.
>   Duty, oh Duty—tis the cherished tie
>   Which binds the sorrowing soul unto the world.

> (ll.121–6; 130–33, *HUP* 1:157)

Certainly, Whig sympathies for Queen Caroline must have been vocalised loudly within the Barrett family circle for even the five-year-old George seems to have taken up the cause, finishing a note to his eldest sister with the declaration 'I am very glad ou is for the Queen and ou say down king for he is very naughty' (*sic*, *BC* 1:118–19). And in her autobiographical essay 'Glimpses', Barrett would openly declare:

> At this period when the base & servile aristocracy of my beloved country overwhelm with insults our magnanimous and unfortunate Queen I cannot restrain my indignation I cannot controul my enthusiasm—The dearest wish of my heart would [be] to serve her . . to serve the glorious Queen of my native ilse [*sic*].

> (*BC* 1:353)

At this early age, then, as Barrett herself said, she was 'fiery in politics', a fieriness which would remain throughout her life and, as subsequent chapters will show, would inflect through much of her poetic writings. It is little wonder, then, that in 1821 Mary Barrett could suggest that her eldest daughter was suffering from 'the infection of politics' (*BC* 1:131), an image which wonderfully rewrites the mythologised image of the sickly poet.

EMBRACING DISSENT

Bound up with the Barrett family's Whiggish political persuasions was the issue of their religious convictions as non-conformists. The term 'non-conformist' was given to any nineteenth-century religious group which was outside the established Tory-aligned Church of England and which therefore sought to break away from the entrenched associations between church and state (see Chapter Six for further discussion). Edward Barrett regularly took his family to the nearby Anglican church, but he aligned himself far more with the dissenting Congregationalist (or Independent) sect, which emphasised faith as more of a *personal* encounter with God and argued that each congregation should be able to act independently and be free to manage its own affairs without submission to a higher theological authority. In its promotion of spiritual autonomy, therefore, Congregationalism, like the other religious sects which were part of the Evangelical Revivals of the late eighteenth and early nineteenth centuries, set itself up in opposition to the structured hierarchy of state-endorsed religion and thus became increasingly aligned with the Whig and, later, the emerging Liberal party.

Elizabeth Barrett herself was deeply religious from an early age, although frequently sceptical of established religious practices and services and the clergy in general. As she recorded in 'Glimpses', around the onset of puberty a religious fervour seemed to be taking her in a completely personal direction:

> At twelve [...] I was in great danger of becoming the founder of a religion of my own. I revolted at the idea of an established religion—my faith was sincere but my religion was founded solely on the imagination. It was not the deep persuasion of the mild Christian but the wild visions of an enthusiast. I worshipped God heart and soul but I forgot that my prayers should be pure & simple as the Father I adored[.] They were composed extempore & full of figurative & florid apostrophes.

> (*BC* 1:351)

Before long, however, Barrett returned to a more moderate devotion ('not so ardent but perhaps more reasonable than formerly', *BC* 1:353), and yet the sense of independent thinking and the individual's right to a personal approach to God and Christ remained with her throughout her life. While at Hope End, she at times attended both the Anglican and Congregationalist churches with her father, although she was to emphasise repeatedly the dullness and misguided preaching of the Anglican services in her diary:

> Went to Church, & took the sacrament. I wish the sacramental service were shortened, & weeded of its expressions '*holy mysteries*' &c. What mystery is there, can there be, in this simple rite? Are there not many weak brethren who shrink back from holy *mysteries*, and who wd. hurry on with a trembling joy to 'do this in remembrance' of their Lord?

> (*D* 139)

Consequently, therefore, Barrett took up the firm dissenting stand of staying at home to read and interpret the gospels by herself, conducting, as her protagonist in *Aurora Leigh* puts it, 'My prayers without the vicar' (*AL* 1:700). Indeed, she increasingly turned further away from any established doctrine and towards the idea of an all-inclusive church, devoid of segregation and theological conflict. As she wrote to Boyd in September 1834:

> I am so weary of controversy in religion [....] The command is—not, 'argue with one another.'—but, 'love one another'. It is better to love than to convince. They who lie on the bosom of Jesus, must lie there TOGETHER!
>
> (*BC* 3:98)

Similarly she wrote to Lady Margaret Cocks the same year, 'Should not Christians [...] cling to each other & love each other, for His sake who first loved them, whether they are dressed in white black or grey?' (*BC* 3:79). And by the early 1840s, Barrett was engaging in theological debate with the religious writer William Merry, a friend of Mary Russell Mitford, to whom she articulated her belief in a Universal Church of Christ, 'pure and undivided in the midst of the sects', meaning that any believer, 'dissenter or not, is *safe* in Christ' (*BC* 8:149).

Such openness about religion would ultimately lead to Barrett Browning's keen interest in spiritualism when she was living in Italy in the 1850s, but in a wider perspective, her early support for dissenting religion, as with her support for Whig politics, was bound up with that challenge to received ideas and the commitment to the freedom and dignity of the individual which she increasingly saw as fundamental to her life and writing. And yet, given certain darker elements in the Barrett family history, such a stance could not be completely unproblematic or unambiguous.

SKELETONS IN THE BARRETT CLOSET

Probably the most disturbing element of the Barrett family's history was the source of their substantial wealth: sugar plantations in Jamaica which were worked by slaves. For several generations, the family had been owners of plantations covering almost all the northern side of the island of Jamaica, including Barrett Town, which had originally been built up by Elizabeth's great-grandfather, known as Edward of Cinnamon Hill. On his death in 1798, Edward had bequeathed his empire to his grandsons, Elizabeth's father and her uncle Samuel, since all his own sons had died before him, and they continued to work the business for the next three decades. Similarly, the Graham-Clarkes, the line of Elizabeth's mother, also owned sugar plantations in the West Indies as well as a fleet of ships sailing between there and England. The beauty of Hope End, therefore, was incongruously founded upon systems of exploitation and massive disregard for human life.

Throughout much of Barrett's youth and early womanhood, her father travelled back and forth to Jamaica to supervise the plantations. But as Kelley and Hudson note, it is wrong to suggest that he was without any concern at all for the welfare of his slaves. In a letter to his estate manager, for example, he expressed his worry that the 'poor Negroes . . . should suffer any species of cruelty' and was clearly relieved to hear that they are being 'well taken care of and made to bear no unnecessary hardship' (*BC* 1:xxix). Of course, this concern could only be relative, for as Edward Barrett's words imply, the slaves would still suffer what was considered 'necessary' hardship. Indeed, as Forster has detailed in her biography of the poet, the brutality of the floggings and slave hunts on the Jamaican plantations was often horrific (Forster, 1988: 4–8).

The will of Edward of Cinnamon Hill which left the plantations to his legitimate grandsons was not unchallenged, however, and legal wrangling over its terms took thirty-six years. As Julia Markus has recently emphasised, the contesters were actually Edward of Cinnamon Hill's *illegitimate* children, six of whom were quadroon (Markus, 1995: 101), and in the early 1830s a double disaster struck the poet's father. Firstly, the legal wrangling over the will was finally settled, with the decision going against Edward Barrett, and secondly, the push for total slave emancipation which had started with the abolition act of 1807 was finally completed with slavery in the colonies being formally abolished. The results for the family were devastating. Edward lost a considerable amount of money and in order to survive on a lower income, he was forced to sell Hope End and move away from Herefordshire (the family would stay first in Sidmouth and then move to London in 1835).

At the time of the passing of the emancipation bill, Elizabeth Barrett wrote to her friend Julia Martin: 'Of course you know that the late bill has ruined the [white] West Indians. That is settled. The consternation here is very great.' Significantly, however, she added, 'Nevertheless I am glad, and always shall be, that the negroes are—virtually—free!' (*BC* 3:86). Barrett was always extremely concerned about the treatment of the slaves on which her own family's wealth was based, writing to Lady Margaret Cocks, for example, of the '*white* savages' in Jamaica (*BC* 3:101), and in a later letter to Robert during their courtship she expressed further her worries concerning her family's background: 'I would give ten towns in Norfolk (if I had them) to own some purer lineage than that of the blood of the slave! Cursed we are from generation to generation!' (*BC* 11:252)

This suggestion of slave blood within the family has recently been taken up by Julia Markus as a reason for Edward Barrett's tyrannical refusal to allow any of his children to marry. Markus argues that Edward feared that any slave blood which had entered the family line through the involvement of one of his ancestors with a black female plantation worker might reveal itself in any offspring his own children had (see Markus, 1995: 105–15). Although this might be seen as rather a tentative theory, it *is* true to say that the family's dependence on the exploitation of slaves was something which Elizabeth Barrett, given her Whiggish commitment to the rights of the individual, found extremely problematic and which she constantly tried to work through in her writings. Most obviously, of course, these issues would be dealt with in her powerful dramatic monologue 'The Runaway Slave at Pilgrim's Point', the first poem she wrote after running away to Italy with Robert (see Chapter Four). However, the issues of liberty and oppression which slavery raised and focused would be ones which would inflect through much of her thinking throughout her life.

READING THE DISSENTING BODY

Throughout this chapter, I have emphasised Elizabeth Barrett as a strong, powerful, dissenting thinker who frequently resisted established ideologies and who constantly chose to follow her own path. But how do we reconcile this narrative with the narrative of her sickening body and failing health? *Can* we reconcile them? In the introduction I suggested how Barrett's frail, disease-stricken, almost corpse-like body is central to her mythologisation. But as with many myths, there is also an element of truth here for throughout much of her life Barrett suffered a number of severely debilitating illnesses which at times left her unable to leave her bed or her room. These illnesses appear to have started in early 1821, when Barrett was just fifteen. All three female Barrett children almost simultaneously fell ill at this time but whereas Henrietta and Arabella soon recovered, Elizabeth continued to suffer from fainting, sickness and severe chest pain. A series of doctors and 'treatments' followed, which included Barrett being subjected to leeching, faecal examinations, and being strung up in a crib two feet off the floor following her complaints of a swollen spine. However, at this stage, as Forster has shown, the medical establishment appears to have had little sense of what really ailed Barrett and so set out to treat her '*as for* a diseased spine' (in Forster, 1988: 24; my italics). For her family, however, Barrett's first bout of illness seems to have taken on semi-mythic proportions. In a poem which Mary wrote for her daughter's birthday, for example, she constructs Barrett as a combination of an anguished poet laureate and the crucified Christ, enduring with patience 'the sad sufferings [which] entwine/ The cheering laurel, with thy couch of thorn' (*BC* 1:152), and as late as 1825, when Barrett's status as semi-invalid within the house seems to have become confirmed, Mary was still referring to the undiagnosed situation as '*the mystery*', reflecting that 'it must be impenetrable. Time seems to have no effect in unravelling it' (*BC* 1:229).

During the rest of her life, however, the illness *was*, at least in part, unravelled and became centred upon Barrett's lungs. The poet's breathing became severely affected by the fog in London, for example, and eventually resulted in her being sent to Torquay to convalesce at the end of the 1830s. Her health and the need for good air was also partly behind the choice of Italy as a home for herself and Robert once they were married. And yet in the pre-marriage years, it could be argued that her illness also offered her an opportunity to develop intellectually. I am not suggesting that Barrett's undiagnosed illnesses were psychosomatic in origin – the evidence of the harsh physical realities is far too strong for that. But it is true to say that the protracted nature of the recuperation freed her from many domestic concerns and social duties, and despite the recommendations of the medical establishment and the concerns of her family, she was able to continue reading and studying in her room, an opportunity denied many nineteenth-century women writers (compare Jane Austen hiding her manuscript each time the drawing-room door creaked open, for example, or the Brontë sisters' relegation of literary creativity to the hours after their father had retired to bed). Indeed, as Dennis argues, the situation 'gave her an excellent, if rarely acknowledged justification for her reluctance to take part in the obligations of Victorian women in the upper middle classes' (Dennis, 1996: 41). Barrett wrote to Boyd in December 1832, for instance, when she had nearly read the whole of the Bible in Hebrew tucked away in her room, '[Papa] does not know anything of my studying the little Hebrew which I do study, or I should be well scolded for it. Bro teaches Henry & Daisy their Latin, now' (*BC* 3:26). Furthermore, as time passed, her parents raised no questions when she did leave her room to go to church or visit Boyd. Between 1822 and 1837, when the illness struck heavily again, Barrett was able to live a relatively healthy and mobile life, but by then the family were used to their daughter's studious existence and left her to it unchallenged.

In this model of reading, therefore, Barrett's illness, while horrific at times in both its symptoms and treatment, also gave her valuable space for writing and study. Ironically, by being placed in an extreme version of the stereotype of weak femininity, she was able to propel herself out of such stereotypes through intellectual endeavour. The young advocate of Mary Wollstonecraft's theories was still very much alive and kicking within the dissenting body.

2
AUDACIOUS BEGINNINGS: ELIZABETH BARRETT'S EARLY WRITINGS

SIMON AVERY

In her autobiographical essay 'Glimpses into My Own Life and Literary Character' (1821), Elizabeth Barrett recorded how she was dedicated to poetry almost from the time she could write: 'At four I first mounted Pegasus [the horse which was the classical symbol of poetry] but at six I thought myself privileged to show off feats of horsemanship' (*BC* 1:349). At first these 'feats' expressed themselves in birthday poems written for members of her family, thereby allowing Barrett to fulfil the role of '*Poet laureat* [*sic*] *of Hope End*', as her father christened her (*BC* 1:350; see Chapter One). These works are usually highly derivative, their content stylised and drawing upon many of the images and conventions which Barrett has taken from her reading of Augustan and Romantic poets. Lute and lyre, muse and cherub, bower and 'hill of verdant green' (*BC* 1:93), along with a host of mythological referents and personified abstractions, predominate throughout, thereby belying the poet's assertion to her father that within her 'lowly lay[s],/ No studied tropes, or hacknied types appear' (*BC* 1:125).

Remarkably, Barrett continued to write these inter-textual, self-referential poems for over fourteen years, only ceasing with the death of her mother in 1828 – 'nascent odes [. . .] crying aloud on obsolete Muses from childish lips', as she later disparagingly termed them (*BC* 7:353). At the same time, however, she was beginning to write short poems focusing on those areas which would interest her throughout her life: politics and gender. I have already discussed Barrett's early poetic drama on Queen Caroline and her 'Essay on Woman' in Chapter One, but contained within H. Buxton Forman's 1914 collection, *Hitherto Unpublished Poems and Stories of Elizabeth Barrett Browning*, are a number of other works of interest which have been ignored in recent criticism. One of Barrett's very first poems, for example, written some time before 1814 according to Buxton's structuring of the material, focuses on 'The Cruelty of Forcement to Man; Alluding to the Press Gang':

Ah! the poor lad in yonder boat
Forced from his Wife, his Friends, his home,
Now gentle Maiden how can you
Look at the misery of his doom?

(*HUP* 1:31)

While this is, of course, an extremely rudimentary work, it nevertheless
points to the concern with personal liberty which, in various forms, Barrett
would interrogate throughout her career and which is also reflected in those
poems in this collection which relate to the position of women. Time and
again female figures are depicted living at the margins of society – 'Loft on
the top of that high hill a lonely cottage stood' (*HUP* 1:33), 'Upon the
boundaries of a lofty Wood' (1:33) – or roaming 'the hungry deserts' as with
the women and children survivors in 'On the Eruption of Mount Etna, 8th
May 1814' (significantly there are no men in this poem). Where a woman
might attempt to claim independence for herself, almost invariably she is
dead by the poem's close, as in the following piece of August 1814:

Down in the Vale, a little cottage stood,
Surrounded by a spacious Wood,
Where Anna lived in blooming pride,
And on her Maker only, she relied.
When wandering out, one early Morn,
Thro' the Wood, and tangled thorn;
The ushering birds sang in the day,
For it was then the month of May. . . .
Now hours passed on, the dark night drew,
She heard a rustling noise—she flew,
But in her breast a dagger felt,
When falling on her knees—she knelt—
'Thy will be done, great God', she said,
'Of grim death I am not afraid,
'During life, I've done Thy will,
'And now in Death I love Thee still.'
Then gently fell her head—she sighed,
And falling on the earth—she died!

(*HUP* 1:55–6)

The bathos of the final two lines here suggests that Barrett might be satirising a standard trope of Romantic sentimental verse, but embedded in the
rest of the poem appears to be a warning against female transgression contained within a fairy-tale-like narrative. For there certainly seems to be a clear

connection being drawn in this poem between Anna's pride and staunch independence and her final fate at the hands of the evil within the woods. Despite her attempt to justify her life to God, she dies a violent death in an environment which, as in many fairy tales, seems to be associated with a psychological wilderness.

Of course, these poems are early experiments as the young poet attempts to discover a voice for herself, but the concerns with independence, politics and gender which they raise were to become central to Elizabeth Barrett's entire *oeuvre*. In the remainder of this chapter, then, I will investigate how these specific concerns were developed in Barrett's first three formal volumes: *The Battle of Marathon* (1820), *An Essay on Mind, and Other Poems* (1826) and *Prometheus Bound, and Miscellaneous Poems* (1833). These volumes have often been overlooked in studies of Barrett's work, with a number of critics viewing them as mere apprentice pieces before the poet finally found her true voice in the highly acclaimed collection *Poems*, published in 1844 (see Chapter Four). What I want to suggest here, however, is that there is far more of a *continuity* between these volumes and the later work than has often been suggested and that it is these earliest works which provide the foundation for Barrett's subsequent development into one of the nineteenth century's most powerful poets.

BATTLING WITH HOMER

Elizabeth Barrett's first major literary work, *The Battle of Marathon*, was privately printed at her father's expense in 1820, when she was just fourteen years old. To begin publishing at so young an age was not uncommon for nineteenth-century women poets – Felicia Hemans published her first volume at fifteen years old, for example, and Christina Rossetti published hers at seventeen – and yet there is a clear difference which marks out Barrett's work from those of her poetic sisters. For rather than the short lyrics on love, nature and religion which make up the majority of Hemans and Rossetti's volumes, Barrett's first work is nothing less than a four-book epic of over fourteen hundred lines which takes as its focus one of the crucial military campaigns of ancient Greece, the Athenian victory over the tyrannical imperialism of the Persian Empire on the plains of Marathon in 490BC.

Clearly this was a remarkable and audacious beginning for a young girl and one which arose out of Barrett's increasing love of the language and literature of ancient Greece (see Chapter One). Specifically, the main inspiration for *The Battle of Marathon* came from Barrett's reading of Alexander Pope's translation of Homer's *The Iliad* (1726), a text which became central to the renaissance in Homer scholarship at the end of the eighteenth century and which was subsequently admired by many of the Romantic poets. As Barrett wrote to Richard Hengist Horne in 1843, the images of Pope's *Iliad* caught her imagination so completely that '[t]he Greeks were my demi-gods, & haunted me [...] until I dreamt oftener of Agamemnon than of Moses [my] black poney [*sic*] (*BC* 7:353). Indeed, as the Preface to *The Battle of Marathon* indicates, through the *Iliad* she came to consider Homer 'the sublime Poet of antiquity' and Pope 'that magnificent translator' who combines 'elegance with strength, and sublimity with beauty' (*CW* 1:4; 8).

In the same letter to Horne, however, Barrett laments that Pope's influence so overpowered her own work that *Battle* proved to be little more than 'a Pope's Homer done over again ... or rather *undone*' (*BC* 7:353), a reading which has often been taken up by critics as a way of dismissing the poem as mere juvenilia or the kind of imitation exercise which Harold Bloom in *The Anxiety of Influence* (1973) suggests forms the first stage of a writer's literary development. Already by 1888, for example, John Ingram could argue that *Battle* 'can scarcely be taken into account in any chronicle of her literary deeds' (11), while in the late twentieth century Deirdre David termed the poem 'highly derivative' (1987: 100) and Pam Hirsch called it one of several 'rehashes of works by male authors' thought to constitute Barrett's early works (1995: 121).

What is missing from these assessments, however, is any consideration of the ways in which Barrett repeatedly downplayed her writings both privately and publicly as a means of locating herself within the literary marketplace and masking the subversive potential of many of her pieces. In the preface to *Battle*, for example, she repeatedly castigates the work as 'my little poem' (*CW* 1:7; 10) and a 'humble attempt' offered to those who might 'condescend' to read it (1:3), a strategy she would use time and again in her prefaces. Equally important, however, is the way in which such condemnation of *Battle* as mere imitation ignores the fact that her subject is itself an original one, drawn from Barrett's own readings in Herodotus' *Histories* and Charles Rollin's *Ancient History* (originally published, 1730–38). Rather than Homer's concentration on the final moments of the Trojan War in the epic dark ages, then, Barrett chooses to focus on a central moment in Greece's transition to a democratic state as the Athenians defend their city against invasion in an unprecedented show of solidarity.

Barrett's choice of this particular subject at this particular historical moment was highly significant, for during the first two decades of the nineteenth century the political situation in Greece was an issue of great concern across Europe. Since the fifteenth century the country had been under Turkish rule, at first benignly as the Ottoman administration permitted various freedoms in terms of commerce, education and religion, but then in

the eighteenth century the Turks became increasingly authoritarian and corrupt. From the 1770s onwards a number of small uprisings marked Greece's
growing discontent, and following the spread of nationalist ideals initiated
by the French Revolution, greater moves were made towards independence both in Greece itself through political awareness and education, and in
other countries through the formation of societies such as the *Philiki Etairia*
(Greek Friendly Society of Odessa), which worked to collect funds and send
volunteers to Greece in order to achieve, in the *Philiki Etairia*'s rallying call,
liberation of the 'Motherland' (Clogg, 1992: 32).

This wider European philhellenism was driven in large part by liberal
intellectuals seeking to assist the plight of the country which they associated
with the world of their classical studies and which they still considered to be
one of the centres and origins of Western culture. In particular, many poets
were important in the spreading of philhellenic ideas, including Percy Shelley
(*Hellas*), Byron (*Childe Harold's Pilgrimage*) and Felicia Hemans (*Modern
Greece*), and I would argue that we should include the young Barrett within
this grouping given the focus of a number of her early works. For although
there are no direct references to contemporary Greece in *The Battle of
Marathon*, the poem centres upon a pivotal moment of Greek democratic
and martial glory and would therefore clearly reflect upon the lamentable
state of the country's present decline. Indeed, that Barrett identified this
connection is evident in a letter to her mother in 1819 where she writes:

> Mr McSwiney believes Greece to surpass Rome in every respect but in con-
> quests he says that tho she is trodden under foot by the Turks yet even in the
> countenance of the inhabitan[t]s she bears the marks of her former greatness
> of soul virtue & grandeur he says she is conquered but still 'virtue' is not
> banished what can be more favourable to my DARLING project.

> (*BC* 1:70–1)

In the preface to the poem, too, Barrett would express her sense of the
enormous resonances which her subject matter would have for its readers:

> Who can be indifferent, who can preserve his tranquillity, when he hears
> of one little city rising undaunted, and daring her innumerable enemies, in
> defence of her freedom—of a handful of men overthrowing the invaders,
> who sought to molest their rights and to destroy their liberties? Who can hear
> unmoved of such an example of heroic virtue, of patriotic spirit, which seems
> to be crying from the ruins of Athens for honour and immortality?

> (*CW* 1:6)

From the very start of her career, then, Barrett's work had a strong political dimension and the choice of epic as the form for *The Battle of Marathon* only served to reinforce this. For in its pure Hellenistic origins, as well as later European reconfigurations, the epic traditionally focused on a male hero who saves the fate of a nation or race through a series of arduous tasks. The genre is therefore highly androcentric, almost celebrating what could be termed a cult of masculinity, and this, together with its traditional status as one of the most revered of literary forms, meant that it was viewed by most male critics as being beyond the capabilities of a woman. Indeed, relatively few nineteenth-century women poets attempted to write an epic, even at the height of their powers. Two exceptions to this rule of silence are Caroline Bowles, who wrote *A Birthday* (1836), an epic based on the development of a woman writer, and Mathilde Blind, who wrote *The Ascent of Man* (1889), an epic based on evolutionary theory, but both have been all but forgotten by literary history (see Avery 2000). Of course, it would be Elizabeth Barrett herself who would make the most significant contribution to women's epic writing in the nineteenth century with *Aurora Leigh* (1856), but it is arguable that this poem could not have been so impressively written had she not first schooled herself in the traditional conventions and structures of epic at the early stage of *The Battle of Marathon* where invocations to the muse, epic similes, the machinery of the gods, and stock scenes such as the hero's preparation for battle all figure. This fact alone demands that we rethink her earliest work, but interestingly, what is also revealed in *Battle* is an initial attempt by Barrett to undercut the overtly androcentric world of her epic inheritance. For in this poem, the young writer offers an incisive interrogation and critique of the pre-democratic battle culture of Homeric epic, and explores the means by which a new, more democratic leadership can be brought about by a substantial reconfiguring of dominant ideologies. As the poem makes explicit, however, this progression to a new democratic civic state is far from a simple process.

TOWARDS A NEW DEMOCRACY

In *The Battle of Marathon*'s opening invocation to the muse, a convention which traditionally summarises the poem's events, a seemingly clear-cut binary is established between the Athenians and the invading Persians, constructing the Athenians in terms of martial glory, honour and artistic excellence, and the Persians in terms of barbarity, violence and tyranny. This binary is then reasserted in the closing pages of the poem and yet throughout much of the intervening narrative, these oppositions keep threatening to break down in ways which serve to remind the reader, and the Greeks themselves, of the former power systems out of which, and against which, Athenian democracy is trying to define itself. In Book One of the poem, for example, a messenger arrives from Darius, the Persian king, seeking earth and water from the Greeks as symbols of submission to Darius' rule. Instead of merely receiving a rebuke, however, he is promptly executed by Aristides, the Athenian leader, in a scene of graphic vividness which highlights the masculinist codes of violence, rather than diplomacy and negotiation, which still underlie Athenian military thought:

'Hence, from yon gulf the earth and water bring
And crown with victory your mighty King.'
He [Aristides] said—and where the gulf of death appeared
Where raging waves, with rocks sublimely reared,
He hurled the wretch at once of hope bereaved;
Struggling he fell, the roaring flood received.
E'en now for life his shrieks, his groans implore,
And now death's latent agony is o'er,
He struggling sinks, and sinks to rise no more.

(ll.259–67)

In Book Two of the poem, Barrett builds on this scene by foregrounding the fact that such violence lies at the very heart of the Athenian political world, the Senate itself, when one of the generals, Clombrutus, incites an attack against authority on little more than a whim. On his calling the other warriors to arms in an act of rebellion, 'Ten thousand swords [. . .] in one instant raised,/ Sublime they danced aloft, and midst the Senate blazed' (ll.489–90).

It is this omnipresent mentality of violence which must be worked through, the poem suggests, if the progress to democracy and a new civic state is to be achieved. The way forward, Barrett argues, is through the actions of a persuasive leader who can bring about unity of thought and purpose among the *popularis* and thereby lead the Athenians out of the confusion and barbarity associated with the older, fragmented Hellenistic order: in short, the type of hero figure which, promoted by Thomas Carlyle in his lectures on Heroes and Hero-Worship, would become central to Barrett's social and political thinking in her later writing (see Chapters Four and Seven, for example).

One of the Athenian leaders who takes a central role in *The Battle of Marathon* is Miltiades, a figure who, Barrett Browning would have known from her reading of Herodotus (*Histories* VI:46–51), had previously been in the service of the Persian king, acting as a tyrannical imperial ruler over the

Greeks in Thrace. By the opening of *Battle*, however, Miltiades has been resident in Athens for a number of years, renowned as an elderly statesman and a great sage who will subsequently become the architect of the Marathon victory. From the basis of tyranny and authoritarianism, Barrett appears to imply here, can emerge the fruits of justice and democracy through wisdom and diplomacy.

More specifically, however, the path to democracy lies, the poem suggests, with a greater fluidity of traditional gender characteristics. In Chapter One I explored how Barrett reacted against the restrictions associated with pre-scribed models of gendered behaviour from an early age. The need for the reconfiguration of gender stereotypes would then become central to much of her work and is evident, albeit in a rudimentary form, even in the early *Battle of Marathon* where the achievement of a new democracy appears to be specifically linked to the generals' readiness to express emotion through tears. The shedding of tears by the epic hero was not, of course, outside the scope of epic conventions, but whereas Homer only allows Achilles in the *Iliad* to cry when alone and at the margins of society, Barrett brings the act centre-stage, right into the very heart of society, with both Aristides and Themistocles breaking down in tears in public in a way which signals a new empathy with the people. Along the same lines, Aristides moves further from the earlier barbarity of the scene where he killed the messenger by developing a more nurturing stance, offering himself to the *popularis* in the combined roles of 'Chief, Guardian, Father, Friend' (l.540). Throughout, these recon-figurations are importantly seen to *complement* masculinity and heroic status rather than detract from it, and are usually celebrated by the other warriors as a collective shift in thinking occurs.

Significantly, however, Elizabeth Barrett also uses *female* figures to challenge socially endorsed gender roles in this text. In traditional Hellenic epic, women were never major protagonists but were often constructed as sorceresses or temptresses (for example, Circe in *The Odyssey*), forsaken lovers (Dido in *The Iliad*), or shadowy, peripheral figures. Many of the women in *The Battle of Marathon* follow similar trajectories, being cast into roles as dutiful wives and the bearers of (male) offspring, or incarcerated in marginalised social spaces which represent their ostracisation from the political structures of Athens:

> The gates, the heroes pass, th'Athenian dames
> Bend from their towers, and bid them save from flames
> Their walls, their infant heirs, and fill the skies
> With shouts, entreaties, prayers, and plaintive cries . . .

(ll.908–11)

Women are granted a voice in the public sphere, these lines suggest, only to remind men of their positions of power. And yet out of the communal 'shouts . . . and . . . cries' of the women rises the voice of the 'matron chief' Delopeia (l.727), whose persuasive rhetoric and rational arguments are more effective than any male voice in convincing Miltiades and the other generals of the necessity of swiftly issuing to battle against the Persians:

> Oh Son of Cimon, for the Grecians raise
> To heaven, thy fame, thy honour, and thy praise.
> Thus—thus—shall Athens and her heroes fall,
> Shall thus one ruin seize and bury all?
> Say, shall these babes be strangers then to fame,
> And be but Greeks in spirit and in name?
> Oh first, ye Gods! and hear a mother's prayer,
> First let them glorious fall in ranks of war!
> If Asia triumph, then shall Hippias reign
> And Athens' free-born Sons be slaves again!
> Oh Son of Cimon! let thy influence call
> The souls of Greeks to triumph or to fall!
> And guard their own, their children's, country's name,
> From foul dishonour, and eternal shame!

(ll.731–44)

In this powerful speech, Delopeia argues that the honour and renown of Greece should not be compromised through lack of action, adding weight to her oration by holding her baby in the air as she speaks and therefore transforming her maternal role into a political one (a reversal of Aristides' tempering his public political role with a more nurturing stance). This technique of using children and motherhood to reflect upon contemporary political issues was one which Barrett, along with a number of other nineteenth-century women poets, would employ throughout her writings (compare 'The Cry of the Children' and Casa Guidi Windows, for example), and although Delopeia here attempts to draw attention away from her powerful polemics by stressing that her rhetoric is nothing more than a 'mother's prayer' (l.730), her political awareness is clearly highlighted. As the narrative voice comments, 'The mother wept, but 'twas the Patriot spoke' (l.746), a political model which is clearly far more positive in Barrett's thinking than overwhelming masculinist violence.

It is possible, therefore, to take issue with the limited readings of The Battle of Marathon which argue that it 'seems in every way an act of homage to male values and male culture' (Mermin, 1989: 24) or that the female poetics evident in Barrett's later works are 'singularly absent' here (Stone, 1995:

Battle may be an early poem by a girl aged only fourteen but even at this stage Barrett is starting to work with some of the more unconventional ideas about gender roles and power structures which characterised her understanding of the world. Indeed, in her depiction of the supernatural realm and the epic machinery of the gods, Barrett specifically celebrates the figure of Minerva, the patron deity of the Athenians who occupies a cross-gendered position as the goddess of warfare, wisdom and intelligence, *and* spinning and weaving, thereby reinforcing Barrett's thesis that successful engagement in the political sphere is linked to a successful combining of traditionally 'male' and 'female' characteristics. Certainly the figures of Delopeia and Minerva point the way towards the more explicitly revolutionary female protagonists such as Aurora Leigh found in Barrett's later work.

The Battle of Marathon therefore maps out a movement towards greater tolerance and liberty and a new collective consciousness embodied within a democratic framework. This is eventually achieved within the final book of the poem which depicts the actual battle itself on the plains of Marathon. Here, a much clearer distinction is drawn between the Persians and the Athenians than has previously been evident. While the Persians rampage round the battlefield, constructed by Barrett through images of terror and anarchy (Darius 'whirls his chariot over heaps of dead/ . . . /For blood he gasps', ll.1400–2), the Athenians are presented with a new collective and democratic identity as they pull together under the tolerant and judicious leadership of Aristides, who has been reconfigured into the type of Carlylean hero Barrett would favour in her later writings. And even on the battlefield, that most masculinised arena of traditional Hellenic epic, Barrett reiterates the importance of female qualities through both the presence and guidance of Minerva and the topography itself, which is figured as a 'labouring plain' that 'groans', an image pattern suggesting an expectant mother in the throes \f giving birth. This early recourse to the gendering of landscape and the use ʻhe kind of 'women's figures' which would become crucial to *Aurora Leigh* ꞈsts that the delivery of a new political state is no easy task. As Barrett in this first major poem, as she would throughout her subsequent this can only be achieved by a commitment to humanitarianism, ᴜnd political and sexual egalitarianism.

꞉E BATTLES OF MARATHON AND PETERLOO

previous section that *The Battle of Marathon* can be ʻhellenic text, for in articulating the emergence of a new democracy, the poem could be seen to reflect upon the qualities needed by a successful leader of modern Greece if the goal of independence is to be achieved. However, the poem also takes on other resonances if we consider events which were occurring in Britain at the time of its composition, for Barrett was predominantly writing and editing this poem during 1819, a year of major political crisis.

The years since the end of the Napoleonic Wars in 1815 had been marked in Britain by economic hardship and increasing agitation for wider suffrage and parliamentary and legislative reform, with demonstrations frequently occurring across the country. In August 1819, one of these demonstrations was organised at St Peter's Field, Manchester, and was attended by over 60,000 people. All was progressing peacefully until Henry 'Orator' Hunt, a known radical, took the stand to call for wider freedoms, at which point the Manchester magistrates panicked and ordered in the yeomanry to disperse the demonstrators. In the turmoil which ensued from the yeomanry's brutal attack, eleven people lost their lives and over four hundred were wounded.

The event became known as the Peterloo Massacre, in an obvious parody of Waterloo, and it sent shockwaves throughout the country. Many radicals viewed Peterloo as nothing less than the final call to take up weapons against an oppressive establishment, while the Whigs, whose party had become increasingly fragmented in recent years, were brought back into a cohesive group in their challenge to the government over the incident. Subsequently, Liverpool's Tory administration, fearing the beginnings of something akin to the French Revolution, responded by implementing the infamous Six Acts, some of the most draconian and repressive legislation of the nineteenth century, which prohibited public gatherings without the permission of local authorities, gave magistrates increased powers to search private property for arms, and imposed further restrictions on the freedom of the press by banning any publication likely to incite hatred or contempt of the government. It was, as all parties quickly realised, an opportunity for the ruling powers to close down freedom of speech and deny fundamental aspects of human liberty.

Nevertheless, as James Chandler has shown in his study *England in 1819*, the year of Peterloo was exceptional for the volume of literary work published, much of it founded upon a 'new and urgent sense of contemporaneity' as it struggled to find new ways of representing the historical moment (Chandler, 1998: 2; xv). In particular, of course, 1819 was the year of Shelley's writing of *Prometheus Unbound*, *The Cenci*, 'Ode to the West Wind', 'The Mask of Anarchy' and perhaps that most (in)famous representation of the year, his sonnet 'England in 1819'. It is within this framework that I would suggest we can also re-read Elizabeth Barrett's *The Battle of*

Marathon, for the young politically alert Whig supporter is likely to have drawn the connection between contemporary events in Britain conducted by a government acting in increasingly authoritarian fashion, and the ancient nation she was writing about rising up in solidarity to overcome another example of tyrannous authoritarianism. Certainly, in returning to the events in the Attic state which she explores in *Battle*, Barrett would have been able to reflect and covertly pass judgement upon the political position of her own country.

Through these lines of argument, then, it is possible to recover *The Battle of Marathon* from its position on the margins of Barrett's *oeuvre* and resituate it as an initial political text which interrogates many of the concerns Barrett would continue to explore throughout her career: the fight for democracy and liberty from tyrannical oppressors, the nature of leadership, and the need for gender equality if society is to function healthily. It is these issues which she would return to in a more contemporary setting in her next published work.

THE LYRIC VOICE OF GREEK INDEPENDENCE

As *The Battle of Marathon* was being printed in 1820, much of continental Europe was entering a new revolutionary phase as insurrectionary groups in Spain, Naples and Portugal rose up against their oppressors in a bid for national independence. Each of these uprisings was defeated but in 1821 the one revolution which would eventually succeed began to take shape in Greece. The Greek War of Independence was to continue until 1830 and, given Barrett's hatred of one country occupying another by force and her love of all things Hellenic, it is hardly surprising that she was gripped by the revolutionary events from the start. Indeed, as Barrett would later write to Boyd, she had trouble understanding why *any* enlightened person wouldn't be rushing to support the Greeks in their bid for liberty:

> Really, when you call the Greeks 'savage monsters' and profess a total want of interest in their emancipation from the Turkish yoke I wonder Æschylus does not let loose his Furies upon you. They must be *snoring* VERY hard! [....] The Greeks are Greeks by name & soil & descent [....] I have a regard for the very earth & air—& would not have tyrants breathe where poets stand,—or slaves tread in the footsteps of heroes!—

(*BC* 2:108–9)

The role which Barrett believed she should adopt in relation to these political events is reflected in the short semi-autobiographical prose piece on Beth which she wrote in the early 1840s. I have already discussed part of this piece in relation to issues of femininity in Chapter One, but connected to Beth's anti-establishment stance are her two specifically philhellenic ambitions. The first of these is to become nothing less than the greatest woman poet who ever lived, what she terms 'the feminine of Homer', or even, she smirks, 'a little taller than Homer if anything' (*BC* 1:361). Her second ambition is then to use this position of powerful poet for specifically *political* ends. As she details, she will

> arm herself in complete steel (Beth always thought of a suit of armour & never of a red coat) & ride on a steed, along the banks of the Danube [...] sing[ing] her own poetry all the way she went . . . [and] attracting to her side many warriors—so that by the time she reached Stambol, Beth wd. be the chief of a battalion & she wd. destroy the Turkish empire, & deliver 'Greece the glorious'.
>
> (*BC* 1:361)

Beth's ambitions here are clearly analogous to Barrett's own ambitions in the early 1820s: to march in the front line of political debate, urging others to join her cause through the medium of her song/poetry, and thus help to restore the liberty of 'Greece the glorious'. Certainly, given that it is the men who are 'led' in Beth's narrative, this was an arena in which Barrett felt women could make a significant contribution.

It is highly significant, therefore, that Barrett's first formally published poems deal explicitly with the Greek War of Independence. 'Stanzas, excited by some reflections on the present state of Greece', which appeared in the May 1821 edition of the Whiggish *New Monthly Magazine* just two months after the outbreak of the war, and 'Thoughts awakened by contemplating a piece of palm which grows on the summit of the Athenian Acropolis', which appeared in the July edition, both lament the decline of the country which was once 'The Conqueror of the World, the Parent of the Free' ('Thoughts'), depicting her as a dying woman bound in chains, her heroic and mythical figures long departed and her native muses silenced. (Interestingly, Barrett would later condemn such images when used in relation to Italy's oppression by the Austrians in *Casa Guidi Windows*: see Chapter Seven.) Despite the fact that these poems are heavily stylised in their use of such philhellenic tropes, Barrett's voice has an urgency which reveals her strong commitment to the Greek cause:

Yes! I have loved thee [Greece]—and my youthful soul
    Hath wildly dreamt of glory, and of thee—
Burst the proud links of man's severe controul,
    And sprung to sojourn with the great and free!
Oh! who would not thy vot'ry, Grecia, be?
    And I have hung upon th'enchanted page
Entranced,—and wept thy fallen liberty—
    Till my breast thrill'd with all the patriot's rage,
    And soar'd aloft, to greet the hero, poet, sage.

(ll.10–18)

Barrett's third published poem on the Greek war, however, opens up further debates concerning her view of her role as political commentator at this time, for it commemorates the death of one of her greatest heroes and influences, George Gordon, Lord Byron. Like Barrett herself, Byron was from a privileged background and committed to the Whig party. He was also the greatest English champion of the Greek cause, which he explored over a number of years in the Cantos of his epic *Childe Harold*, a work which Barrett argued possessed great 'imaginative passion & invention' (*BC* 2:132), before he travelled to Greece in person in order to help defeat the Turks.

Byron's subsequent death in Missolongi in April 1824 marked him out as a liberal hero-martyr and further roused European sympathy for the Greeks. Indeed, as Wallace argues, 'his idealised symbolic death was more powerful than all the thousands dying on real battlefields' (1997: 192). Certainly Barrett's 'Stanzas on the Death of Lord Byron', a work which was originally published in *The Globe and Traveller*, almost deifies the poet-politician, equating him with his own hero Childe Harold ('Harold's pilgrimage at last is o'er', l.3) and constructing him as 'the great Deliv'rer' (l.7) who arrives, myth-like, riding the Ægean waves before 'Expiring in the land he only lived to save!' (l.9). At his death, Barrett suggests, Greece is left 'widow'd' (l.10) and the power of language, communication and song is withdrawn from the land ('Mute the impassioned tongue, and tuneful shell', l.4). In her elegy, therefore, Barrett equates the death of Byron with the death of the Greek spirit itself.

Although Barrett later told Boyd that these early poems on Greece were 'much too interjectional, & too little comprehensible' (*BC* 2:225), she was already clearly setting herself up as a commentator on contemporary Greek affairs – and this when still only in her mid-teens. And it was this role which she would subsequently develop in her major work of the 1820s, *An Essay on Mind*, where both the figure of Byron and the Hellenic question became part of a wider exploration of the issues of intellectual and physical liberty.

THE POWER OF LIBERAL KNOWLEDGE:
AN ESSAY ON MIND

An Essay on Mind is an astonishingly complex poem, nearly thirteen hundred lines long, in which Barrett sets herself the task of producing nothing less than an exploration of genius, that 'Prometheus of our earth' as she terms it (*CW* 1:64). In its length and erudition, the poem clearly reveals a young poet affirming her vocation and starting to establish an original voice, and although Barrett would later dismiss the work, lamenting its 'imitative form', she nevertheless argued, using an apt birthing image, that the volume was 'not without traces of an individual thinking and feeling—the bird pecks through the shell of it' (*BC* 7:354).

The form which Barrett uses for this poem is not the mini-epic or the lyric she had previously employed, but the poetic essay which Pope had developed in the eighteenth century as a vehicle for philosophical discussion. Just as much as Byron, therefore, Pope was one of Barrett's earliest influences, both as translator and original poet, and she adapts his essay form here in order to undertake a comparative assessment of the disciplines of history, science, philosophy and poetry. The range and depth of allusions to practitioners in these fields is startling, revealing Barrett's vast reading and learning, but this is no abstract survey lacking an overarching argument, for underlying Barrett's explorations is a specific concern with the power and politics of knowledge. In particular, Barrett suggests how intellectual flexibility and freedom of the mind can lead to liberal political thought and how this, in turn, can help bring about *physical* freedom from oppressive regimes. The overall movement of the poem, therefore, is from narrow introspection to more wide-ranging, synthesising thought, from a mind concerned only with the local to a mind concerned with the political.

The poem begins by offering a series of strategies for empowering the mind and celebrating the freedom of thought which can itself be transgressive and 'revolutionary'. In Book One, then, Barrett is particularly concerned with warning individuals to be wary of received wisdoms and to question, like she herself constantly questioned, anything which might be paraded as 'Truth', since Truth, she points out, is always relative and often presented 'in masquerade' (1.345). As I noted in Chapter One, for example, Barrett's discussion of the nature of history in this poem emphasises the value of learning moral messages from the past ('let the dead instruct thee how to live', 1.225), but simultaneously warns readers to be attentive to the biases of historians who, through an allegiance to their own 'peculiar school' (1.306), might 'use the truth to illustrate a lie' (1.267).

At the centre of these debates is Barrett's insistence throughout the text on the need to see a wider picture, to assess ideas in their broadest terms and see their interconnections rather than getting caught up in detail. '*Dwell not on parts!*' she counsels before using an apt image of imprisonment to argue that 'parts contract the mind' (l.535). Rather, she emphasises that we should question, judge, evaluate, contest, and thereby achieve independence of thought and more perceptive, even original, ways of viewing the world. As Barrett wrote to Boyd the year after *Essay* was published, 'I should be sorry to walk on a beaten path merely because it was *beaten*' (*BC* 2:35).

In the second half of Book One and the first part of Book Two, then, Barrett expands on this thesis through a range of examples of scholars who suffered from partiality, from too fixed an idea or from intellectual hubris. Scientists, according to Barrett, seem to be particularly prone to this, as she cites the examples of Archimedes being killed because of his lack of awareness of anything outside his own work or the German physicians Spurzheim and Gall whose work in the field of phrenology she dismisses with a scoff of ridicule ('Will reasoning curs leave logic for a bone?' l.738). Scientists all too often 'Interpret parts, and misconceive the whole' and yet they are not alone, for metaphysicians too can be so caught up in limited debates that they are unaware of 'the crash of worlds,—the fall of kings' (l.611).

Out of this condemnation of narrow thinking, however, arise three men whom Barrett applauds for their impartiality, daring and intellectual flexibility, those qualities which she would always align with the hero figure. After critiquing scientists in general, she concludes Book One of the poem by pointing to the exceptional example of 'Divinest Newton' (l.589), whom she honours for his humanitarianism and modesty: 'Too wise, to think his human folly less;/ Too great, to doubt his proper littleness;/ . . . /Endow'd with all of Science—but its pride' (ll.595–600). The Enlightenment poets often attacked Newton for destroying the mystery of the universe (see, for example, Keats' 'Lamia'), but Barrett, following her own agenda, sees a wider picture and praises Newton as the 'bright example' of scientific disinterestedness (l.592). Similarly, she praises Bacon as the 'Sublime Columbus of the realms of mind' (l.869), using the kind of exploratory image she often employed in depicting liberal thinking, and John Locke, 'noblest in my song' (l.893), whom she commends for his refusal to 'rise by faction, or to crouch to power' (l.883). Barrett had already read *An Essay Concerning Human Understanding* (see 'My Own Character', *BC* 1:347), and both Locke's position as the father of Whiggism and his emphasis on the need for independence of mind would only increase her admiration.

Barrett's investigation into the disciplines in *An Essay on Mind*, perhaps unsurprisingly, assigns the highest status to poetry since poets in Barrett's view produce 'elevation of the *reasoning* mind' (l.945, my italics). As the poem's summary titles suggest, essential to the poet's work is a 'generous sympathy' (empathy) with others and a dedication to 'the voice of Freedom'

(*CW* 1:259), and this naturally leads Barrett back to the figure who looms largest over her poetic and psychological landscape during this period: Byron. In Book One of *An Essay on Mind*, Byron is the first figure of genius in the poem to receive an extended description as Barrett constructs him in subliminal and mythological terms as the 'Mont Blanc of intellect' at whose feet all nature throngs and in whose presence 'Terror's spirit . . . shrieks' (l.70; 76). Viewing Byron as nothing short of an heroic god figure, therefore, a spiritual and humanitarian leader, Barrett returns full circle to him in the closing pages of *Essay* as if he is the culminating point of all the best qualities of the other 'heroes' she has mapped out in the poem. Certainly, he is presented here as the ideal trope of the poet dedicated to liberty through his actions in revolutionary Greece, the 'pilgrim bard, who lived, and died' for his adopted Hellenic homeland (l.1191), and Barrett uses him to initiate a call for others to become involved in the process of liberating the land which she identifies as the 'country of my soul' (l.1147). Given that *An Essay on Mind* appeared in 1826 when the Greek civil war was flagging due to two years of civil war and factionalism among the revolutionaries, Barrett might here be calling for a refocusing of efforts in order to break the Ottoman stranglehold.

As with *The Battle of Marathon*, *An Essay on Mind* has had a mixed reception in recent studies with Dorothy Hewlett dismissing it as 'a heavy lump' (1953: 7), Virginia Radley arguing that its 'ponderous' nature 'does little to convince us of [Barrett's] ability as a poet' (1972: 31), and Angela Leighton (1986) and Helen Cooper (1988) ignoring it. Mermin and Stone consider it more carefully – Mermin calls *An Essay on Mind* Barrett's 'threshold' work, arguing that it demonstrates 'remarkable self-confidence' (1989: 33; 34), while Stone reads it as one of Barrett's initial explorations in 'Romantic Revisionism' (1995: 61–3) – and yet even here there is little concern with the *revolutionary* thought embodied in the work. For rather than being 'lumpy' or 'ponderous', *An Essay on Mind* constitutes a call for an intellectual revolution as the young poet, using terms which almost prefigure the 1840s Chartist movement, urges 'Men! claim your charter! spurn th'unjust controul,/And shake the bondage from the free-born soul!' (ll.811–812). Barrett's version of Blake's breaking of the 'mind-forg'd manacles' is fundamental, in the logic of the poem, to the physical fight for liberty from oppressive regimes, a concept Barrett would return to time and again in her writings (see, for example, *Casa Guidi Windows*). And again this is clearly a place where Barrett felt women could make a contribution, for although there is a singular absence of women in the roll call of genii she maps out in *An Essay on Mind*, it is a young woman who sifts and weighs them with an ability and astuteness that is startling. At age twenty, Aurora Leigh, 'Woman and artist— either incomplete' (*AL* 2:4), crowns herself with ivy in her garden as a symbol of her desire to achieve poetic stature. At the same age, Elizabeth Barrett is far nearer to reaching this stature in a work that engages with and challenges the bastions of male learning and which advocates a liberal politics which would become central to her developing aesthetic.

ROMANTIC HISTORIES

An Essay on Mind is, of course, the lead poem to a collection and although Mermin argues that the fourteen additional poems are 'an ill-assorted whole' (1989: 33), I would argue that there is more of a coherence among them and the ideas of the title poem than Mermin suggests. The figure of Byron is carried through in the reprinting of 'Stanzas on the Death of Lord Byron' in this collection and the dramatic lyric 'Stanzas occasioned by a Passage in Mr Emerson's Journal' which details the anguish of one Captain Demetrius on hearing of Byron's death ('I could not love my Country's fame,/ And not my Country's Friend', ll.15–16). But the concern with political heroes is also picked up in two other works here: 'Riga's Last Song' and 'On a Picture of Riego's Widow'.

The first of these, the powerful 'Riga's Last Song', commemorates an earlier – and some argue, the first – martyr to the Greek cause, Rhigas Pheraios, an outspoken advocate of republicanism who was betrayed to the Habsburg authorities and subsequently handed over to the Turks for execution. Barrett's poem is a dramatic lyric in which Riga delivers his final speech before his execution, full of patriotic fervour as he records a journey through his country focusing on sites of past political independence and martial glory (Souli, Marathon, Thermophylæ) and locating hope for the future, as Barrett herself would later do in *Casa Guidi Windows*, with children and his oppressed countrymen: 'I gazed on peasants hurrying by,—/The dark Greek pride crouched in their eye' (ll.25–6). 'On a Picture of Riego's Widow', in contrast, is the only depiction of a woman associated with heroism in this volume and focuses on Teresa del Riego, the wife of the Spanish revolutionary. Although this poem might be seen as problematic in its depiction of a woman who dies of grief for her dead husband and is then 'objectified' into an art work, the overriding impression of this poem, and the later 'Death-Bed of Teresa Del Riego' published in *Prometheus Bound, and Miscellaneous Poems* (1833), is of a strong woman who, in her refusal to show grief publicly and in her loyalty to her husband's memory aligns herself with revolutionary thinking and against brutal systems of absolutism. Indeed, her significance is clearly portrayed in her symbolic and iconic stance as 'Daughter of Spain' on whose face viewers can 'read the Patriot's woe' (l.1; 8).

The other short poems appended to *An Essay on Mind* deal with varying subjects: Barrett's relations with her father and Bro ('To My Father', 'Verses to My Brother'), a dream where the speaker returns to ancient Greece, Egypt and then the Garden of Eden ('The Dream: A Fragment', 'Memory' and 'The Past'). Common to them all, however, is a concern with history and the way in which history shapes and acts upon the present, an issue which Barrett would interrogate throughout her writing career. Certainly, the collapsing of private and public histories recorded in this volume as a whole was important in an age which, as Talmon notes, was fascinated with history as a political tool and which saw an unprecedented 'flowering of the historical discipline' (Talmon, 1967: 101).

In the preface to this collection, Barrett makes a strong argument for using poetry to explore ideas and theories: 'We do not deem the imaginative incompatible with the philosophic, for the name of Bacon is on our lips; then why should we expel the argumentative from the limits of the poetic?' (*CW* 1:56). By the time she was twenty, Barrett was clearly demonstrating how this would be one of the underlying principles of her mature aesthetics.

PROMETHEAN POLITICS

Elizabeth Barrett's third volume, *Prometheus Bound, and Miscellaneous Poems*, the last of her volumes to be published anonymously, appeared seven years after *An Essay on Mind*. During the intervening period, Barrett had been pursuing her classical studies with Boyd and had spent considerable time reading and translating the major Greek tragedians. One of the texts which she was particularly drawn to was Æschylus' *Prometheus Bound*, a work which she described as 'an exquisite creation' (*D* 91), and it was a translation of this, rather than one of her own original compositions, which she subsequently used as the lead work of her 1833 collection. *Prometheus Bound* would be the only translated work that Barrett would publish in her poetry collections so we need to consider *why* she drew on it at this particular stage of her career and at this particular historical moment.

Æschylus' play is the most famous version of the myth of the Titan Prometheus, who steals fire from the gods and gives it to humankind in what is essentially a humanitarian act. As punishment for this transgression against divine power, however, Jove (later called Zeus in Barrett's second translation of the poem) commands that Prometheus is forever chained to a rock in 'th'unpeopled wilderness' at 'the utmost bound of the earth' as Barrett translated it in 1833 (1.1–2). And yet Jove is also fascinated by Prometheus since Prometheus possesses secret knowledge concerning the means by which he will be brought down from his position of power in the future. It is Prometheus' defiance in refusing to share this knowledge which results, as the final speeches of the play indicate, in his having his liver ripped out each day by a vulture.

The myth is therefore one of extreme violence and this is a distinguishing feature of Æschylus' play and Barrett's translation of it. The opening scene focuses on Prometheus being riven to the rock by Jove's henchmen, 'Erect, unslumb'ring, bending not the knee' (l.32), in a posture reminiscent of the Crucifixion. It is, as Vulcan says, 'A spectacle . . . sad to see' (l.69). After this first brutality, however, the text has little action, being constructed mainly through a series of conversations and monologues where the nature of leadership and kingship is carefully scrutinised. In particular, the construction of Jove is used both to explore the psychopathology of an authoritarian figure who rules by cruelty and who 'hath/ For his sole justice, his own will' (ll.86–7), and to reflect upon the tyranny often perpetrated by those new to positions of power: 'ever cruel is a new-made king' (l.35). But as Prometheus reveals, just as Jove killed his own father in order to win the seat of power from him in a titanic Oedipal struggle, so will he himself be defeated by a son who will be 'his sire's superior' (l.767). The warning to those in positions of power who arrogantly think they inhabit 'citadels impregnable' (l.960) is therefore forcibly made here as authoritarianism is connected with unending cycles of destruction.

Elizabeth Barrett completed her translation of Æschylus' play in just two weeks in February 1832, often translating more than a hundred lines a day, as she notes in her diary. This is clearly a remarkable accomplishment and sees Barrett joining a tradition of Romantic artists, including Byron, Mary Shelley, Percy Bysshe Shelley and Beethoven, who were fascinated by the challenges to authority which Prometheus represents. However, as a number of feminist critics have highlighted (Cooper, 1988: 26; Mermin, 1989: 51; Stone, 1995: 72), Prometheus might have been even more attractive to Barrett because he occupies a more traditionally feminine structural position in the text as the passive victim of patriarchal power systems. And yet in his secret knowledge, he also possesses a means of shaking the establishment to the core. From his position of seeming powerlessness, then, Prometheus/ woman, the text suggests, can speak back to authority in ways which challenge and undermine it.

I would like to suggest a further reason for Barrett's choice of Æschylus' play, however, which relates to the precise historical moment at which Barrett was translating the work. For despite her move with *Prometheus Bound* to a concern with large mythic narratives – an interest she would develop in the lead poems of her next two volumes, *The Seraphim* (1838) and *A Drama of Exile* (1844) – Barrett is still clearly grounding her work here in critiques of undemocratic power politics and tyrannical authoritarianism. It therefore seems highly significant, particularly given Barrett's commitment to Whig politics, that she chose to translate this play at such a heated pace during the period of intense debate preceding the passing of the Great Reform Act in 1832, that major piece of early nineteenth-century Whig legislation which sought to produce a better representation of the people in the House of Commons by reducing rotten boroughs, redistributing parliamentary seats to include larger industrial towns such as Birmingham, Manchester, Leeds and Sheffield, and extending the franchise. The Act was seen by many as a major move in the extension of fundamental civil rights and, as I noted in the last chapter, the Barrett family were actively engaging in campaigning for its passage through Parliament.

As with *The Battle of Marathon*, therefore, Barrett's *Prometheus Bound* provides another example of the poet drawing upon classical events or texts in order to draw analogies with contemporary political situations. In the play's interrogation of Jove who rules by his whim and who represents 'a rank disease' in the authority of the heavens (l.225), Barrett might be seen to be reflecting on the Tory administrations which in her youth had implemented the Six Acts and which more recently had been vehemently opposed to reform. In such a context, Prometheus thus becomes a version of the liberal hero who, like the figures of Byron, Rigas and Riego in the *An Essay on Mind* volume, attempts to initiate a more democratic way of thinking.

When *Prometheus Bound* was published, the reviews were mostly condemnatory, particularly since another, less literal translation by Thomas Medwin had been published in December 1832, a work which Barrett considered 'an awful rival' (*BC* 3:78). Indeed, reviewers found Barrett's translation weak and too quickly done, a critic in the *Athenaeum*, for example, using it to warn 'those who adventure in the hazardous lists of poetic translation to touch anyone rather than Æschylus' (*HUP* 2:144). Several years later, Barrett herself would also condemn it, regarding it as 'cold stiff & meagre, unfaithful to the genius if servile to the letter of the great poet' (*BC* 5:297). Her conviction that this was 'a Prometheus *twice* bound' (*BC* 5:27), however, did not stop her from translating the tragedy again in the 1840s and including it, with a slightly revised version of the 1833 preface, in her *Poems of 1850* (see Chapter Four). In the 1833 version, however, Barrett had clearly locked on to a number of issues – authority, the destructive nature of power, the (female) rebel – which she would return to in her future work.

Throughout her first three volumes, then, Barrett had transformed herself from the Poet Laureate of Hope End into a competent woman artist with a strong and often challenging voice. Although these early works do not always have the greater poetic originality and assurance of her later works, they nonetheless raise a range of concerns which would become central to her mature aesthetics, including the fight against oppressive systems, the need for greater democracy in both thought and action, and the transformative potential of both the Carlylean hero figure and the individual woman to bring about political change. Far from these volumes being mere 'rehashes' of other poets' works (Hirsch, 1995: 21), then, a more attentive reading reveals that they possess an astonishing degree of consistency with the preoccupations of the maturer poems and that they should be seen as part of an overall trajectory of poetic development. As Barrett herself said when speaking of *An Essay on Mind*, there is strong evidence of 'an individual thinking and feeling' in these early works (*BC* 7:354), and as we will see in subsequent chapters, this would provide a firm foundation for the works she would produce throughout the rest of her career.

3

THE CULTURE OF THE SOUL: ELIZABETH BARRETT BROWNING'S POETICS

REBECCA STOTT

Nay, if there's room for poets in this world
A little overgrown, (I think there is),
Their sole work is to represent the age,
Their age, not Charlemagne's, – this live, throbbing age,
That brawls, cheats, maddens, calculates, aspires,
And spends more passion, more heroic heat,
Betwixt the mirrors of its drawing-rooms,
Than Roland with his knights at Roncesvalles.

(*AL* 5:200–7)

Elizabeth Barrett began writing poetry in what we conveniently now label as the late Romantic period and she died hailed as one of the greatest Victorian poets. Throughout the period in which she wrote, poets, reviewers and intellectuals argued about the definition and role of the poet, in a post-revolutionary, swiftly advancing, industry-dominated age. Was the poet a genius, a prophet or seer, with special powers of perception and intuition, perhaps even divinely possessed, as Samuel Taylor Coleridge had argued, or was he simply 'a man speaking to men', feet firmly on the ground, as William Wordsworth claimed, a man with special powers of expression and feeling perhaps but distinguished from the common man only by differences of degree not of kind (Woolford and Karlin, 1996: 64–73). I use the word 'man' here to describe the poet, not because there were no women poets, of course, but because the romantic conceptions and models of the poet, quarrelled over in these very public debates, were almost always premised upon a *male* model of the poet. Women wrote poetry, but it was assumed by many that for them it was an 'accomplishment' rather than a vocation. Other writers and reviewers sometimes claimed that for complex reasons, based upon differences of education, biology and experience, the vision of women was profoundly different from that of men – the poetry at which women excelled was beautiful, small-scale and exquisite.

When Aurora expresses her poetic manifesto in Book 5 of *Aurora Leigh* (1856) her voice is, as it so often is in the poem as a whole, assured, even zealous. The poet is to speak for her age, explore the drama of the Victorian drawing room, not the squabbles of medieval courts. Although it is important not to conflate Aurora and her author, for Aurora is made up of auto-biographical fragments of Barrett Browning's life and opinions but also much more, we know from Barrett Browning's private writings that Aurora's views are her own here. However, without a knowledge of Elizabeth Barrett's early poetry and especially her Prefaces, it is all too easy to read this as a manifesto of a poet who by her mature years had found her voice. It is also important to remember that Elizabeth Barrett made her debut as a poet taking a stand on these subjects, staking out her ground, and she continued to do so throughout her life, often using the Prefaces to her collections in order to take up new positions or modify old ones. She was only thirteen when she first put her opinions on this subject into print in the Preface to *The Battle of Marathon* (1820; the Preface was written in 1819) and her voice here, though more tentative than the voice of *Aurora Leigh*, is no less sure that she is right.

So many critics of Elizabeth Barrett Browning's life and work have presented it as one overshadowed by her struggle to find a voice in a world dominated by male poets and by the overbearing presence of her own father. Some even go so far as to argue that she only really found this voice in her very late poems. Helen Cooper, for example, claims that 'by the time Elizabeth Barrett wrote *Casa Guidi Windows* (1851) and *Aurora Leigh* (1856) she possessed an authoritative poetic I' (Cooper, 1988: 10). In this chapter I want to present an alternative figure of Elizabeth Barrett Browning, a woman in full possession of her 'poetic I' from the moment she ventured into print as a young girl, but one who, for complex reasons not unlike those faced by her male counterparts, chose to experiment with that 'I'. I seek to recover, as Marjorie Stone does in exploring Barrett Browning the fire-thief (Stone, 1995), the consistently ambitious and audacious Elizabeth Barrett, the young woman who wrote in 1841 to Horne: 'Ah, when I was ten years old, I beat you & Napoleon & all, in ambition' (*BC* 5:110).

As I have claimed, Elizabeth Barrett Browning's subtly shifting opinions about the function of poetry and the role of the poet, published over a period of some forty years, provide important insights into the changing debates about poetry from the late Romantic period when she began to write to the mid-Victorian period when she died. What was poetry? And who was the poet? She was fascinated by such questions and what others had to say about them and her statements are always in dialogue with her contemporaries who were also trying to formulate their own views in a rapidly changing culture and society. In these Prefaces, we therefore hear not just her own voice but those of a generation, for her Prefaces are discursive; they are often absolute in their clarity of position and simultaneously looking for other voices with which to engage in dialogue and debate. In the words of Vivienne Rundle, 'she daringly places herself within the forefront of Romantic and Victorian aesthetic experimentation' (Rundle, 1996: 248). Unlike others who had views on the subject, she often brought a classical perspective to bear, quoting Roman or Greek writers drawn from her classical learning as if they too were seated around the discussion table. The evolution of her opinions on the role and function of poetry, as expressed in the Prefaces, also provides the modern reader with a way of reading and understanding her own poetry.

The thirteen-year-old Elizabeth Barrett opened her very first Preface with the following confident claim:

> That Poetry is the first, and most celebrated of all the fine arts, has not been denied in any age, or by any philosopher. The culture of the soul, which Sallust so nobly describes, is necessary to those refined pleasures, and elegant enjoyments, in which man displays his superiority to the brutes.

> (CW 1:2)

In her very first published (but privately printed) sentence, then, she places herself at the centre of a consensus which she claims is shared by all writers and philosophers of all ages: poetry is the greatest of all the fine arts and thus poets are the greatest artists. In making this claim she both shows herself to be familiar with writings on this subject from classical times to her own day and places herself among this assembly of the greatest artists. Poetry, she continues, elevates, cultures, civilises. It is what marks humanity's superiority above the brutes; without the poet, there is only barbarism. She goes even further when she claims that it was Homer who lifted Greece out of its darkness and degradation and into the beginnings of civilised democracy, using imagery which is reminiscent of the Creation Story with Homer as God bringing light to the world or, if perhaps not God himself, the medium through which God has chosen to work:

> then it was that the unenlightened soul of the savage rose above the degradation which assimilated him to the brute creation, and discovered the first rays of social independence, and of limited freedom; not the freedom of barbarism,

but that of a state enlightened by a wise jurisdiction, and restrained by civil
laws

(*CW* 1:4)

Barrett's alignment here of poetic imagination with social justice and political freedom is important because it places her in a Shelleyan tradition
expressed in poems such as 'Prometheus Unbound', 'The Mask of Anarchy',
'Ode to Liberty' and 'Ode to the West Wind'. If Barrett is ambitious for
herself here, she is ambitious for all poets.

The second major claim that she makes in the Preface, and one that
perhaps would not have endeared her to many literary readers, is that
few poets of her own time have the ability to fulfil this role as creator and
arbiter of civilisation. She disparages the way in which 'the press pours forth
profusion' and 'the overwhelming abundance of contemporary authors'.
The sheer number of writers, she claims, has brought about a decline in
literary taste for the 'flowers are mingled with weeds' and the eye of the critic
and reader 'frequently mistakes the flower for the weed, and the weed for the
flower'(*CW* 1:3–4). She names only three living poets as exceptions: Lord
Byron, Sir Walter Scott and Thomas Moore. These are revealing choices,
spanning England, Scotland and Ireland: Lord Byron, English poet, had
a reputation as a free spirit and adventurer, was passionately committed
to liberty and prepared to fight for it; Sir Walter Scott was a Scottish poet
of verse romances and ballads as well as historical novels; and Thomas
Moore, though less well known today, was an Irish writer who had recently
published *Lalla Rookh* to critical acclaim, a series of oriental tales in verse
connected by a story in prose. So while she is ambitious for all poets, only a
very few writers fit her criteria of great poets.

POET AS HISTORIAN

Interestingly, given that she is writing about the superior status of poetry
above all other arts, the first authority Barrett draws upon in the Preface
to *The Battle of Marathon*, Gaius Sallust (85–36 BC), was not a poet but
a *historian*. But this is part of her point. For as chronicler of the 'Battle
of Marathon' in verse, she is both its poet and its historian. As a battle for
liberty and civilisation, it is, she claims, appropriate subject matter for the
poet, because it is 'formed to call forth the feelings of the heart, to awake
the strongest passions of the soul' (*CW* 1:6). It will elevate the reader. She
considers herself alongside the great historian-poets Virgil and Homer and

claims that a poet when writing on historical subjects should be allowed to enlarge upon her subject. A historian must be dedicated to truth, but a poet-historian can add invention, judgement and imagination to this truth. This assimilation of poetry and history was characteristic of her writing throughout her career.

POET AS RHETORICIAN AND PHILOSOPHER

Elizabeth Barrett took on the subject of the role of the poet again, but this time she took the issue beyond the Preface and into a poem itself, a long discursive, philosophical poem published in 1826 called *An Essay on Mind*. She was now twenty and the poem is an extraordinary testimony to the range of her reading and the sophistication of her intellectual development by this point, for she engages in dialogue with a series of metaphysicians including John Locke (philosopher), Rene Descartes (philosopher), the Comte de Buffon (natural historian and evolutionary thinker), Gottfried Wilhelm Leibnitz (mathematician), George Berkeley (philosopher) and Etienne Bonnot de Condillac (philosopher) as well as Byron whom she calls 'the Mont Blanc of intellect' (1.70), in order to determine an understanding of the operations of the mind. In terms of form, the poem follows in the tradition of Pope's 'Essay on Criticism' (1711) or 'Essay on Man' (1732–4), verse poems written in heroic couplets on philosophical subjects.

In the Preface to *An Essay on Mind* Barrett claims that ethical poetry is the highest of all poetic forms and that contrary to some opinions, poetry should be able to encompass argument and persuasion. Once again that was exactly what she was doing in the poem itself. Just as she had brought together history and poetry in *The Battle of Marathon*, here she fuses intellectual history, philosophy and poetry. It is almost as if she was putting herself through an ambitious apprenticeship in these first poems, with Homer and Pope as her masters in the first published poem and Milton and Pope as her masters in the second. Many critics, led by Elizabeth Barrett's own claims in her thirties that she spent a good deal of her early years dreaming of dressing up in male clothes in order to escape the restrictions of her girlhood, have tended to dismiss these early poems and Prefaces as the work of a girl impersonating men. Marjorie Stone, for instance, claims that *An Essay on Mind* is a work of 'metaphorical transvestism or male impersonation' (Stone, 1995: 33). But while Elizabeth Barrett may borrow an authority of tone in order to speak here, the opinions and the conclusions that she reaches from an extraordinary reading programme are no less her own. They are not borrowed, nor parroted. Though she was herself later critical of the imitative nature of some of her early works, she also claimed that *An Essay on Mind* was 'not without traces of an individual thinking & feeling — the bird pecks through the shell in it' (*BC* 7:354).

It is also important to remember that before she wrote the Preface to *The Battle of Marathon* Barrett read Mary Wollstonecraft's *A Vindication of the Rights of Woman* (1792), a passionate argument about the slavery and bondage of women expressed by a female voice of great confidence and assertion, who sought on every page to balance passion and reason. So if there is a degree of impersonation it is not just male impersonation. Wollstonecraft, who was called a 'hyena in petticoats' by Horace Walpole, was a great dissenting rhetorician who single-handedly took on a whole assembly of respected philosophers and intellectuals as well as established ideas in the *Vindication*:

> It is plain from the history of all nations, that women cannot be confined to merely domestic pursuits, for they will not fulfill family duties, unless their minds take a wider range, and whilst they are kept in ignorance they become in the same proportion the slaves of pleasure as they are the slaves of man.

> (Wollstonecraft, 1983: 299)

In *An Essay on Mind* itself, Barrett also champions breadth of knowledge for both men and women, for, she claims, it is only with this breadth of vision achieved by wide reading and thinking that the mind is able to transcend detail to see the larger patterns at work in the universe:

> 'Tis easy, as Experience may aver,
> To pass from general to particular.
> But most laborious to direct the soul
> From studying parts, to reason on the whole:
> Thoughts, train'd on narrow subjects, to let fall;
> And learn the unison of each with all.

> (ll.545–50)

Again her vision of the importance of the synthesising mind, which is able to connect parts, extends to the role of the poet. The poet is the great connector. It is not enough for the poet to describe the world in all its beauty as a series of parts, she/he must draw the reader's mind to the patterns and laws of nature. So by the beginning of the 1830s Elizabeth Barrett was consistently championing a poetics of *transcendence*. The poet's role was, she believed, to *elevate* her reader, to take the reader beyond the detail and beauty of the world to the larger patterns in nature, because essentially the poet was a visionary, her work was to civilise and cultivate the soul. It wasn't enough for the poet to take the reader out of the world, she must also aid the reader to see it anew, revealing patterns and connections through a kind of bird's-eye view or aerial mapping.

THROUGH SERAPHIC EYES: PLAYING AT ANGELS

It is in this context that we might look at the role of the angel in Elizabeth Barrett's poetry of the 1830s and early 1840s, most particularly in two dramatic lyric poems called *The Seraphim* (1838) and *A Drama of Exile* (1844), both of which are title poems to collections. In the Preface to *The Seraphim* Barrett claims that her aim in writing the title poem, a dramatic dialogue between two angels at the gates of heaven looking down to earth during the Crucifixion, was to

> gather some vision of the supreme spectacle under a less usual aspect, — to glance at it, as dilated in seraphic eyes, and darkened and deepened by the near association with blessedness and Heaven. Are we not too apt to measure the depth of the Saviour's humiliation from the common estate of man, instead of from His own peculiar and primeval one? To avoid which error, I have endeavoured to count some steps of the ladder at Bethel, – a very few steps, and as seen between the clouds.

> (*CW* 1:167)

She claims here that in order to give the reader a new vantage point of the Crucifixion, she, the poet, will climb into the clouds and provide an angel-eye view of it. By doing so she will get closer to the truth about the 'depth of the Saviour's humiliation', the 'voluntary debasement of Him who became lower than the angels'. But the poem is also about how ugly and fearful the earth looks like to an angel who, being pure and sinless, fears corruption. By inhabiting an angel, and expressing its horror and fear, she is able to cast a different light on the courage of the Christ figure, who, also pure and sinless, was prepared to live among this corruption and to die in order to redeem it. In taking this view she will elevate her readers to a new vantage point, a transformative one.

Although the influence of Milton on the poem is incontrovertible, this is an extraordinarily original and ambitious poem in both subject matter and form. In addition, it is metaphysically and philosophically demanding in that the angels discuss the nature of grace and sin. Furthermore, Elizabeth Barrett experiments with the dramatic lyric, again using a form that brings together two genres, the lyric and the drama. However, a further important aspect of the poem is undoubtedly her use of voice. Instead of speaking directly here in her own voice as either epic historian (*The Battle of Marathon*) or as philosopher-poet (*An Essay on Mind*), she impersonates angels, and is therefore able to explore and dramatise conflictual thoughts and feelings by using a mask, or rather *two* masks for she plays and ventriloquises both angels. Moreover, despite a single, brief reference to the departure of the other 'brother angels', the two angels who speak in the poem, Zerah and Ador, are distinctly androgynous in a Miltonic tradition and their voices are similarly androgynous. They have more in common with Blake's paintings of muscular androgynous beings than they do with many of the sentimentalised and feminised angels which people the paintings of Victorian art. I want to suggest, firstly, that Elizabeth Barrett is using voice here in new ways to explore the nature of the poet as prophet or as transcendent being, and secondly that in using two voices she can dramatise conflict and disagreement in ways that avoid gendered positions.

Interestingly, these angels are on the edge of heaven looking down. They are neither in heaven nor on earth; they are on the threshold between the two worlds. She also sets *A Drama of Exile* on a threshold, telling us in the stage direction of the first lines that the scene is 'the outer side of the gate of Eden shut fast with cloud' (*CW* 2:149); it is also set on the edge of night and day, a kind of extended twilight, an important aspect of the poem which Elizabeth Barrett draws attention to in her Preface. Her subject here is newly fallen humanity and her cast is much more ambitious in number than in *The Seraphim*, including Lucifer, the angel Gabriel, Adam, Eve, various nature spirits, invisible angels, the morning star and Christ. Her angels are again only tacitly gendered. Her interest here is in the nature and pain of exile, an experience which, shared by both Adam and Eve, transcends gender. In choosing androgynous angels who are neither explicitly male nor female but encompass both, in choosing a place with is neither inside nor out but on the edge of both, by choosing in *A Drama of Exile* a time which is again neither day nor night but on the edge of both, Elizabeth Barrett seems to be exploring these great binaries by looking from the vantage point of the threshold itself at the same time as she explores being able to move between different gendered voices. Here in the dramatic lyric she can be both Lucifer and Eve, see through their eyes, feel through their experience. In so doing she releases herself from the weight of finding a direct voice for herself, expressing her own personal emotion or opinions.

It was at about this point that two other important poets of the nineteenth century were finding similar solutions to the burden of speaking with the direct – and perhaps constraining – confessional voice of the romantic lyric and finding their own ways of defining and developing their roles as poets at the beginning of what many hailed as a new era in British poetry. Both Alfred Tennyson and Robert Browning had published collections of poems by the date of the publication of Elizabeth Barrett's *A Drama of Exile* in 1844. Both had been experimenting since the 1830s with the dramatic monologue for different reasons and both were struggling to define their poetics within the terms set out by the Romantic poets – the poet as seer and the poet as man speaking to men. I will explore the context of this emerging *form* of the dramatic monologue in more detail in the later chapter on genre, but here I want to argue that Elizabeth Barrett came to the dramatisation of voice for similar reasons to those of her two major male contemporaries. I want to question those critics who have stressed Elizabeth Barrett's struggle to find a voice within a male-dominated cultural tradition. I do not want to deny that she struggled but rather to suggest that her struggle was of her time and that her male counterparts also battled to find a voice and that sometimes for them the burden of tradition and inheritance was similarly both seductive and problematic. And throughout the Victorian period the business of gender and the poet, whether the poet was manly enough, or the female poet womanly enough to speak, was a terrain that had to be negotiated by poets of both sexes as Joseph Bristow and Herbert Sussman in particular have shown us (Bristow, 1987; Sussman, 1995).

Isobel Armstrong has shown in *Victorian Scrutinies* that the issues raised by the publication of Tennyson's early poetry helped to reshape questions about the role of the poet for decades to come. Tennyson's ability to impersonate was remarked upon in the first reviews of his first collection and particularly by William Fox in 1831:

He seems to obtain entrance into a mind as he would make his way into a landscape; he climbs the pineal gland as if it were a hill in the centre of the scene; looks around on objects with their varieties of form, their movements, their shades of colour, and their mutual relations and influences; and forthwith produces as graphic a delineation in the one case as Wilson or Gainsborough could have done in the other, to the great enrichment of our gallery of intellectual scenery ... The author personates (he can personate anything from an angel to a grasshopper) [...] Our author has the secret of the transmigration of the soul. He can cast his own spirit into any living thing, real or imaginary. Scarcely Vishnu himself becomes incarnate more easily, frequently or perfectly. [. . .] He does not merely assume their external shapes, and exhibit his own mind masquerading. He takes their senses, feelings, nerves, and brain, along with their names and local habitations; still it is himself in them.

(William Johnson Fox in Armstrong, 1972: 76)

For Fox there were two new areas for poetry to explore: the drama of the modern world and the new developments in psychology. The poet can enter and map the landscape of the mind as if it were a new world to be conquered. Again it is the poet's vision that is prioritised here with an extraordinary range of scopic references which shift uneasily between interior and exterior, microscopic and telescopic, and which play around with scale. The poet 'climbs the pineal gland as if it were a hill' – the poet is both a scientist looking through a microscope at a gland and climbing a hill to look down with the eyes of a landscape painter. We must also bear in mind that the privileging of sight over other senses in much Victorian culture is shaped at least in part by the enormous advances in optic technology which had made it possible to see into creatures in a drop of water through a microscope and to map the planets with increasingly powerful telescopes. In a world in which more and more was being brought into the range of the visible – from nerves to planets – the poet must have a role in *making known the still invisible*, the world of the senses, of the mind, and of the metaphysical. There was still an unknown world despite the efforts of science to reduce all mental phenomena to laws of sensation and association.

Fox and others saw a role for the poet in Tennyson's supposedly unique ability to project himself into other beings as a way of extending the realm of imaginative experience for both poet and reader and binding human society together through feeling and understanding. Tennyson could impersonate anything from an angel to a grasshopper but he was particularly drawn to impersonating women. Twentieth-century critics have pointed out a pattern of feminine identification and personification in Tennyson's poetry, particularly in his early poetry, just as critics have pointed out such a pattern of male impersonation in the early work of Elizabeth Barrett. Furthermore they have suggested that Tennyson felt drawn to impersonating or exploring female characters because it gave him a realm of experience and an opportunity for expressive feeling that was in many ways closed to him as a Victorian man but a realm he could move in and out of as a Victorian male poet (see Sinfield, 1986). The same is also true for Elizabeth Barrett's supposed impersonation of male voices. Tennyson found his way through to the dramatic lyric or dramatic monologue as a way of broadening the range of his poetry and the minds, feelings and opinions he sought to express in poetic form. Just as Elizabeth Barrett found her way up the stairs to the gates of heaven so that she could imaginatively enter the body of an angel and look down at the world through his/ her eyes, so Tennyson found his way up the steps of a tower and into the body of a weaving woman so that he could see the world from the vantage point of a woman imprisoned and in love, divided against herself, the Lady of Shalott. For different reasons again, Robert Browning, fascinated by the darkest sides of the human psyche, had begun to explore imaginatively the minds of murderers and madmen in his first dramatic monologues 'Porphyria's Lover' and 'Johannes Agricola' both published in 1836 under the title *Madhouse Cells*.

The 1830s were politically volatile: a new queen was crowned and political unrest and unease focused upon the new reform bill which enfranchised the property-owning middle classes but continued to exclude the working classes. During this decade, poets, reviewers and intellectuals continued to try to forge or redefine a new role for the poet for a new age. John Stuart Mill, a distinguished intellectual and philosopher, published two influential essays on this issue in the 1830s which helped to refocus cultural attention on the subject. Mill rejected the idea of the poet as *vates* or prophet, speaking to a nation, helping to shape historical events, and instead claimed that 'all poetry is the nature of soliloquy'. It must be distinguished from eloquence for 'eloquence is *heard*, poetry is *over*heard'.

> Poetry is feeling confessing itself to itself in moments of solitude, and embodying itself in symbols, which are the nearest possible representations of the feeling in the exact shape in which it exists in the poet's mind. Eloquence is feeling pouring itself out to other minds, courting their sympathy, or endeavouring to influence their belief, or move them to passion or to action.

> (Mill in Bristow, 1987: 349)

Elizabeth Barrett Browning, however, was passionately committed to the eloquent, rhetorical and persuasive powers of poetry. She explored the dangers of the self-exiled, isolated poet for example in 'A Poet's Vow' in which a poet makes a vow to break 'the bondage ... /That knits me to my kind' and to 'forswear' the human in the hope that his vision and understanding will be enhanced thereby (ll.90–1; 93). Instead he becomes 'an awful thing that feared itself' (l.276) and the woman who loves him pines away and dies, leaving behind a 'scroll' on which is written a powerful indictment of the poet's denial of life and love. He wails with the 'weeping wild of a reckless child/ From a proud man's broken heart' (l.475), but the poet's tears, which confirm his emotional redemption and the return of his human connectedness, come too late to save him; when they come to fetch her coffin they find his dead body by her side. The poem testifies to Barrett's developing rejection of the poet of the margins, a rejection powerfully intensified for her by her correspondence with Mary Mitford and with Robert Browning in the 1840s.

FEELING AND GENDER

The realm of the feelings was heavily feminised in the nineteenth century as part of a set of binaries which included public and private, reason and feeling, male and female. And if poets were to open up this new world of the mind and of private feeling, they risked being relegated to the woman's sphere and marginalised as both Joseph Bristow and Alan Sinfield have shown:

> in its concentration on individual states of mind, Victorian poetry found itself doing two things at once: first, it demanded greater attention to the uniqueness of human character in opposition to the stultifying forces of the 'march on mind' (industrial 'Progress' and the utilitarian values underpinning it) and, second, it discovered that this focus of interests (on the private self) actually evacuated it from the space it wished to occupy – the centre of culture.

> (Bristow, 1987: 8)

And the more poetry was associated with women and feminine feeling, the less influential it became. Elizabeth Barrett consistently refused to be confined to the drawing room of feeling, it was too constraining for the poet. She saw a much wider range of appropriate subject matter for poetry: already she has claimed history and philosophy as appropriate subjects, and argued that ethical subjects are the highest form of poetry. Eloquence and rhetoric could be accommodated by a poet concerned with truth. She even seems to suggest that it is *desirable* for poets to be eloquent for in so doing they encourage not only emotional but also philosophical and intellectual transcendence. It is therefore important that one of her first manifestoes on poetics claims that feeling (so often assigned to women and so much privileged by the male Romantic poets) needs to be tempered by reason (so often assigned to the masculine sphere):

> Sensation is a stream with dashing spray,
> That shoots in idle speed its arrowy way;
> When lo! the mill arrests its waters' course,
> Turning to use their unproductive force:

The cunning wheels by foamy currents sped,
Reflection triumphs, — and mankind is fed!

(*An Essay on Mind*, ll.759–64)

If Bristow is right to argue that there were two dominant models of the
poet in the nineteenth century – the poet as *vates* (poet-prophet) speaking
at the centre of culture to an audience and seeking to influence that audience, or the poet of the margins, confessing itself to itself in moments of
solitude – Elizabeth Barrett was always the vociferous champion of the *vates*
model. Like Wollstonecraft, Barrett Browning experienced unrestrained
feeling as a problem throughout her poetic career and it was one with which
she struggled both as a woman (and therefore socialised and constructed as a
creature of feeling) and as a poet. As her poetry developed she showed herself
to be increasingly suspicious of *untempered* emotion as an unquestionable
truth in itself. It is tempting to see her own suspicion of extreme feeling
as shaped by its essentialist association with women and at the same time
perhaps coloured by experience of the tyranny of emotions enacted within
the walls of the Barrett household, in which her father's passionate opinions
were never to be questioned in part because they were passionate. 'To A
Poet's Child' attests to her growing distrust of the privileging of emotion
above reason as she warns the orphaned female child of a poet to:

Feel not too warmly: lest thou be
Too like Cyrene's waters free,
Which burn at night, when all around
In darkness and in chill is found. . . .

And, as a flame springs clear and bright,
Yet leaveth ashes 'stead of light;
So genius (fatal gift!) is doom'd
To leave the heart it fired, consumed.

(ll.45–8; 53–6)

Apart from questioning the Romantic privileging of feeling above all other
human responses, there are other ways in which Elizabeth Barrett's emergence on to the stage of aesthetic debate strikes a discordant and iconoclastic
note in the early years. The language used by the most revered Romantic
poets might have advocated a new, quasi-religious and to-be-welcomed role
for the poet, but it was very much a men's club, this group of would-be
prophets with vatic status. Samuel Taylor Coleridge presented himself as
what he called a 'Bard', a poet-prophet. But how many female prophets were

there in the Western world who might present a role model for a teenage female poet who aspired to such a role? Would Elizabeth Barrett have to continually make herself forget or deny her sex in order to join this vatic brotherhood or were there ways in which she could find a female role within it?

In 1843 she wrote to her friend, Mary Mitford, that at the age of ten she had aspired to be Byron's page and there are many references to cross-dressing in her early writings which make it easy to assert that Elizabeth Barrett was somehow subsuming her femininity into a fantasy world in which she could imagine herself in a whole series of male roles and adopt male voice after male voice. But I would like to argue that Elizabeth Barrett did not simply imagine herself a man in order to resolve this problem but sought to negotiate between and redefine the characteristics and ideologies that her generation asserted were exclusively and essentially either male or female. That is why I argue in this chapter, and in the subsequent chapter on genre, that she is a boundary crosser, someone who from the very first words she uttered sought to reconcile in her poetics a whole series of binaries which her generation told her were absolutely gendered: reason and feeling in particular.

POET AS HERO

Elizabeth Barrett was not alone in championing a vatic public role for the poet and rejecting Mill's emphasis on poetry as private feeling. In 1840 Thomas Carlyle gave a lecture entitled 'The Hero as Poet' as part of a formulation of a clutch of ideas on heroism and the nature of the hero in the modern age. His book *On Heroes, Hero-worship and the Heroic in History* would influence a generation and make heroism a preoccupation of the century. As Elizabeth Barrett had done in her very first Preface published twenty years earlier, he lamented the demise of poetry. There were all too few prophet-poets left in the world, he claimed, at a time when the world needed such figures perhaps more than it ever had:

> Poet and Prophet differ greatly in our loose sense of them. In some old languages, again the titles are synonymous: *Vates* means both Prophet and Poet: and indeed at all times, Prophet and Poet, well understood, have had much kindred of meaning. Fundamentally, indeed, they are still the same; in this most important respect especially, that they have penetrated both of them into the sacred mystery of the Universe: what Goethe calls the 'open secret'. 'Which is the great secret?' asks one.—'The open secret'—open to all, seen by almost none! . . . But now, I say, who ever may forget this divine mystery, the

Vates, whether Prophet or Poet, has penetrated into it; is a man sent hither to make it more impressively known to us. That always is his message; he is to reveal that to us,—that sacred mystery which he more than others lives ever present with. While others forget it, he knows it:—I might say, he has been driven to know it; without consent asked of him, he finds himself living in it, bound to live in it.

(Carlyle in Bristow, 1987: 64–70)

Once again what is at stake here is the nature of vision itself – the poet reveals the world to man; he is sent here to reveal the sacred mystery which is open to all and 'seen by almost none'. I have quoted from Carlyle's lecture at some length because it so interestingly complements and extends Elizabeth Barrett's views on the subject and because I believe Carlyle's views about the role of the poet carried her aesthetic views into a new phase. In an article which she co-wrote with Richard Hengist Horne for *The Spirit of the Age* only four years after Carlyle published these ideas about heroism, Elizabeth Barrett praised Carlyle as a man of genius who has 'knocked out his window from the blind wall of his century' (Reynolds, 1996: 393), the writer of a soul-language 'a still grave music issuing like smoke from the clefts of the rock' (Reynolds, 1996: 393). But she insists none of Carlyle's ideas is original – he is a renewer not an originator, 'but his reiterations startle and astonish us like informations' (Reynolds, 1996: 396). More than anyone perhaps, she must have felt that Carlyle was reiterating the views she had expressed in her writing, for had she not herself written in *An Essay on Mind*:

None read, but Poets, Nature's poetry!
Its characters are trac'd in mystic hand,
And all may gaze, but few can understand.

(ll.1029–31)

So while she is able to applaud Carlyle for his views, she will not grant him originality:

We 'have souls' he tells us. Who doubted it in the nineteenth century; yet who thought of it in the roar of the steam-engine? He tells us that work is every man's duty. Who doubted that among the factory-masters?—or among the charity children, when spelling from the catechism of the national church, that they will 'do their duty in the state of life to which it will please God to call them'? Yet how deep and like a new sound, do the words 'soul', 'work', 'duty,' strike down upon the flashing anvils of the age, till the whole age vibrates! . . . . And again—[he tells us] 'Truth is a good thing'. Is that new? . . . .

Yet we thrill at the words, as if some new thunder of divine instruction ruffled the starry air,—as if an angel's foot sounded down it, step by step, coming with a message.

(Cited in Reynolds, 1996: 396–7)

It is not surprising, given Elizabeth Barrett's impersonation of angels and experimentation with the vantage point of the angel as a correlative to the aerial vision of the poet-prophet, that she should hear in Carlyle's voice the rustle of angel wings and the step of an angel foot 'coming with a message' for she saw that Carlyle himself, though no writer of verse, was the very embodiment of the *vates*. More importantly, she hears the sound of the *vates* descending: 'an angel's foot sounded *down* it, step by step.'

By the mid-1840s Elizabeth Barrett made a major shift in her poetic philosophy: she did not abandon her conviction that the poet had a public role to play but she did change her views about *where the poet should stand* in order to occupy that central position in culture. If she had consistently championed a poetry of transcendence until the 1840s, from about 1844 she begins to adopt the language of descent. Aerial views are no longer either valuable or viable.

However, although Barrett may have committed herself to writing poetry about her own world in the 1840s, throughout her life this question about the appropriate viewpoint for a poet remained an issue, as it did for other Victorian poets. Should the poet look on from afar – even from above – or immerse him or herself in the hustle and bustle of the contemporary world? And did the poet have a different kind of sight from other men? For Carlyle the answer was that the poet-hero remained essentially other-worldly in that he had 'penetrated . . . into the sacred mystery of the Universe', but had been sent into the world 'to make [divine mysteries] more impressively known to us'. He was a revealer, an unveiler. He could exist on two planes but chose to live in one.

WHERE ANGELS FEAR TO TREAD: ENTERING THE DRAWING ROOM

Marjorie Stone argues that in the early 1840s Elizabeth Barrett's relationship with Romanticism came to a head, and that around 1843 in particular Barrett came to call for a poetry of the present, turning away from poetic and vatic transcendence and towards a poetry more rooted in the world around her (Stone, 1995: 23–34). She singles out Mary Mitford as having a key role in

Barrett's shift of positions from the aerial to the earthly, for the correspondence between the two women shows that Mitford was challenging Elizabeth Barrett to experiment with the poetry of the here and now. I have also suggested that Carlyle's writing on the hero as poet had a part to play in this shift of aesthetics and renewed interest in experimentation with form and with voice. Significantly, it was around 1844, the period in which Elizabeth Barrett was writing reviews and perspective pieces for *The Spirit of the Age*, that she began to think about and plan a long novel in verse, which would be almost twelve years in the making and would be published in 1856 as *Aurora Leigh*. She wrote to Mary Mitford in 1844:

> And now tell me, . . . where is the obstacle to making as interesting a story of a poem as of a prose work . . . Conversations & events, why may they not be given as rapidly & passionately & lucidly in verse as in prose?
>
> (*MRM* 3:49)

She explains that her intention is

> to go on & touch this real everyday life of our age, & hold it with my two hands [. . .] I want to write a poem of a new class
>
> (*MRM* 3:49)

The following year she wrote to Robert Browning:

> my chief intention just now is the writing of a sort of novel-poem . . . running into the midst of our conventions, & rushing into drawing-rooms & the like, 'where angels fear to tread' & so, meeting face to face & without mask, the Humanity of the age and speaking the truth as I conceive of it out plainly.
>
> (Cited in Reynolds, 1996: 330)

'Where angels fear to tread': her angels in *The Seraphim* were also interestingly fearful of the world of men, disdainful of all things mortal. Christ, however, had lived and preached among men, conquering his fear of earthly corruptions. Elizabeth Barrett here announces to her fellow poet that she too will go 'where angels fear to tread', she will unmask and take her place in the drawing room. So her new poetics are formed through a resituating in the present moment and in the commonplace, thereby forming a new vantage point.

If 1843 was a turning point, the Preface of the *Poems* of 1844 attests to this change of position and the influence of Carlyle in that shift, for the language she uses incorporates some of the Carlylean mantras of work, suffering and duty which she had celebrated in her essay on Carlyle only two years earlier as well as deploying a distinctively Carlylean metaphor of incrustation:

> In the eyes of the living generation, the poet is at once a richer and a poorer man than he used to be; he wears better broadcloth but speaks no more oracles: and the evil of this social incrustation over a great idea is eating deeper and deeper and more fatally into our literature than either readers or writers may apprehend fully. I have attempted to express in this poem my view of the mission of the poet, of the self-abnegation implied in it, of the great work involved in it . . .

> (CW 2:147)

In 'A Vision of Poets', where the title implies both a vision *of* poets and *by* poets, Elizabeth Barrett explores the poetics of suffering and martyrdom as a qualification for genius, as the mission of the poet. As a poet wracked by personal loss and the sufferings of a sick body, it was a qualification Barrett had in abundance. In the poem, the sleepless poet, in despair about the lack of value given to poetry, is taken by a lady dressed in white to see the true worth of poets. At the altar of a great church in which 'mist and marble seemed to blend' (l.241), the poet sees an angel surrounded by a 'strange company' (l.271), the assembly of dead great poets. They are all bleeding and the sound of the falling blood '[tolls] the silence as a bell' (l.510). The angel once again carries the message of the poem – that the poet and Christ are joined as both fellow sufferers and fellow martyrs:

> . . . these were poets true,
> Who died for Beauty as martyrs do
> For Truth

> (ll. 289–91)

And that as martyrs their power is formed from suffering:

> "If every vatic word that sweeps
> To change the world, must pale their lips,
> And leave their own souls in eclipse, –

> (ll.529–31)

The angel reminds the strange company to remember the sacrifice of Christ and challenges them to 'refuse this baptism in salt water' (tears) (l.551) and to choose instead 'Calm breasts, mute lips, and labour loose' (l.552). The poets concede to this role:

Content! it sounded like *Amen*
Said by a choir of mourning men;
An affirmation full of pain

(ll.559–61)

It is interesting to see here in this poem , that while she might have been suspicious about assigning the poet to the realm of untempered feeling, suffering has a legitimacy and grandeur validated by religious visions and visionaries. It was what Christ chose to do in leaving the heavens to live among men; it was what Barrett herself was symbolically doing in leaving the world of angels, Homer and Milton, and entering the world of the drawing room.

While Barrett *began* planning *Aurora Leigh* in the 1840s, its writing is shaped by her experience of the 1850s, and of the best part of a decade of living in the world with Robert Browning. It proved to be far from the world of suffering which she had written for herself in 'A Vision of Poets', but perhaps she had suffered enough by this point to receive her full qualification as poet. She had also arrived, hailed in the reviews of the 1844 collection as a genius by many of the sages she most admired including Thomas Carlyle and Harriet Martineau. By the time Barrett Browning was ready to give Aurora the words of her poetic manifesto, then, the statement was so rich and honed after a lifetime's reflections that it is very much a synthesis of current ideas as well as an implicit rejection of others. Her artistic philosophy may have shifted in terms of vantage point and in terms of what she considered to be appropriate subject matter for poetry, but she remained consistently within the vatic tradition at the centre of culture rather than at its margins throughout her life.

In *Aurora Leigh*, Elizabeth Barrett Browning is still concerned with the poet's vision, insisting here that the poet must have a synthesising vision, a double vision. Now she does not reject the long, aerial, seraphic view, but instead she claims that in order to be able to see at all the poet must reconcile the long view and the close up, to move between the microscopic and the telescopic or panoramic, see things close up as if seen from afar, in order to reveal Carlyle's 'unknown known' for the first time: ' "The open secret" – open to all, seen by almost none!':

Every age,
Through being beheld too close, is ill-discerned
By those who have not lived past it. . . .
　　　　　　Tis even thus

With times we live in, – evermore too great
To be apprehended near.
                            But poets should
Exert a double vision; should have eyes
To see near things as comprehensively
As if afar they took their point of sight,
And distant things as intimately deep
As if they touched them. Let us strive for this.

                                            (*AL* 5:166–8;181–8)

The object of the poet's vision had therefore changed significantly in her view
by 1856. At a time when Tennyson was still writing his sequence of connected
Arthurian poems *The Idylls of the King* and the British people were excited by
all things medieval as a kind of nostalgic yearning for a pre-industrial past,
Barrett Browning insisted on a poetry of the here and now:

I do distrust the poet who discerns
No character or glory in his times,
And trundles back his soul five hundred years,
Past moat and drawbridge, into a castle-court. . . .
Nay, if there's room for poets in this world
A little overgrown, (I think there is)
Their sole work is to represent the age,
Their age, not Charlemagne's – this live, throbbing age,
That brawls, cheats, maddens, calculates, aspires,
And spends more passion, more heroic heat,
Betwixt the mirrors of its drawing-rooms,
Than Roland with his knights at Roncesvalles.

                        Never flinch,
But still, unscrupulously epic, catch
Upon the burning lava of a song
The full-veined, heaving, double-breasted Age

                                    (*AL* 5:189–192; 200–7; 213–16)

In the poem itself these poetics of the unmasked poet with which Barrett
had been playing since the mid-1840s are developed into the full aesthetics
that characterised the second phase of her writing career. In this cult of the
real, Elizabeth Barrett Browning's aesthetics were in line with those of George
Eliot who would publish her aesthetic manifesto in Chapter 17 of *Adam
Bede* only two years later in 1859: 'Let us always have men ready to give the
loving pains of a life to the faithful representing of commonplace things, and

delight in showing how kindly the light of heaven falls on them' (Eliot, 1985: 180). Elizabeth Barrett and George Eliot arrived at similar positions at about the same time. Both were dismayed by the silliness of so much writing by women and both felt there was a line to be walked between the soaring vatic utterances of the Romantic models of the writer and the poetics of the common life.

4

THE VOICE OF A DECADE:
ELIZABETH BARRETT'S POLITICAL
WRITINGS OF THE 1840s

SIMON AVERY

THE GREAT SHAMES OF GREAT NATIONS

In 1851, Elizabeth Barrett and Robert Browning, who had been married for five years, returned to London from their Italian home in Florence's Casa Guidi to visit members of their families and renew contact with a wide range of artistic friends, including Mary Russell Mitford, Thomas Carlyle and the art historian Anna Jameson. This year, however, London was even more crowded than usual since 1851 saw the hosting of the Great Exhibition, a large-scale celebration of recent achievements and developments in industrial manufacturing and artistic endeavour. The brainchild of Prince Albert, the Great Exhibition – or Crystal Palace Exhibition as it was also known due to the vast construction of glass and iron designed to house it – extended over 800,000 square feet in Hyde Park and juxtaposed hydraulic presses, agricultural machinery and printing technology with fabrics and furniture, china and ornaments, in displays which were brought from nearly every European country and as far and wide as Canada, the United States and Egypt. Visited by more than six million people, this 'Great Exhibition of the Works of Industry of all Nations' quickly became a symbol of Victorian pride in progress and an embodiment of the national and racial supremacy much of contemporary British society believed it had achieved.

Elizabeth Barrett Browning was not quite so impressed, however. Indeed, writing to Mrs Ogilvy, her Florentine neighbour, the day after she had visited the Exhibition, she recorded how she felt 'disappointed' at the whole event (*MDO 1849–1861 – 49*). But then this reaction is hardly surprising given that Barrett Browning had already sharply critiqued what she saw as the Exhibition's ideological hypocrisies in the second part of her long poem on Italian politics, *Casa Guidi Windows*:

> Imperial England draws
> The flowing ends of the earth from Fez, Canton,
>   Delhi and Stockholm, Athens and Madrid
> The Russias and the vast Americas [. . . .]
>   All trailing in their splendours through the door
> Of the gorgeous Crystal Palace [. . . .]
>   O Magi of the east and of the west,
> Your incense, gold and myrrh are excellent!—
>   What gifts for Christ, then, bring ye with the rest?
> Your hands have worked well: is your courage spent
>   In handiwork only?

> (*Casa Guidi Windows* Part Two, ll.578–632)

To Barrett Browning the 'gorgeous Crystal Palace' was an illusory façade, the celebration of material wealth which it embodied – the 'trailing in [of] splendours' – only masking a range of social ills which these supposedly 'civilised' countries had failed to address:

>   . . . no light
> Of teaching, liberal nations, for the poor
>   Who sit in darkness when it is not night?
> No cure for wicked children? Christ,—no cure!
>   No help for women sobbing out of sight
> Because men made the laws? no brothel-lure
>   Burnt out by popular lightnings? Hast thou found
> No remedy, my England for such woes? [. . .]
>   Alas, great nations have great shames, I say.

> (2:634–41; 648)

Like many of her contemporaries, then, such as Dickens, Carlyle and Elizabeth Gaskell, Barrett Browning was acutely aware of the systems of abuse and oppression which the seeming 'progress' suggested by the Great Exhibition was founded upon. For the preceding decade, the revolutionary or 'Hungry' forties, had witnessed some of the worst poverty and exploitation and some of the most potent political debate that the nineteenth century was to see. The impact of industrialism, the employment and living conditions of those in factories or down the mines, the implementation and repeal of the Corn Laws, the abuse of the Poor Laws, the devastation of the Irish potato famine, and the socially endorsed roles assigned to women were all hotly debated and argued over, creating great tension and unease in political circles and throughout society generally. Indeed, the decade which opened with the national celebrations of Victoria's marriage to Albert ended with the fear that the revolutions sweeping across continental Europe throughout 1848 were about to erupt in Britain.

In this chapter I will explore how Barrett Browning engaged with a number of these issues and firmly established herself in the eyes of many of her contemporaries as an astute commentator on political affairs. What role did she believe poetry should have in political debate? What techniques did she employ to articulate her concerns regarding contemporary social problems? How did she reflect upon and critique the established power systems she witnessed around her? And how did gender issues influence her views?

THE STATUS OF *POEMS* (1844)

At the beginning of the 1840s Elizabeth Barrett was staying in Torquay where she had been convalescing from illness since August 1838. This treatment seemed to be having positive effects until her beloved brother Bro, who had left London to join her, was tragically drowned in a sailing accident. This loss of her dearest companion, 'he who added pleasure to every cherished object' (*BC* 1:358), was by all accounts the greatest tragedy of Barrett's life and it would be fourteen months before her doctors thought her strong enough to cope with the journey back to Wimpole Street. In September 1841, however, she returned to London as a crucial first move in her psychological recovery after the events of the preceding year. Yet this return was also important on another level, since it placed Barrett at the very heart of the British political and literary circles with which she increasingly sought to engage. Although the idea of Barrett as a solitary recluse was already starting to develop – her friend Richard Hengist Horne, much to her horror, described her in *A New Spirit of the Age* as '[c]onfined entirely to her own apartment, and almost hermetically sealed, in consequence of some extremely delicate state of health' (Horne, 1844: 134) – in reality she remained as alert as ever to developments in social and political as well as literary and artistic thinking, and kept herself well informed of current affairs and contemporary events through visits to friends, epistolary relationships, and extensive reading in newspapers, journals and books. It was this commitment to the modern and to contemporary affairs that would be crucial both to Barrett's development as a poet during the 1840s and to much of the success of the two-volume *Poems* of 1844 and the revised and expanded edition of *Poems* published in 1850.

Before the publication of *Aurora Leigh* in 1856, *Poems* (1844), published simultaneously in America as *A Drama of Exile, and Other Poems*, was arguably Barrett's most ground-breaking and original work. Barrett had been working on the collection for five years and on its publication *Blackwood's Magazine* praised its scope as rare among the work of women poets. The poems ranged, the reviewer wrote, 'over a wider and profounder range of thought and feeling, than ever before fell within the intellectual compass of any of the softer sex' (*BC* 9:350). Indeed, the collection was diverse both generically and thematically. Beginning with a long religious narrative work, *Poems* also draws upon and experiments with the genres of the sonnet, ballad, lyric, devotional meditation and political verse, with the subjects ranging from Adam and Eve's expulsion from Eden to the brutality of industrialism, from the sexual betrayal of women to the leadership strategies of Napoleon, from the irrelevance of classical deities in the modern world to child labour, and from reflections upon Hugh Stuart Boyd, Mary Russell Mitford and Flush to condemnation of slavery in a variety of forms. Clearly, then, this collection signalled a major development in the poet's technique and intellectual endeavour. Indeed, as Stone argues, *Poems* marked a 'poetic awakening' where Barrett's 'youthful audacity of authorship resurfaced with renewed force' (1995: 58), and Mermin similarly suggests that here Barrett was 'in fuller possession of her powers than ever before', speaking with 'a new confidence, as if she really trust[ed] her own voice' (1989: 86–7). Certainly, Barrett herself seems to have felt this when she wrote to Boyd that 'It seems to me that I have more *reach*, whether in thought or language. . . . All the life and strength which are in me seem to have passed into my poetry' (in Forster, 1988: 131).

What is clearly evident in these volumes is that something of a paradigm shift is occurring in Barrett's thinking about the role of poetry, for as she continued to align herself with the Romantic model of poet as sage or *vates* (see Chapter Three), she increasingly turned to commentaries on and critiques of the political and social injustices she saw around her. This is not, of course, to argue that this is a new occurrence – as we have seen, Barrett was drawing upon political subject matters from the beginning of her writing career – but as the remainder of this chapter will argue, her work of the 1840s emphasised the engagement with contemporary social debates to a far greater extent than before as the poet searched out new territories and sought new, more rigorous means of reflecting upon 'the great shames of great nations'. The success with which she achieved this can be measured, at least in part, by the fact that by the close of the decade the then Elizabeth Barrett Browning (she married Robert in 1846) would have developed a growing international reputation and, following the death of Wordsworth in 1850, would be seriously considered for the post of new Poet Laureate of 'this live, throbbing age' (*AL* 5:203).

WOMAN AS EXILE

One of the areas where *Poems* (1844) represents a thematic continuity with the earlier work most evidently is in Barrett's perpetual fascination with power and the politics of power – its construction and deconstruction, its legitimacy and abuse. In particular, Barrett's work of this period overtly engages with and resists what the twentieth-century French theorist Michel Foucault termed 'discursive practices', the ideologies and mindsets endorsed by the establishment in order to maintain the status quo. Of course, much of this engagement on Barrett's part is bound up with her interrogation of traditional gender roles and this is particularly significant in this volume where, as Mermin argues, Barrett 'began covertly to inspect and dismantle the barriers set in her path by gender' (Mermin, 1989: 3) – only sometimes that inspection and dismantling is more overt than Mermin suggests. Indeed, from the lead poem onwards, such concerns are acutely in evidence with *A Drama of Exile* rehearsing the biblical narrative of the expulsion from Eden but through Eve's perspective rather than Adam's. Barrett's collection therefore begins with her rewriting the androcentric tradition of epic as constructed by Milton's *Paradise Lost*, a task which she argued a woman poet was more qualified to undertake (*CW* 2:144). The result, as Stone suggests, is a 'de-centring' of Milton through processes which can be seen as proto-feminist 'revisionist mythmaking' (Stone, 1995: 77). (It is possible here to draw a connection with Barrett's 'de-centring' of Homeric epic in *The Battle of Marathon* – see Chapter Two.)

Barrett's agenda, therefore, is to give a voice to women's oppression as she saw it by refocusing on the first woman, the woman whom conventional religious thought and rhetoric continued to blame for the loosing of sin upon the world, and to use this figure to depict a more generic concern with woman's 'alloted [*sic*] grief', by which she meant 'the self-sacrifice [which] belonged to her womanhood' (*CW* 2:143–4). As Antony Harrison has demonstrated, *A Drama of Exile* was to influence later nineteenth-century women poets such as Christina Rossetti to rewrite the biblical narrative of Eve along similar revisionary lines (see Harrison, 1990: 127–34), but for Barrett herself, this principal concern with woman's 'grief' was to continue throughout *Poems* and, indeed, much of her later work as well (see, in particular, Chapter Eight on *Aurora Leigh*).

Equally important, however, is the way in which this lead poem establishes another political keynote of Barrett's work: the construction of the exile figure. As Barrett writes in the Preface, 'I took pleasure in driving in, like a pile, stroke upon stroke, the Idea of EXILE' (*CW* 2:144), thereby developing a concern which had emerged from earlier works such as 'Riga's Last

Song' and 'The Vision of Fame' (1826), *The Seraphim*, 'Cowper's Grave' and 'The Exile's Return' (1838). Certainly the politics of exclusion and alienation which the exile figure embodies became increasingly fundamental to Barrett's writings and were a dominant characteristic of her work of the 1840s where, as this chapter will demonstrate, not only women but working-class figures, children and slaves are constructed as political exiles forced to negotiate as best they can potentially destructive power systems of 'alien tyranny' (*A Drama of Exile*, l.1865).

WOMAN ENTERING THE PUBLIC SPHERE

Barrett explores the issue of women being exiled from the centres of authority and control in the public space in one of her most popular works in *Poems*, 'The Romaunt of the Page'. This is one of the female-centred ballads which Barrett wrote to accompany pictures supplied by Mary Russell Mitford for her editions of *Findens' Tableaux*, a journal marketed for a predominantly female readership. As Stone has argued, however, many of Barrett's ballads challenged dominant gender expectations by focusing on female independence and agency on the one hand, and exposing systems of exploitation and betrayal on the other (1995: 94–133). Therefore, the reprinting of these ballads in *Poems* (1844) extended Barrett's commitment to writing of 'Eve's alloted grief' (*CW* 2:143). In Chapter Five, we explore the ways in which Barrett manipulated the conventions of the ballad form in order to develop this new gynocentric perspective, but here I want to focus principally on how 'The Romaunt of the Page' reconfigures the relations between women and the public world.

'The Romaunt of the Page' rehearses the narrative of a newly wedded woman who follows her husband, the knight Sir Hubert, into the holy wars in Palestine dressed as his male page. Due to the hasty nature of the marriage, Sir Hubert has never seen his wife's face, thereby allowing her in disguise to question him on his views on marriage and woman's place. The 'page' – another example of Barrett's fascination with physical and psychological cross-dressing – subsequently listens while Hubert asserts that should his wife follow him to battle, he would consider her 'Unwomaned' (l.196) and although he may forgive her, he could then only think of her as 'my servitor' and 'little as my wife' (l.228–9).

It is therefore ironic that throughout the poem Hubert praises the battle skills of his wife/page who has already saved his life three times: 'Thou fearest not to steep in blood/The curls upon thy brow' (ll.9–10). Indeed, the poem concludes with the page once again saving Hubert's life for as she hears danger approaching, she sends the knight away to safety while she succumbs to a violent death which she almost seems to relish:

> She felt the scimitar gleam down,
>   And met it from beneath
> With smile more bright in victory
>   Than any sword from sheath,—

(ll.323–6)

A number of commentators have suggested that despite the female heroism which 'The Romaunt of the Page' records, the poem's closure only reaffirms conventional gender politics. Angela Leighton, for instance, argues that 'In the end . . . this heroine is as cruelly betrayed as any Sappho or Corrine' (1992: 83–4), while Dorothy Mermin argues that the page finally 'chooses a woman's fate—unrecognised, self-sacrificing death' (1989: 92). According to these arguments, any subversion of the status quo in the body of the text is closed down at the end. However, throughout the text the page's independence is consistently highlighted and I would interpret the closure as an articulation of the woman's desire to play an active role in the public world and assert her autonomy, even if the result is her seemingly inevitable death.

Although set in the past, the poem's use of the settings, costumes and props of the Middle Ages, as with Tennyson's *Idylls of the King* or Morris' 'Haystack in the Floods', makes it typical of the emerging Victorian interest in medievalism which, as Bernard Richards argues, allowed 'an exercise in self-definition and self-knowledge' as the past became 'a theatre in which [contemporary] problems could be acted out' (Richards, 1988: 99; 100). For Barrett, these problems clearly involved women's choice to enter the public sphere, an issue which was increasingly foregrounded throughout *Poems*. As with Eve in *A Drama of Exile*, then, the page is also constructed as an exiled figure who is subsequently able to critique woman's restricted role from the margins.

Barrett would return to cross-dressing as a trope to explore women's access to the public sphere elsewhere, of course, the device recurring again in the two sonnets in this collection addressed to George Sand (1804–76), one of Barrett's greatest literary heroes. Known during her lifetime as much for dressing like a man and smoking in public as for her art, Sand was one of the most controversial authors of her day whose strong feminist and socialist beliefs resulted in a series of novels such as *Indiana* (1832), *Lélia* (1833), *Maurprat* (1837), *Horace* (1842) and *Consuelo* (1843) which openly critiqued the institution of marriage, the systematised oppression of women, sexual hypocrisy, the archaic hierarchy of the French class system and the failures of established religion, and which therefore accorded with many of Barrett's own political ideas. Indeed, when Barrett finally met Sand in Paris in February 1852, her thrill far exceeded even that of her earlier meeting in 1836 with her poet-hero Wordsworth.

Barrett had always been drawn to Sand as one of the iconoclastic French writers she enthusiastically read and discussed with Mitford, and in many ways Sand's challenging political views and the incorporation of these views into her fiction influenced Barrett's own work; indeed, it is possible that Barrett even sought to commemorate Sand, whose real name was Aurore, in her most revolutionary protagonist. In the sonnets to George Sand, written in the form most usually associated with expressions of heterosexual love, Barrett both celebrates Sand's work and critiques the society which condemned her for her views:

Thou large-brained woman and large-hearted man,
Self-called George Sand! whose soul, amid the lions
Of thy tumultuous senses, moans defiance
And answers roar for roar, as spirits can:
I would some mild miraculous thunder ran
Above the applauded circus, in appliance
Of thine own noble nature's strength and science,
Drawing two pinions, white as wings of swan,
From thy strong shoulders, to amaze the place
With holier light! that thou to woman's claim,
And man's, mightst join beside the angel's grace
Of a pure genius sanctified from blame,
Till child and maiden pressed to thine embrace
To kiss upon thy lips a stainless fame.

('To George Sand: A Desire)

Here Barrett turns Sand's borderline cross-dressing existence into a creative hybridity, constructing her as 'large-brained woman and large-hearted man' and thereby suggesting that Sand's success as both thinker and writer is partly derived from a form of the androgynous state which Virginia Woolf, writing in her feminist classic *A Room of One's Own* (1929), would argue was fundamental for great art. The first quatrain, therefore, emphasises Sand's power and agency in breaking traditional models of femininity. She is 'Self-called', suggesting a conscious choice over her own identity and a celebration of it in terms not dissimilar to Napoleon's famous crowning of himself as Emperor (an image which possibly also lies behind Aurora's self-crowning of herself as poet in Book Two of *Aurora Leigh*). Moreover, she has a defiant soul which, lion-like, claims equality, 'answer[ing] roar for roar'.

The remainder of the sonnet, however, considers how Sand's power and originality is received by the society in which she lives. Barrett suggests that Sand is like an animal in a circus entertainment, but rather than the mild 'applause' she might receive from the public, Barrett argues that Sand should be transfigured by some 'miraculous thunder' into an angel, wings emerging from her 'strong shoulders, to amaze the place/ With holier light', a trans-figuration which would allow Sand's genius to be recognised 'sanctified from blame' and her reputation and fame to become 'stainless'.

This is a complex poem which raises many issues concerning the reactions to a woman wishing to enter and engage with the public sphere. Barrett celebrates an androgynous boundary crossing which leads to greater intellectual power and understanding, suggesting that this hybridity of traditionally male and female qualities is necessary for a woman if she is to successfully negotiate the established gender power differentials associated with public and private spaces, centres and margins. Indeed, she repeats this idea in 'George Sand: A Recognition' where, in a slightly less optimistic tone than in 'A Desire', she argues that despite Sand's 'manly scorn' (l.2) and 'man's name' (l.9) signifiers of her femininity are still evident: 'Thy woman's hair, my sister, all unshorn/ Floats back dishevelled strength in agony' (ll.7–8). This politics of assimilation is taken further in the *form* of these sonnets, of course, with Barrett casting herself in the traditional role of the male speaker of the sonnet and then addressing a cross-dressing woman. Such unsettling of conventions therefore acts to question all essentialist categories. In the next section we will explore how Barrett related these ideas to the most important public woman of nineteenth-century Britain, Queen Victoria herself.

STUDIES IN LEADERSHIP: VICTORIA

Barrett was fascinated by leaders and leadership throughout her life. As we saw in Chapters One and Two, this stemmed from both a Whig concern with, and resistance to, authority and dominant power structures, and a version of nineteenth-century hero-worship as it was articulated and theorised by Carlyle. Barrett's work of the 1840s continued to interrogate leadership, particularly in two poems paired by their titles, 'Crowned and Wedded' and 'Crowned and Buried', poems which contrast two very different national leaders: the young Queen Victoria and the French Emperor Napoleon.

Despite her fundamentally republican beliefs, Barrett was always greatly interested in Victoria and the complex nexus of ideas concerning power and gender which Victoria's role embodied. In a society where the dominant ideology concerning femininity would result a few years later in such influential and far-reaching works as Coventry Patmore's *The Angel in the House* (1854–62) and John Ruskin's 'Of Queen's Gardens' (1865), how could a woman be a ruler and still negotiate gender expectations? So concerned was Barrett with this question that she had already started to explore her responses to it in two poems published in *The Athenaeum* in 1837, 'The Young Queen' and 'Victoria's Tears'. In the first, written a month after Victoria's accession, Barrett emphasises both the weight of duty and the pressures of an inherited tradition of male monarchs faced by the young woman by using the image of a 'deathly scented crown' which '[w]eighs her shining ringlets down' (ll.22–3). Aurora Leigh would later use the image of cutting her ringlets to signify a bid for independence from male dominance, but in 'The Young Queen' Victoria achieves her self-agency by rather 'lift[ing] her trusting face, and call[ing] upon God' (l.24) and developing an enabling reciprocal relationship with the country which places her in a nurturing, maternal role:

> A nation looks to thee
> For steadfast sympathy:
> Make room within thy bright clear eyes for all its gathered tears.
>
> And so the grateful isles
> Shall give thee back their smiles,
> And as thy mother joys in thee, in them shalt *thou* rejoice . . .

(ll.46–51)

The power to be derived from traditionally feminine positions is similarly highlighted in 'Victoria's Tears' which depicts her as a ballad-like 'maiden' (l.1) who turns away from the crowds cheering for the monarch as 'She wept, to wear a crown!' (l.30). Throughout the poem, Victoria's weeping both emphasises her femininity and, as with the leaders in *The Battle of Marathon*, serves to complement her public status, acting as a signifier of her integrity: 'The tyrant's sceptre cannot move,/ As those pure tears have moved' (ll.33–4). Indeed, the logic of the poem works to suggest that such integrity will be eventually rewarded by Victoria's accession to heaven where she will receive the ultimate 'heavenly crown' (l.50).

Barrett drew upon and developed the ideas explored in these two earlier poems in the more substantial 'Crowned and Wedded' where, as the title indicates, she focuses on both Victoria's coronation and her wedding in the kind of work she might have been called upon to write had she succeeded to the laureateship in 1850. In the opening stanzas Barrett depicts the ceremonial splendour of the coronation where Victoria swears a number of oaths which place her in traditionally masculine roles of responsibility and power:

> a princely vow—to rule;
> A priestly vow—to rule by grace of God the pitiful;
> A very godlike vow—to rule in right and righteousness,
> And with the law and for the land!

> (ll.5–8)

Witnessed by representatives 'from countries east and west' (l.14), Victoria is here celebrated in her public role as the head of a (supposedly) unified Empire and the country's moral guardian, but in the final two sections of the poem, Barrett switches the focus to emphasise instead Victoria's role as wife, calling directly upon Albert to 'Esteem that wedded hand less dear for sceptre than for ring,/ And hold her uncrowned womanhood to be the royal thing' (ll.57–8). Through the structuring unity of 'Crowned and Wedded', therefore, Barrett suggests that Victoria's success as a leader on the world's political stage derives from the combination of her able statesmanship and her femininity, a combination which prevents her succumbing to the potentially emotionally stultifying effects of authority as Barrett outlined them to Mitford:

> There is something hardening, I fear, in power [. . .] and the coldnesses of state etiquette gather too nearly round the heart, not to chill it, often! But our young Queen wears still a very tender heart! and long may its natural emotions lie warm within it!—

> (BC 3:261)

Barrett's poems on Victoria have remained relatively neglected in recent feminist recovery work with only Hayter referring to them and then to dismiss them as 'among the worst and most embarrassing of all her poems' (1962: 125). What is missing from this condemnation, however, is any consideration of the way in which Barrett uses Victoria as a trope with which to consider women's relations to structures of power and authority in the political sphere, for the three Victoria poems serve to reinforce the idea, repeatedly present in Barrett's writings, that good leadership involves the successful negotiation of public and private personas and a strong commitment to moral responsibility, emotional honesty, and personal and social integrity, qualities which are often gendered in nineteenth-century discourses as feminine. Indeed, the crucial status of these qualities for leadership is highlighted by the pairing of this poem with 'Crowned and Buried', Barrett's most detailed analysis of her ambivalent views on Napoleon Bonaparte.

STUDIES IN LEADERSHIP: NAPOLEON

Throughout her life Barrett's interest in the politics of France was every bit as lively as her interest in the politics of England, Greece or Italy. By the age of nine, following the reopening of the Continent after the end of the Napoleonic Wars, she had visited France with her parents and seen a number of the sites associated with the country's recent revolutionary past, including the Palais Bourbon and the site of Louis XVI's execution (see *HUP* 1:165–73). And as we have already noted, she was to continue her interest by studying the language and reading widely in French novels and histories. In particular, her concern with French politics was firmly rooted in her fascination with the figure of Napoleon Bonaparte, whom she hero-worshipped to a large degree for his meteoric rise, his determination and energy, his military victories, and his routing of corrupt European monarchs which she figures in 'Crowned and Buried' as 'lightning . . . /Scathing the cedars of the world' (ll.4–5). Originally published under the title 'Napoleon's Return' in *The Athenaeum* in 1840, the poem describes the return of Napoleon's ashes from St Helena for burial in Paris, using this elegiac trope to reflect upon his life and reign. As with her earlier treatments of Byron and Riga in the 1826 volume, Barrett here interrogates the powerful resonances of Napoleon's name, how '[t]he world's face changed to hear it' (l.31) and how it called up devotion from a wide range of people – 'children small/ Leapt up to greet it', 'Priests blest it from their altars', 'dying men on trampled battle-sods/ Near their last silence, uttered it for God's' (ll.11–16).

Interspersed with this praise, however, is clear condemnation of Napoleon's dictatorship which sacrificed the democratic principles which the French republic had originally meant to embody, for personal gain. For in establishing his siblings as new state leaders, Barrett argues, Napoleon constructed an overwhelmingly autocratic 'composite of thrones' (l.36), and the French people themselves clearly suffered as many losses as gains through their emperor's Machiavellian machinations; their hands may be 'toward freedom stretched' but they eventually drop 'paralysed' since freedom is never actually forthcoming (l.53). Indeed, as Barrett indicates, Napoleon operated principally through strategies of deception since the 'frequent streams/ Of triumph' (ll.56–7) through Paris are a mere showcase which rather 'magnified/ The image of the freedom [Napoleon] denied' (ll.149–50).

Despite this recognition of autocracy, however, Barrett remains ambivalent about Napoleon's legacy and his position in history. For as soon as he signed his abdication of power at Fontainbleau in April 1814, she writes, 'kings crept out again to feel the sun' (l.66) and many of the old orders of absolutist power – Louis XVII of France, Ferdinand of Spain, the King of Sicily and the Pope – were restored by the allies and subsequently reinstated systems of government which were equally as tyrannical, if not worse, than Napoleon's reign. In the final stanzas, then, she asserts 'I do not praise this man' (l.157) but nevertheless she ultimately leaves the text open with indecision:

> I think this grave stronger than thrones. But whether
> The crowned Napoleon or the buried clay
> Be worthier, I discern not: angels may.

> (ll.166–8)

Barrett was to remain fascinated by Napoleon and his successors (see Chapter Seven) and seriously considered Mary Russell Mitford's suggestion that the planned epic she wanted to write, which would eventually become *Aurora Leigh*, should be based on the French dictator's life. Indeed, as she wrote to Mitford in 1844:

> No man, better than Napoleon, understood the heroic poetry of situation. He was always equal to his position, whatever that might be, . . Austerlitz, Moscow, Fontainbleau. Napoleon was cast in the heroic mould, & fell naturally into the heroic gesture. His very great surtout does not dress him out of the heroic! He is as statuesque as Hercules, though in boots!

> (*MRM* 2:454)

The purposeful pairing of 'Crowned and Buried' with 'Crowned and Wedded' in *Poems*, however, eventually works to emphasise the destructive bases of male-dominated political systems and the potential embedded in more female-dominant systems. Certainly it is the qualities that the young Queen Victoria is made to stand for – morality, honesty, integrity, love, honour, compassion and empathy – which Barrett would increasingly turn to as solutions to wider social ills, 'the great shames of great nations', which she was to figure in two other paired poems in the 1844 volumes: 'The Cry of the Children' and 'The Cry of the Human'.

CYCLES OF EXPLOITATION

'The Cry of the Children', one of Barrett's most well-known and widely debated political poems, is a powerful attack on child labour. First published in *Blackwood's Magazine* in 1843, it was inspired, Barrett's correspondence indicates, by her reading of the 1843 *Report of the Royal Commission on the Employment of Children and Very Young Persons in Mines and Factories*, which was produced in part by her friend Richard Hengist Horne. Horrified by the report's details of the systematic exploitation of children by the new mechanisms of the Industrial Revolution, the excessively long hours they were expected to work (up to fourteen) and the numerous risks to health they faced through accidents, insufficient food, overcrowding and lack of light and air, Barrett immediately set out to make these social ills more widely known through her now well-established position as poetic *vates*. Indeed, so passionately did she feel about this subject that she later told Hugh Stuart Boyd that the first stanza of 'The Cry of the Children' 'came into my head in a hurricane' (*BC* 7:331).

There was, of course, already a substantial body of literary work tackling the humanitarian problems associated with industrialism, and poetic precursors such as Blake's *Songs of Innocence and Experience* (1789/1794) with its depiction of the 'dark satanic mills', Caroline Norton's 'A Voice from the Factories' (1836) and Thomas Hood's 'Song of the Shirt' (the 1843 poem with which 'The Cry of the Children' was often compared) may have influenced parts of Barrett's poem. Certainly 'The Cry of the Children' would itself be influential on later literary representations and has often been seen as helping to fuel the political debates which eventually led to the passing of the 1847 'Ten Hours' Factory Act for women and young persons.

Barrett's poem is partly articulated through an authorial voice and partly through the voices of the children themselves. In this respect, then, it is comparable with other works such as 'Riga's Last Song', 'Bertha in the Lane' and 'The Runaway Slave at Pilgrim's Point' which give back a voice to representatives of culturally oppressed groups (political revolutionaries, women, slaves) who have often been silenced by mainstream literary discourse or relegated to the liminal areas of the textual space. Furthermore, Barrett's sociopolitical agenda specifically highlights the humanity and physical conditions of her subjects – aspects which were often erased in official reports or 'Blue Books' of statistics – by an extended contrast between the natural qualities of youth and the unnatural conditions of the children working in the mine and factory. While the children appear 'weeping bitterly' with 'pale and sunken faces' (ll.10; 25), the natural world is associated with freedom in ways which make the common tropes of pastoral poetry into strong political statements: 'The young lambs are bleating in the meadows,/ The young birds are chirping in the nest' (ll.5–6). Constructed as weary, shadowy figures, old before their time, the children long for an early death and therefore stand as poignant images of the sacrifice of humanity to capitalism's 'Mammon-worship', as Carlyle termed it (Carlyle, 1986: 278). The poem's epigraph from Euripides' *Medea* – 'Woe, woe, why do you look upon me with your eyes, my children?' (*CW* 3:363, *Medea* l.1048) – is clearly apt, then, in the suggested comparison with Medea's infanticide.

As the poem develops, this established dichotomy of the industrial and natural worlds becomes increasingly gendered in ways which are consistent with a number of Barrett's other poems. The children are displaced from both their own mothers and mother earth, caught and exploited in the brutal power systems of the ironically defined 'happy Fatherland' (l.24) from which the positive energies of the mother are fiercely eradicated. What remains, therefore, is the 'alienated' state explored in the writings of numerous social commentators such as Thomas Carlyle, Karl Marx, John Ruskin and Matthew Arnold, in which increased mechanisation of industrial processes is seen to result in increased mechanisation of the mind and body. Certainly the monotony of the children's work is effectively caught by Barrett not only in the text's language but also in the rhythmic patterns and the rhyming present participles:

> For all day the wheels are droning, turning;
>   Their wind comes in our faces,
> Till our hearts turn, our heads with pulses burning,
>   And the walls turn in their places:
> Turns the sky in the high window, blank and reeling,
>   Turns the long light that drops adown the wall,
> Turn the black flies that crawl along the ceiling:
>   All are turning, all the day, and we with all.

(ll.78–9)

Displaced from their youth, humanity and nature, even the children's souls are afflicted by 'this cold metallic motion' (l.93) so that the industrial mechanisms work to come between them and God. Significantly, within this overtly masculine world the only religious phrase the children know is 'Our Father' (l.115), and while they desire that God might lift them up to him, they end up questioning his actual existence since 'He is speechless as stone' (l.126). Indeed, as Leighton argues (1992: 94), heaven is seen by the exploited children as nothing more than another part of this oppressive patriarchal order, where even the clouds are 'Dark, wheel-like, turning' (l.130). Subsequently, God is perceived only in grotesquely distorted form through the figure of the factory/mine manager: 'His image is the master/ Who commands us to work on' (ll.127–8). The poem therefore suggests that there can be no escape from the structures of exploitation.

Interestingly, after reading Elizabeth Gaskell's industrial novel *Mary Barton* in 1850, Barrett Browning wrote to Mitford of her disappointment in the work:

> There is power & truth—she can shape & she can pierce—but I wish half the book away, it is so tedious every now & then,—and besides I want more beauty, more air from the universal world—these class-books must always be defective as works of art.

> (*MRM* 3:318)

Contemporary reviews of Barrett's own class-poem, however, were mostly laudatory. *Tait's Edinburgh Review* argued that had Barrett written no other poem 'she must have been recognised as a poetess of a very high class' (*BC* 9:365); *The Broadway Journal* described it as 'full of a nervous unflinching energy—a horror sublime in its simplicity—of which a far greater than Dante might have been proud' (*BC* 10:352); while *The Dublin University Magazine* proclaimed that 'It stands alone for tenderness, fervour, and force, among all the outpourings of the spirit of humanity of our time' and, in a clear indication of the gendering of this type of poem, commented that 'It is essentially the protest of a woman on behalf of that infancy of which woman is the proper protectress and advocate' (*BC* 10:364). However, *The League*, an Anti-Corn Law circular, highlighted different problems, arguing that

> Miss Barrett joins in the mistaken clamour which has been raised against the factory system; she never has visited one . . . and has taken their description on trust. . . . The benevolence [here is] . . . tinged by that cant of sentimentalism which is one of the evils of the day.

> (*BC* 9:379–80)

Similarly, a number of recent critics have asked how Barrett, brought up in a highly privileged background, could give an adequate and accurate voice to the working classes and their experiences when her only engagement with them is through mediated literary representations and government reports. Cora Kaplan, for example, argues that the depiction of the working classes in *Aurora Leigh* is crudely handled and stereotypical to the point of being offensive (Kaplan, 1978: 11–12), while Sandra Donaldson has criticised Barrett's portrayal of the children in this poem as flat and two-dimensional (Donaldson, 1980: 55). Indeed, Deirdre David suggests that such problems are inevitable since 'almost all [Barrett's] writing is generated by the reading and writing of other texts' (David, 1987: 101).

While there are inevitable problems with Barrett's representations, her work is actually more typical of the Condition-of-England genre than appears to have been acknowledged. For in the wake of industrialism many Condition-of-England novelists, poets and non-fictional prose writers struggled to find ways of articulating the full horrors of this new method of production and its consequences. Some, like Gaskell and Dickens, had *direct* access to real examples of the problems faced by the urban poor on which to base their work, but many writers did not and still wanted to contribute to the debate. The results may be 'sentimentalism' as *The League* reviewer comments (the same condemnation has been repeatedly thrown at Harriet Beecher Stowe for her depiction of American slaves in *Uncle Tom's Cabin* when she had no first-hand experience of their plight), but that is not to say they are not still effective. Indeed, the power of 'The Cry of the Children' lies in its stark contrasts, reconfiguration of conventional literary tropes, direct language, effective rhythms and emotional power, and this is felt in full force in the final shocking stanza where the children curse Britain as a whole for their maltreatment:

> 'How long,' they say, 'how long, O cruel nation,
>   Will you stand, to move the world, on a child's heart,—
> Stifle down with a mailed heel its palpitation,
>   And tread onward to your throne amid the mart?
> Our blood splashes upward, O gold-heaper,
>   And your purple shows your path!
> But the child's sob in the silence curses deeper
>   Than the strong man in his wrath.'

(ll.153–60)

The effective closure of Condition-of-England texts is often notoriously difficult to achieve: how can an effective, workable solution to the ills of industrialism be brought about? Gaskell's *Mary Barton* (1848) only succeeds in advocating greater commitment to religion or suggesting emigration as the answer for the urban poor, while Dickens' *Hard Times* (1854) posits potential hope in the humanitarian values embodied by the circus which nevertheless remains on Coketown's periphery. Barrett herself was also unable to proffer a solution to the children's cries and instead, through the imagery of the final stanza, she delivers a curse from the children, the impact of which is shocking and forceful and which is only further highlighted in the placing of 'The Cry of the Children' in *Poems* (1844) next to 'A Child Asleep', a text which celebrates childhood in true Romantic fashion as holy, visionary and innocent.

The poem syntactically connected with 'The Cry of the Children', 'The Cry of the Human', is rather more wide-ranging in its critique of the hardships faced by the workers in the Hungry Forties but was partly inspired by Barrett's desire to write something on the horrifying consequences of the Corn Laws. Implemented in 1815, the Corn Laws were originally intended to protect Britain's farmers against foreign competition by imposing duty on imported grain. The result was that bread prices were kept artificially high and many workers could not afford to buy it. The National Anti-Corn Law League was founded in 1839 but by the time the laws were repealed in June 1846, the high bread prices had only served to exacerbate the effects of the Irish potato famine and nearly a million people had died.

Central to Barrett's 'The Cry of the Human', therefore, is the exposure of the ruthlessness of modern capitalist practices which, like the market in Christina Rossetti's *Goblin Market* (1862), even puts a price on humanity and morality:

> The plague of gold strikes far and near,
>   And deep and strong it enters [. . .]
> Our thoughts grow blank, our words grow strange,
>   We cheer the pale gold-diggers,
> Each soul is worth so much on 'Change,
>   And marked, like sheep, with figures.

(ll.37–8; 41–4)

This was a great period of financial speculation through, for example, the new railway mania, where fortunes were being made and lost in a day. But it was also, of course, a time of great poverty and famine and Barrett demonstrates how, within these systems of exploitation, people are effectively de-humanised, alienated from their own consciousness and from language, and reduced to a beast-like status for sale on the open market. It is this Carlylean worship of Mammon as a defining feature of the age that

Barrett then cites as the cause of the implementation of the Corn Laws and the terrible consequences which ensue:

> The curse of gold upon the land
>   The lack of bread enforces;
> The rail-cars snort from strand to strand,
>   Like more of Death's White Horses:
> The rich preach 'rights' and 'future days,'
>   And hear no angel scoffing,
> The poor die mute, with starving gaze
>   On corn-ships in the offing.

(ll.46–53)

Again, as in the conclusion of 'Crowned and Buried' and throughout *A Drama of Exile* and *The Seraphim*, it is the figure of the angel here who ultimately casts judgement upon human activity, 'scoffing' at the self-righteousness of those in positions of authority who use economic status to 'normalise' the structures of society to their own ends. This fits, of course, with the overall agenda of the poem which emphasises that in the face of a range of political and social catastrophes, including battle, disease, poverty and infant mortality as well as the impact of the Corn Laws, people should never stop trusting in God. The poem opens, therefore, with the firm statement '"There is no God," the foolish saith' (1.1) and is punctuated throughout by the refrain 'Be pitiful, O God!'. Indeed, despite the mirroring image with 'The Cry of the Children' of heaven as 'cloud-wheels roll[ing] and grind[ing]' (1.14), the poem ends with the need to embrace God, to 'Look up and triumph' (1.123).

Again, therefore, Barrett situates a solution for social ills in fervent belief in God and greater understanding, reasoning which aligns her with other Condition-of-England commentators. In the meantime, however, she has clearly exposed, and asserted her public voice on, a range of contemporary issues which conflicted with her Whig-influenced beliefs in the fundamental necessity of the dignity and liberty of the individual. Indeed, so successfully did she do this that in early 1845 she was approached by the Anti-Corn Law League to write something further for their cause. In the end, under the influence of her father and brothers who were against the idea, she declined, but her letter to Mitford strikingly demonstrates the strong social role to which she felt it was her duty to aspire:

> Now *I*, you know, am leagues before the rest of my house in essential radicalism, . . & by no means believe in the ruin of farmers being dependent on the preservation of duties on corn, or even in the desirableness of *saving* a farmer & landed proprietor at the expense of the great body of the population.

The people ought to have free trade in corn, & they will have it, . . without duty
& restriction . . whether I write a poem on the actual grievance or not [. . . .]
But to refuse to give or rather to refuse to attempt to give, a voice to a great
public suffering, when I am asked to do it . . & when I recognize the existence
of the suffering . . should THIS be refused?

(*BC* 10:62)

Such giving of a voice to suffering had always been central to Barrett's poetics
and as we will see in Chapters Seven and Eight, this would become the
dominant mode of address in her writings of the 1850s.

THE EMERGING COMMITMENT
TO THE MODERN

Volume One of *Poems* (1844) concludes with a poem in which Barrett
emphasises her emerging commitment to contemporary issues and concerns:
'Lady Geraldine's Courtship'. Written at great speed in order to swell the
size of the volume (Barrett told Boyd that she wrote 140 lines in one day,
BC 9:65), it is constructed in pseudo-epistolary form as Bertram, a poor poet,
writes to a friend of his seemingly unrequited love for Geraldine, the lady of
the manor. After a series of tense scenes between them, however, Geraldine
finally admits her love for Bertram and we are left to presume that they will
marry.

What is particularly important for our arguments here, however, is how
'Lady Geraldine's Courtship' represents a new commitment to the modern
world in Barrett's developing aesthetic. Indeed, the poem can almost be read
as a summary of Barrett's changing ideas about poetry and poetics which
Poems as a whole appears to map out. For as the subtitle makes clear, this is
'A Romance of the Age' which treats, Barrett wrote to Boyd, 'of railroads,
routes, & all manner of "temporalities,"—and in so radical a temper, that
I expect to be reproved for it by the conservative reviews round' (*BC* 9:65).
Within the third stanza alone the poem moves from the lady, knight and
castle associated with traditional ballad poetry to an emphasis on the modern
early Victorian scene:

She has halls among the woodlands, she has castles by the breakers,
She has farms and she has manors, she can threaten and command:
And the palpitating engines snort in steam across her acres,
As they mark upon the blasted heaven the measure of the land.

(ll.9–12)

The poem therefore shifts into a political dimension with its competing referents to the products of Victorian industry and progress. Indeed, right at the very heart of the poem is an extended satire spoken by Bertram on the whole notion of 'progress' in the contemporary world which probably would account, at least in part, for Carlyle's enthusiasm for the work:

> And her custom was to praise me when I said,—'The Age culls simples,
> With a broad clown's back turned broadly to the glory of the stars.
> We are gods by our own reck'ning, and may well shut up the temples,
> And wield on, amid the incense-steam, the thunder of our cars.
>
> 'For we throw out acclamations of self-thanking, self-admiring,
> With, at every mile run faster,—'O the wondrous wondrous age!'
> Little thinking if we work our SOULS as nobly as our iron,
> Or if angels will commend us at the goal of pilgrimage.
>
> 'Why, what *is* this patient entrance into nature's deep resources
> But the child's most gradual learning to walk upright without bane!
> When we drive out, from the cloud of steam, majestical white horses,
> Are we greater than the first men who led black ones by the mane?
>
> 'If we trod the deeps of ocean, if we struck the stars in rising,
> If we wrapped the globe intensely with one hot electric breath,
> 'Twere but power within our tether, no new spirit-power comprising,
> And in life we were not greater men, nor bolder men in death.'

(ll.197–212)

While the poem on one level therefore seems to critique the Victorian notion of 'progress' when it leads to self-congratulatory posturing and the loss of morality, it does, however, also point to positive elements in the modern world in terms of class and gender. For this is another of Barrett's poems which deals explicitly with class issues, working through the differentials between Geraldine and Bertram – 'She was sprung of English nobles, I was born of English peasants' (l.15) – to a stage where barriers are broken down through love and understanding. Moreover, in terms of gender, Geraldine represents a very modern woman who, rather than resembling the statue of Silence at the centre of Wycombe Hall's grounds, possesses intellectual curiosity and self-agency.

The final work which Barrett wrote for *Poems* (1844) therefore draws together many of the strands of the volume, highlighting issues concerning both the positive and alarming aspects of social, political and technological development, and interrogating established structures of class and gender. By placing it as a closing poem, Barrett purposely foregrounded her new commitment to 'the Age' which would be most powerfully explored in the poem for which 'Lady Geraldine's Courtship' stands as something of a prototype and which Barrett would begin conceiving just two years later, her magnum opus, *Aurora Leigh*.

FAMILY POLITICS AND RUNAWAY SLAVES

Two years after the publication of *Poems* (1844), Elizabeth Barrett secretly married Robert Browning, whose work she had already celebrated in 'Lady Geraldine's Courtship' as part of the positive aspects of the modern age, and ran away to Italy. In this act of rebellion, of course, she was herself fighting against a tyranny every bit as oppressive as those tyrannical structures she spent much of her work of the 1840s interrogating and put herself into the position of the exile with which she was perennially fascinated. Significantly, however, she recognised that her father's forbidding his children to marry under any circumstances (Henrietta and Alfred later married too and were similarly disowned) was a deeper problem than the seeming whim of a single Victorian *pater familiaris*. Rather, as she explained to Robert, '[t]he evil is in the system—& he simply takes it to be his duty to rule [. . .] like the Kings of Christendom, by divine right' (*BC* 11:43). Barrett's understanding of the ways in which power systems work and the close links between the abuse of power in public and private domains was always astute, and here she suggests that her father was just as much a victim of the political and social ideologies he felt it necessary to uphold.

It is highly significant, therefore, that the first political poem written by Elizabeth Barrett *Browning* was 'The Runaway Slave at Pilgrim's Point'. We have already discussed the ambiguities of the Barretts' slave-owning background in Chapter One and it is clear that in this work the eldest daughter of the family was overtly critiquing both the exploitative systems upon which her own privileged existence was based and slavery more generally, in America and elsewhere. As with the factory poem, the slavery poem had a long association with women poets since it was believed that this was an area where women could express compassion on a public scale. And yet for many women, of course, the slavery issue was more complex, for repeatedly women constructed their own sense of societal oppression through analogies with the reported experiences of slaves in America and Africa. From Jane Austen's *Mansfield Park* to Harriet Beecher Stowe's *Uncle Tom's Cabin* and through to Toni Morrison's *Beloved* in our own time, the discourses of feminism and slavery have often been interlinked in complex ways. Barrett Browning's family background only served to make that interlinking even more problematic.

'The Runaway Slave' was written in 1845 when the Boston Anti-Slavery Bazaar, which distributed anti-slavery propaganda throughout America, asked Barrett if she would contribute to their radical annual, *The Liberty Bell*. Although the poem only appeared in the 1848 edition, it was already completed by early 1847, just a few months after Barrett had married. At the time, however, she feared that her narrative of a black woman slave who is raped by her masters and who subsequently murders her child might be too extreme for her American editors. Writing to Mitford, for example, she stated that she 'could not help making it bitter' (*MRM* 3:203) and later she confided to Boyd that the work might be 'too ferocious'. Resolutely, however, she continued, 'but they asked for a poem and shall have it' (*HSB* 283).

Ferocious it was, indeed, and remains so. Constructed in the form of a complex dramatic monologue (see Chapter Five on genre), the poem takes place at Pilgrim's Point as the slave makes a last defiant stand against the oppressive white system which has systematically robbed her of her freedom, her identity, her lover, and her right to control her own body and sexuality. Ironically, Pilgrim's Point was the site where the Pilgrim Fathers, fleeing religious persecution in their native England, landed to begin a new life of liberty, but as the slave kneels down to invoke their spirits, she realises that it is their descendants who are now the perpetrators of the systems of tyranny: 'O pilgrims, I have gasped and run/ All night long from the whips of one/ Who in your names works sin and woe!' (ll.12–14). Once again, therefore, Barrett Browning articulates how cycles of abuse are perpetuated from one generation to the next.

As with 'The Cry of the Children', this poem of political protest also works through a dichotomy, but here of black and white images. Throughout, the slave repeatedly emphasises her colour with her bold cry of self-identification 'I am black, I am black!' (l.57), a political signifier of both her pride in her race and that which alienates her from the sources of (white) power and authority. However, as she produces her carefully reasoned argument against these sources of oppression, the slave, who significantly remains nameless throughout, highlights the fact that systems of racial power difference are little more than social fabrications. Indeed, looking around her at the natural world, she observes multiple examples of positive black images in the dark birds, the dark stream and the dark night (ll.31–5). The assignation of specific attributes to the races in the world inhabited by the runaway slave (white = good/ intelligent/ superior, black = evil/ mentally undeveloped/ inferior) is therefore exposed as a stratagem developed by those in control in order to maintain the established economic and social order. In contrast to the freedom of the black creatures in the natural world, the skin colour of slaves 'shuts like prison bars' (l.39).

'The Runaway Slave' achieves a more wide-ranging representation of the horrors of slavery through the slave's articulation of her past narrative and the use of analepsis (flashback). Once, she reports, she was not a victim of fear but one who 'laughed in girlish glee' (l.58) because of her reciprocated love for another slave, and while her lover made verbal affirmations of his love for her, she quietly sang his name 'Over and over' (l.79) as a form of covert rebellion against their captors. As Ann Douglas notes, one of the most distressing abuses of civil rights embodied in the slave system was the forced separation of families and relationships which Harriet Beecher Stowe vividly dramatises in *Uncle Tom's Cabin* (Douglas, 1981: 27). Barrett similarly foregrounds this abuse in the slave's reporting how her lover was brutally taken away from her and possibly murdered ('I crawled to touch/ His blood's mark in the dust', ll.96–7), while she herself became the victim of gang rape by the slave owners:

> Mere grief's too good for such as I:
> So the white men brought the shame ere long
> To strangle the sob of my agony.
> They would not leave me for my dull
> Wet eyes!—it was too merciful
> To let me weep pure tears and die.
>
> I am black, I am black!
> I wore a child upon my breast . . .

(ll.100–7)

As an ultimate act of subjugation, Barrett Browning would return to the issue of rape in *Aurora Leigh* in which she tells the story of Marian's rape and her being sold into prostitution. However, whereas Marian is rescued by Aurora in an act signifying both female solidarity and another dismantling of class barriers, the runaway slave is abandoned and isolated with her child, whose white colour and male gender aligns it with her oppressors. '[T]oo white for me,' the runaway slave argues (l.116), observing in her child's '*master's* look' (l.144) the germ of the next generation of murdering, raping slave owners. Therefore, in a protracted scene which is arguably the most horrifying in all of Barrett Browning's work, she suffocates her child in her shawl until he lay 'a stiffening cold' (l.152).

In his theorisation of the dramatic monologue in *The Poetry of Experience*, Robert Langbaum has argued that there exists a tension between sympathy and judgement in our reactions to the speaker of a dramatic monologue, that we often split off our sympathy from moral judgement since 'we must adopt his [*sic*] viewpoint as our entry into the poem' (Langbaum, 1957: 78). Certainly, despite the horror of the infanticide scene in this poem, an act which would, of course, undercut fundamental nineteenth-century beliefs about woman's 'natural' maternal role, most readers are likely to have understanding and even empathy with the slave's situation. Barrett Browning may have subscribed to the Romantic idea of children representing hope for the future (see Chapter Seven), but here the murder fits the logic of the poem and represents, as David argues, a powerful reversal of the white master/ black slave relationship (David, 1987: 139). Indeed, through the burial of the white child in the black earth where it will decay and be absorbed, the woman is further undercutting the colour-based binaries which deny her power and agency.

Also fundamental to 'The Runaway Slave', of course, is a continuation and development of the critique of the relationship of established religion to the marginalised 'Other' which 'The Cry of the Children' earlier explored. As a number of American literary works of the 1840s and 50s such as Nathaniel Hawthorne's *The Scarlet Letter* and Harriet Beecher Stowe's *Uncle Tom's Cabin* clearly articulated, established religion was often used as an instrument with which to keep down those groups who might be seen as alien or a potential threat to the status quo whether they be women, Indians or slaves. In Barrett Browning's poem, despite the slave's affirmation that God 'has made dark things', he is depicted as aloof and uncommunicative ('nothing didst Thou say', l.88), residing over a heaven of 'fine white angels' (l.157), the colour of which serves to further alienate the black slaves. The runaway slave is therefore betrayed by all society's structures, reaffirming once more Barrett Browning's belief that the fault is in the system. As the poem ends, the slave turns to face the men who have hunted her down and powerfully defies their control over her: 'I throw off your eyes like snakes that sting!' (l.207) she cries, before once again exposing the myth of America, the land of the free, as mere empty rhetoric. As she argues, the black eagle, symbol of American democracy, has rather been 'killed ... at nest' (l.208) and the marks of the ropes on her wrists tell a different narrative of struggle and oppression.

As Helen Cooper notes, the speaker 'never falters in presenting the complexity of her situation' and achieves integrity in part by the shaping of her own discourse (Cooper, 1988: 115). It is highly significant, therefore, that her final gesture before throwing herself off the rock to her death, in what David terms 'a dreadful parody of the liberation achieved by [the] white pilgrims' (David, 1987: 139), is to curse the nation's authorities and to call to other slaves to rise up against oppression: 'from these sands/ Up to the mountains, lift your hands,/ O slaves, and end what I begun!' (ll.229–31). Importantly, therefore, Barrett Browning's final major political poem of the 1840s concludes with the ultimate defiance of, and challenge to, the exploitative patriarchal systems of authority and power which she had spent the decade interrogating, a defiance which Michel Foucault would read as essential to the potential dismantling of dominant discursive practices.

Barrett Browning was not to leave the slavery issue here, however, for in the late 1840s she wrote a sonnet, 'Hiram Powers' "Greek Slave"', which again explores the links between the oppression of slaves and women. The Brownings knew the American sculptor Hiram Powers in Florence and the statue which the sonnet describes was one of the most popular art works of the nineteenth century, even being displayed at the Great Exhibition. Depicting a young naked Greek girl captured by the Turks and put up for sale in the slave market with her wrists enchained, the statue is an embodiment of beautiful, even erotic vulnerability which Barrett Browning was then able to use to launch a more devastating attack on all forms of slavery across Russia, America and the West Indies. As the poem articulates, she certainly saw Power's work as mirroring her own, both of them seeking to expose political and social injustice through 'Art's fiery finger' which can '[p]ierce to the centre' and 'break up ere long/ The serfdom of this world!' (ll.8–10). Indeed, as she later wrote to a female correspondent:

> is it possible that you think a woman has no business with questions like the question of slavery? Then she had better use a pen no more. She had better subside into slavery and concubinage herself, I think, as in the times of old, shut herself up with the Penelopes in the 'women's apartment,' and take no rank among thinkers and speakers.
>
> (in Moers, 1977: 40)

By the end of the 1840s, then, Elizabeth Barrett Browning had clearly joined the ranks of important 'thinkers and speakers' on political matters. She had dedicated herself to using art as a political weapon and had drawn attention to a range of social and political ills she witnessed around her. In 1850, *Poems* (1844) was reissued with some restructuring of the material, the inclusion of works from *The Seraphim, and Other Poems*, and some significant new additions such as the *Sonnets from the Portuguese*, the sonnets to Boyd who had died in 1848, and a new translation of *Prometheus Bound*. Barrett Browning had been particularly uneasy with her earlier translation (see Chapter Two) and so insisted on translating it a second time. Again, however, it is possible to see this endeavour in a wider political context, for just as we can relate Barrett's earlier attraction to the tragedy in the wake of the debates around the First Reform Bill, we can relate this later return to the play in the light of the revolutionary fervour of the 1840s and the increased emphasis on the rights of the individual. Prometheus stands, like her own runaway slave, as a defiant figure who refuses to accept tyrannical power structures and who makes a final stand against them. It was this defiance in the face of contemporary political injustices which Barrett Browning herself would make the hallmark of the remainder of her life's work in *Casa Guidi Windows*, *Aurora Leigh* and *Poems Before Congress*.

5

GENRE: A CHAPTER ON FORM

REBECCA STOTT

As soon as the word genre is sounded, as soon as it is heard, as soon as one attempts to conceive it, a limit is drawn. And when a limit is established, norms and interdictions are not far behind.

(Derrida, 1992: 224)

What form is best for poems? Let me think
Of forms less, and the external. Trust the spirit,
As sovran nature does, to make the form;
For otherwise we only imprison spirit
And not embody. Inward evermore
To outward, – so in life, and so in art
Which still is life.
           Five acts to make a play.
And why not fifteen? why not ten? or seven?
What matter for the number of the leaves,
Supposing the tree lives and grows? exact
The literal unities of time and place,
When 'tis the essence of passion to ignore
Both time and place? Absurd. Keep up the fire,
And leave the generous flames to shape themselves.

(*AL* 5:223–36)

On 30 December 1844, Elizabeth Barrett wrote to her friend Mary Russell Mitford: 'I want to write a poem of a new class, in a measure—a *Don Juan*, without the mockery and impurity, . . under one aspect,—and having unity, as a work of art,—& admitting of as much philosophical dreaming & digression (which is in fact a characteristic of the age) as I like to use. Might it not be done, even if I could not do it? & I think of trying at any rate' (*BC* 9:304).

    A poet is at work planning a poem. She has a shadowy idea of what she wants to write and is now trying to find an appropriate form for it. It is not easy. The form is a problem. She is not confident that she knows what it will be, but in beginning to conjure this form she reaches for the example of another poem – *Don Juan* by her adored poet-mentor, Lord Byron. But Byron's poem does not represent a model that she will follow slavishly; instead it will be a way of helping her think her way through to a *new* form, for there is so much of Byron's model that simply will not do; she adds immediately 'without the mockery and impurity'. In addition, her poem, unlike Byron's, she implies, will have a *unity* as a work of art. By this point in her poetic career, Elizabeth Barrett had used many poetic forms: the ballad, the poetic essay, the dramatic monologue, the lyric, the sonnet, the epic. But none of these will do here. She needs a 'poem of a new class'; she is not confident that she can achieve it, but that anxiety will not prevent her trying.

Elizabeth Barrett's letter foreshadows the voice of the twentieth-century novelist Virginia Woolf, who also struggled against the weight of literary tradition and in particular against the conventional forms of the novel that were available to her in the early twentieth century. The old tools of the realists are no longer adequate, she wrote passionately; rather, new forms must be found by the many writers of her age who shared with her a struggle to portray not the surface clutter of people's lives but their *essence*, their interiority. Addressing her audience in 1927, she asked them to accept her experiment and the experiments of her fellow writers: 'Tolerate the spasmodic, the obscure, the fragmentary, the fail-ure.... For I will make one final and surpassingly rash prediction – we are trembling on the verge of one of the great ages of English literature' (Woolf, 1950: 119).

Virginia Woolf and Elizabeth Barrett Browning were inventors of new literary forms, but not inventors for invention's sake; they struggled to find new forms because the existing forms did not allow them to do what they needed to do; nor did the old forms shape the world adequately. Virginia Woolf's writing made waves; it troubled readers and reviewers precisely because it was sometimes difficult for them to place her work within familiar genres. A work like *A Room of One's Own*, for instance, had pre-cisely the rambling philosophical elasticity that Elizabeth Barrett Browning hungered for in planning *Aurora Leigh*. But as with *A Room of One's Own*, it is very difficult to categorise it: it draws on the conventions of rhetoric, essay, journalism, invective, autobiography and lecture. It is all of these and none of them. Similarly, *Aurora Leigh* proves resistant to genre categorisa-tion: it is part autobiography, part biography, part *Kunstlerroman* (a form that describes the development of an artist), part philosophical rumination, part political invective, part religious discourse, and at once both novel and poem.

Elizabeth Barrett Browning was inventive in an age of poetic invention. In an essay on experiment in Victorian poetry, E. Warwick Slinn has argued that many Victorian poets were driven to 'adapt established styles to contemporary needs', particularly by a common desire to 'combine narrative and speculative commentary with the requirements of aesthetic unity' (Slinn, 2000: 46). Many, like Elizabeth Barrett Browning, found the most flexible and permissive form in the shape of the long poem, one that told a story about a realisable world but allowed for philosophical rumination, as did Tennyson in *In Memoriam*, *The Princess* and *Maud*, and Arthur Hugh Clough in *Amours de Voyage* and *The Bothie of Tober-Na-Vuolich*. After Elizabeth Barrett Browning's death, Robert Browning also used this form in his richly philosophical and poetically innovative *The Ring and the Book*. The long poem allowed for interesting combinations of the three classical genres identified by the Greeks – drama, epic and lyric – which Barrett Browning had, of course, studied. In an exploration of the modern long poem, the poet and critic Smaro Kamboureli writes both about the form's elasticity and the way it enables writers to transgress traditional genre boundaries – an observation that holds for both the nineteenth- and twentieth-century long poem:

> The diverse compositional nature of the long poem illustrates that generic limits are indeed elastic: they can stretch, extend, or fold within and without. Nonetheless, the long poem transgresses not the limits of a single genre but the limits, the frames, of various genres, such as those of the lyric, the epic, the narrative, the drama, the documentary, and the prose poem.

> (Kamboureli, 1991: 100)

Elizabeth Barrett Browning and Virginia Woolf adapted established genres in the same manner as the novelist Angela Carter who celebrated the explosive effects of putting new wine into old bottles: 'I am all for putting new wine in old bottles, especially if the pressure of the new wine makes the old bottles explode' (Carter, 1997: 37). But this reworking and reshaping and 'rebottling' has other effects too, for enshrined in the old forms are old assumptions, pre-scripted plots, socially-determined ways of behaving. Genres embody social norms and expectations as well as aesthetic ones. For instance, the nineteenth-century patterns of closure in the novel so often enshrined marriage as a point of arrival and achievement of social integration. So in reworking the old patterns of poetry, writers unsettle not just poetic forms but also implicitly offer at the same time an 'institutional critique' as E. Warwick Slinn has argued:

when genres are reshaped or recovered (like medieval ballads in the eighteenth century), they may test or expose paradigms of contemporary values (reason, orderliness, universality) as well as aesthetic norms (neoclassical decorum).

(Slinn, 2000: 46–7)

Experimental writing, Slinn argues, is therefore often not just of aesthetic significance but also of cultural significance. In this sense, he continues, 'literary experimentation functions as a form of social dynamism, breaking up the inertia of linguistic habits and, ambiguously, questioning or rehabilitating them' (Slinn, 2000: 47). To return to the example of Virginia Woolf, this novelist rejected the realist novel of her predecessors not just because she wanted to do something different but because its form and the social norms and expectations it scripted were in her view no longer relevant to her world. The world had changed.

In this chapter I want to test Slinn's claims against Elizabeth Barrett Browning's experiments with form, particularly in her use of the sonnet, the ballad and the epic, some of the oldest of all the poetic forms with a set of gendered expectations and traditions which have accrued around them, and her use of a much newer form used by many Victorian poets in inventive ways, the dramatic monologue. But I want to begin with the most formally experimental poem she wrote, which in some ways incorporates all of these genres and more: *Aurora Leigh*.

'TEARS AND SMALL-TALK': *AURORA LEIGH*

Aurora Leigh, one of the greatest literary experiments of the Victorian age, is the generic hybrid that Elizabeth Barrett needed it to be in order to accommodate her planned 'conversations & events' and 'philosophical dreaming & digression'. Another way of describing its eclectic grafting of diverse genres (including autobiography, dialogue, satire, treatise, narrative, prophesy, modern epic and *Kunstlerroman*) is to use the term coined by W. David Shaw, 'generic indeterminacy', by which Shaw means a 'radical failure' to satisfy expectations of closure or the conventions of an established genre (Shaw, 1985: 472). Generic indeterminacy is at the heart of *Aurora Leigh*; one of the effects of this is a degree of liquidity commented on by several reviewers: George Eliot, for instance, described the poem as being a 'full mind pouring itself out in song as its natural and easiest medium', and as having 'the calm, even flow of a broad river' (Eliot in Reynolds, 1996: 408).

Other critics, however, such as H.F. Chorley, writing in *The Athenaeum* in November 1856, commented less favourably on its formal qualities:

> ... we have no experience of such a mingling of what is precious with what is mean – of the voice of clarion and the lyric cadence of harp with the cracked school-room spinet – of tears and small-talk – of eloquent apostrophe and adult speculation – of the grandeur of passion and the pettiness of modes and manners – as we find in these nine books of blank verse.

> (Chorley in Reynolds, 1996: 406)

In the poem itself Barrett Browning uses the metaphor of lava rather than water to describe its molten quality: Aurora, for instance, speaks of poetry as 'the burning lava of a song' (*AL* 5:215). The poem solidifies and melts, opens up and closes down continually as Aurora describes her complex and subtle inner world, 'the soul itself, / Its shifting fancies and celestial lights' (*AL* 5:340–1), and then opens to the outer world in which she writes: the age which 'brawls, cheats, maddens, calculates, aspires' (*AL* 5:204). The poem also oscillates between retrospective narration, everything that has happened in Aurora's life until the actual writing moment, and the present-time unfolding of events written like a poetic journal. The loose form of the poem allows the digressive philosophical rumination which Barrett Browning longed for in planning it but the voice of Aurora, with all its variations of mood and tone and introspection, is what unifies the poetry, holds it all together and channels the volcanic energies of the poem:

> Why what a pettish, petty thing I grow, –
> A mere, mere woman, a mere flaccid nerve,
> A kerchief left out all night in the rain,
> Turned soft so, – overtasked and overstrained
> And overlived in this close London life!
> And yet I should be stronger.

> (*AL* 3:36–41)

AURORA LEIGH AS FEMINISED EPIC

Susan Stanford Friedman and a number of other critics such as Marjorie Stone and Dorothy Mermin have drawn attention to the way Barrett Browning has feminised the epic conventions used in *Aurora Leigh* (for a further discussion of Barrett Browning's use of epic forms see Chapter 3 on the early poems). In comparing the poem with another feminised epic of the early twentieth century, *Helen in Egypt*, by the poet H.D., Friedman shows how both poets moved 'woman' from the margins of the epic to its centre:

> This centrality of women was commonplace in the novel, but the transformation of woman from Being to Doing, from object to subject was a radical re-vision of epic convention.

> (Friedman in Reynolds, 1996: 467)

As a consequence of this shift of position the heroic comes to be redefined in female terms and the scene of heroic action shifts from the public world of battle and conflict to the private domain of the lyric – in Barrett Browning's case, domestic spaces such as the drawing room, the shrubbery, the attic garret and the slum home of Marion Erle as well as to the street life of the great city spaces of the poem in Paris, Florence and London. In addition, the male protagonist, Romney, undergoes a transformation which is essential to the resolution of Aurora's conflict between poetic vocation and love, for it is only when Romney through blinding comes to love Aurora as a poet that that conflict can be resolved. The narrative of the poem remains focused throughout entirely on the development of Aurora. By using the epic form, Barrett Browning makes Aurora the Odysseus or Aeneas of her epic and suggests that her struggle for selfhood is no less heroic than theirs and that domestic spaces contain no less drama than the open seas and unexplored lands of the traditional epic adventure. In all these changes to the form, Barrett Browning is indeed presenting a critique of patriarchy and writing about her own conflict with the dominant ideologies of her time: that within traditional poetics men are heroes, women objects in male dramas, and heroism can only be played out in the public world. *Aurora Leigh*, as Friedman has argued, represents

> a deconstruction of the binary gender system underlying poetic genres, norms personified by Homer as the father of the epic and Sappho as the mother of the lyric. Replacing the father with the mother, Barrett Browning and H.D. brought the discourse of the personal and the marginal into the genre of the public and the patriarchal.

> (Friedman in Reynolds, 1996: 473)

AURORA LEIGH: DIDACTICISM IN DIALOGUE

Although the poem is written in Aurora's voice, the story that she tells encompasses the voices of others and in this it is both rooted in dialogue and didactic at the same time. Throughout the poem Barrett Browning draws on rhetorical techniques in which Aurora's claims are balanced by counter-claims. Aurora may claim, for instance, that the education her aunt gives her is oppressive and pointless, but Barrett Browning is careful to show us that her aunt thinks otherwise. Aurora may claim that being a poet is vocation enough, but Barrett Browning shows us that Romney thinks otherwise: he believes she should put her self to one side and instead work to right social wrongs. Aurora may claim that poetry should be of the age, but Barrett Browning shows us that there are other ways of looking at the question of the role of the poet. Aurora's voice is always in dialogue with others. And her representation of these marshalled counterclaims is always fair, even when she passionately rejects them. When Aurora describes her aunt in Book 1, for instance, she is quick to tell us why her aunt has invested so much in the education she provides for Aurora:

> She had lived
> A sort of cage-bird life, born in a cage,
> Accounting that to leap from perch to perch
> Was act and joy enough for any bird.
> Dear heaven, how silly are the things that live
> In thickets, and eat berries!
> I, alas,
> A wild bird scarcely fledged, was brought to her cage,
> And she was there to meet me. Very kind.
> Bring the clean water, give out the fresh seed.

> (*AL* 1:304–12)

In passages such as this Barrett Browning draws on the rhetorical techniques of the dramatic monologue in inventive ways. Both Aurora and her aunt seem to have burst into impromptu speech here in giving their conflicting perspectives on women's roles: 'Dear heaven, how silly are the things that live in thickets', 'says' the aunt, whereas Aurora, already raised as a 'wild' bird in Italy, cannot adjust to the cage-bird life. The aunt, however, knows of no other way of living. The result is conflict and suffering for Aurora but she is keen to show us through passages of 'spasmodic' dialogue like this, in which one view is juxtaposed with another, that her aunt believes these things because she has been conditioned to do so through her own education and socialisation. She believes she is doing the right thing. It is the only option for her if she is going to fulfil her sense of duty to the child. The cutting ironic tone caught in the last two lines perfectly expresses Aurora's bitterness about, and simultaneously resignation to, her oppressive socialisation.

In this way the poem builds up book by book, episode by episode, as a space in which Aurora's voice is heard in conversation and in often impassioned debate. In certain parts the poem is a series of clustered arguments about the role of women, of poets, of social reformers, the place of education, social change and duty in a modern world. It is a poem, in Barrett Browning's words, that concerns its own 'live, throbbing age' (*AL* 5:203).

Just as Aurora is in dialogue with other characters in the verse-novel, so Elizabeth Barrett Browning uses the poem as a way of engaging in conversation with fellow poets and writers, living and dead. Cora Kaplan in her introductory essay to the 1978 edition of *Aurora Leigh* writes:

> *Aurora Leigh* should be read as an overlapping sequence of dialogues with other texts, other writers. None of these debates are finished, some pursue contradictory arguments. . . . The text's unity is that adult voice that does not permit interruption as it tells us how things should be: its unintegrated remarks and pointed silences remind us that the 'knowledge' of any one age is constantly open to rupture and revision.

(Kaplan, 1978: 16–17)

In a later chapter on *Aurora Leigh* I will deal with the *thematic* borrowings of the poem, but here I am concerned primarily with the aspects of form Barrett Browning borrowed from earlier writers. She admitted to using Byron's long poem *Don Juan* as a model for *Aurora Leigh* but Wordsworth's *The Prelude* probably also gave her ideas for writing a long poem about the growth of a poet. The discursive, apparently fragmented form of Milton's *Paradise Lost* provided another starting point. In terms of dialogue with other literary texts of Barrett Browning's time, Kaplan demonstrates that in *Aurora Leigh* the poet was engaging with issues about class and the position of women also being explored in other novels and verse-novels of the early nineteenth century, in particular de Staël's *Corinne* (1807), Tennyson's *The Princess* (1847), Clough's *The Bothie of Tober-Na-Vuolich* (1848), Kingsley's *Alton Locke* (1851) and Elizabeth Gaskell's *Ruth* (1853).

On one level, then, the voice of Aurora, and behind it the voice of Elizabeth Barrett Browning, is didactic, often deafeningly so – we are never in doubt about Aurora's opinions – but by placing those opinions in clusters of counter-arguments, Barrett Browning, as Kaplan has argued, reminds us that 'the "knowledge" of any one age is constantly open to rupture and revision', that truth is multi-sided and that conversation and debate are central to exploring that multi-sidedness. To return, then, to Slinn's proposition that experiment in poetry needs to be considered both in terms of how it unsettles cultural as well as aesthetic norms, how do we approach the experiment of

Aurora Leigh? One answer is that Barrett Browning's experiment with form has brought together didacticism and dialogue, or rather has placed didactic argument *within* dialogue. We see Aurora's strong opinions forming through conversation with herself and others, so that the views the poem champions are passionately championed, yet never held up as the *only* views. Truth, the poem implies, is indeed many sided and reached as often in everyday conversation with ordinary people as in the debating chambers of politicians or the philosophical exchange of great men.

SONNETS FROM THE PORTUGUESE

Rhetorical structures and dialogue are also at the centre of the sonnet form as used by Barrett Browning. She wrote sonnets throughout her life but it is the sonnet sequence she wrote during the two-year correspondence leading up to her marriage to Robert Browning for which she is best known. Although she did not show the forty-four sonnets of *Sonnets from the Portuguese* to Browning until after their marriage and they were not published until 1850, the poems themselves grew out of and through the extraordinary corres-pondence between Barrett and Browning written between 1844 and 1846. These letters are also worthy of study in terms of rhetoric, as the critic Eric Griffiths has noted when he praises '[t]he intensity with which they imagine absent interlocutors, their probing of what the other might reply, the devel-oping sense of how the letters continued the talks they had developed in a different and complicated medium' (Griffiths, 1989: 201). In many ways, the letters of Barrett and Browning are comparable to the spoken voice of the dramatic monologues they wrote: the monologues also assume a specified listener and create a degree of intimacy of discourse which builds up over time; like the letters, the monologues often seem confessional and whispered. Griffiths even suggests that Robert Browning continued to develop his use of the dramatic monologue through his experience of writing these letters:

> he learned . . . some of the profundity of the form as they developed their intimacy through the interchange of meetings and letters, in the accumulation of ardent scanning and re-audition, glossing each other's words, eliciting the voice of personality from fragments of conversation and comment.

> (Griffiths, 1989: 202)

The written yet intensely conversational quality of the courtship letters also appears to have directly influenced Elizabeth Barrett's use of the sonnet which, written at the same time as the letters, also seems conversational and with this unique overlap between written and spoken discourse. What Griffiths claims about the letters when he writes about 'these wonderful, affectionately palimpsest letters, sprawling with vows and cajolery, interjections, cross-references and private jokes' also describes the poems themselves which can be difficult to read because they so 'closely approach the condition of speech' (Griffiths, 1989: 203).

In undertaking to write a sonnet sequence, Elizabeth Barrett chose one of the tightest and most circumscribed of poetic forms with a long history and established set of conventions. The sonnet usually follows one of two main patterns. The first is the Italian or Petrarchan sonnet (named after the Italian fourteenth-century poet Petrarch) which has an octave (eight lines) rhyming *abbaabba* followed by a sestet (six lines) rhyming *cdecde* or some variant, such as *cdccdc*. The second is the English or Shakespearean sonnet, developed by poets in the sixteenth century, in which the sonnet falls into four sections rather than two: three quatrains (four lines) followed by a concluding couplet thereby rhyming *abba cdcd efef gg*. The success of the form depends to some extent upon the tension between the exploration of a complex problem or proposition or feeling and its containment within a tightly circumscribed structural pattern of rhyme and metre. In some of the most powerful love sonnets the feelings expressed are pushing constantly against their confines.

Although the Petrarchan sonnet usually moves towards some kind of resolution of the problem in the sestet, the English sonnet often fails to resolve the problem or paradox, moving instead to a new formulation of that problem in the final couplet, as a kind of encapsulation of the problem. The English sonnet then tends to be tighter, turned back on itself, spiralling; Peter Fuller calls it 'three turns of the screw so to speak, before the point is driven home in the final couplet' (Fuller, 1972: 17). In all sonnets rhetorical forms and techniques are evident to a lesser or greater extent in that the problem/ proposition/ paradox is explored through a series of questions, claims and counterclaims embodied, for instance, in the opening question of one of Shakespeare's most famous sonnets 'Shall I compare thee to a summer's day?' or the opening paradox of Sir Philip Sydney's sonnet: 'What may words say, or what may words not say,/ Where truth itself must speak like flattery?'

Rhetorical speculation is ever-present in *Sonnets from the Portuguese*. Perhaps the most famous line of all the sonnets in the sequence is the opening line of Sonnet 43: 'How do I love thee? Let me count the ways' – a question and answer contained within a single line. The intermittent use of rhetorical questions in the opening lines: 'What can I give thee back . . . ?' (Sonnet 8), 'How do I love thee?' (Sonnet 43), 'Is it indeed so?' (Sonnet 23), the direct address, the interjections and metrical freedoms and deliberate elisions, the claims and counterclaims, the pairing of paradoxes, the puns, all contribute to the sense of an intimate and intense ongoing conversation between the speaker and imagined interlocutors who are both an alternative self (in that she argues with different sides of herself) and the lover. One of the finest of the sequence uses cuckoo-song as its central conceit, as the speaker petitions for her lover to reiterate his love, to return her call like the cuckoo, for the repetition of the cuckoo serves to usher in spring. The poem is a marvellous orchestration of voices and calls:

> Say over again, and yet once over again,
> That thou dost love me. Though the word repeated
> Should seem 'a cuckoo song,' as thou dost treat it,
> Remember, never to the hill or plain,
> Valley and wood, without her cuckoo-strain
> Comes the fresh Spring in all her green completed.
> Belovèd, I, amid the darkness greeted
> By a doubtful spirit-voice, in that doubt's pain
> Cry, 'Speak once more — thou lovest!' Who can fear
> Too many stars, though each in heaven shall roll,
> Too many flowers, though each shall crown the year?
> Say thou dost love me, love me, love me—toll
> The silver iterance!—only minding, Dear,
> To love me also in silence with thy soul.

> (*Sonnet 21*)

Isobel Armstrong argues that in Barrett Browning's sonnets 'the late caesuras and enjambement declare an attempt to dissolve the customary forms and restrictions' (Armstrong, 1993: 356) but Barrett Browning's success is that she adapts the form to what she has to say, so that she both holds its shape and adjusts it simultaneously, putting new wine into old bottles in such a way as to make the old bottles explode, in Angela Carter's words. 'Language goes into a flux, as if enacting the dissolution of categories,' Armstrong continues. 'The effect is of expansion, a going beyond the limit of definition. . . . The sonnets chart the struggle of the feminine subject to take up a new position which is free of dependency. They struggle with their own dissolve as they try to break into new areas of being' (Armstrong, 1993: 356). Armstrong also points out that doors and thresholds dominate the imagery of these poems as they do in Sonnet 24, for instance:

> Let the world's sharpness, like a clasping knife,
> Shut in upon itself and do no harm
> In this close hand of Love, now soft and warm,
> And let us hear no sound of human strife
> After the click of the shutting.

> (*Sonnet 24*, ll.1–5)

But the barrier, the frontier, the locked and enclosed space are also some of the challenges for the sonnet writer, so often part of the paradoxes presented in the poem – infinite feeling expressed by finite rationed words.

Barrett Browning plays with the conventions and constraints of the sonnet throughout the sequences, allowing some of the sonnets to spill over into others, beginning some as if they were the unfinished conversations of others or answers, just as spoken conversation constantly spills over the grammatical structures of sentences. The first words of so many of the sonnets exemplify this spillage, establishing conversational and rhetorical echoes that resound across the boundaries of individual poems; several begin, for instance, with words such as 'yet' or 'and yet', 'indeed', 'but' or even 'oh yes!'. Often the rhythmical patterns of the lines break down, again like conversation, breaking momentarily into ellipsis, the characteristic three dots that intersperse the poems, showing for a moment the struggle with words, the catch of the imagined voice, pausing before it begins again.

One of the remarkable features of these sonnets is their studied spontaneity. The lines mimic the cut and thrust of internal monologue or spoken conversation with all its fragmentary, elliptical qualities and questions and answers turning in and back upon themselves, yet Barrett Browning achieves this spontaneity within the discipline of a tight rhyme scheme which is consistent throughout the poems. Throughout the sequence she merges features of the Italian and English sonnets, as if they were grafted together. Let's take Sonnet 36 as an example, a poem which explores the nature of romantic expectation and the perilous and thrilling insubstantiality of new love:

When we met first and loved, I did not build	(a)
Upon the event with marble. Could it mean	(b)
To last, a love set pendulous between	(b)
Sorrow and sorrow? Nay, I rather thrilled,	(a)
Distrusting every light that seemed to gild	(a)
The onward path, and feared to overlean	(b)
A finger even. And, though I have grown serene	(b)
And strong since then, I think that God has willed	(a)
A still renewable fear . . . O love, O troth . . .	(c)
Lest these enclaspèd hands should never hold,	(d)
This mutual kiss drop down between us both	(c)
As an unowned thing, once the lips being cold.	(d)
And Love, be false! if *he*, to keep one oath,	(c)
Must lose one joy, by his life's star foretold.	(d)

The rhyme scheme is regular and follows a pattern used often in Petrarchan sonnets, *abbaabba cdcdcd* which sets up an expectation that the poem will have two parts: an octave and a sestet. But the readers' expectations of a 'volta' (turning point) at the beginning of line nine are unsettled when the first of several voltas arrives halfway through line four as the first statement finishes and is countered by a 'Nay'. The next turn arrives one-third of the way through line seven beginning with 'And'. The final turn then comes just before the last two lines, giving the form of a couplet without the rhyme scheme to support it. It is as if the shadows of both Italian and English forms are overlaid on each other: a Petrarchan rhyme scheme holding within it a version of an English sonnet structure with three parts followed by a final couplet. This form which sets up expectations of recognisable structures only to dissolve or unsettle them, perfectly compliments and expresses the subject matter of the poem which turns on intangibility and solidity, expectation and lack of expectation. The speaker begins by describing the way in which she first felt about love: that it might not last, that it is as evanescent as light itself. Far from wanting to make something solid of it like marble or gilding, she thrills at its pendulousness and fears to touch ('feared to overlean/ A finger even'). The poem enacts these tensions and sensations.

UNSETTLING THE FORM

The great sonnet sequences written before the nineteenth century had all been written by men: William Shakespeare, Edmund Spenser, Philip Sydney, John Donne and John Milton. The speaker of the sonnet, then, had been exclusively male for centuries and he invariably expressed an unrequited love for a resistant or elusive female mistress. Elizabeth Barrett's *Sonnets from the Portuguese* play with these gendered conventions and expectations in subtle and inventive ways. The very fact that these are sonnets written by a woman and in the voice of a woman unsettled the form, which is not to say that women poets did not use the sonnet but rather that centuries of dominance by the male voice conditioned the expectations of readers to hear a male subject speaking to a female object.

There are several ways in which Barrett Browning 'troubles' the form of the sonnet. One of the established scenarios of the love sonnet sequence, for instance, as used by Shakespeare, Spenser and Sydney was that of the lover standing outside the mistress's locked door asking to be allowed entry. Barrett plays with this convention in *Sonnets from the Portuguese* by having the speaking voice speaking not from the outside to an elusive mistress inside, but from the *inside* to a passionate lover outside. In Sonnet 4 for instance, the speaker tells the lover outside that his music has worked, for she has heard him and 'weeps . . . as thou must sing . . . alone aloof':

And dost thou lift this house's latch too poor
For hand of thine? and canst thou think and bear
To let thy music drop here unaware
In folds of golden fulness at my door?
Look up and see the casement broken in,
The bats and owlets builders in the roof!

(ll.5–10)

This woman is not manipulatively elusive, but instead enthusiastic and impassioned, even baffled by her conviction that the man she loves is too good for her and she too sorrowful and close to death for him.

In using the sonnet form, then, Barrett was indeed transgressing long-established romantic expectations of the male speaking subject and the silent female object of desire. But her transgression was to level rather than simply reverse or invert. Here the addressee is given a voice and a subjectivity within the conversational form of the poem – Barrett's speaker is replying to a set of words already spoken. The speaker's voice is strong and assertive yet at the same time speaks of her limitations; at all times she is frank, honest and never elusive. As this voice speaks, it shakes off the shadow of the silent, coy mistress of the traditional love sonnet replacing it with the forthright voice of a self-assured woman. Barrett has turned the sonnet sequence into something of a duet, as voice counterpoints voice inside and outside, yet the individuality of the two speakers is always maintained: significantly too the sequence begins with the word 'I' and ends with the word 'mine'. The new love of equals is no less problematic or tortured – it too, like the love of the Elizabethan sonneteers, is circumscribed by paradox, by mortality, illness, doubt, intangibility, the inadequacies of language, yet it is a love based on dialogue and conversation and shared thoughts and preoccupations.

Barrett Browning did not only use the sonnet to express love, but also to explore complex abstractions, mirrored in the other titles of her love sonnets such as 'Substitution', 'Grief', 'Finite and Infinite', Exaggeration', 'Adequacy'. She also used the form to express her admiration for the French female novelist who took the name of George Sand in two sonnets called 'To George Sand: A Desire' and 'To George Sand: A Recognition'. These two sonnets are hybrid in form, crossing the form of the encomiastic ode (meaning eulogistic or laudatory in subject matter) with the sonnet, in that they are elevated in style and written to praise and glorify the novelist. In this Barrett shows her allegiances to the Romantic poets, and particularly to the odes of Shelley, Keats and Wordsworth. They are passionate meditations upon a feeling or a paradox or a person, even upon, in one case, her dog, Flush. Each begins with an object of contemplation and turns on an attempt to solve a personal or universal emotional problem. In the George Sand sonnets she uses the example of George Sand as 'large-brained woman and large-hearted man' ('George Sand: A Desire', l.1) to meditate upon the nature of gender and its effect upon the creative powers when qualities considered 'male' and 'female' are united in a single writer. As a woman poet she uses the sonnet form to express her love for another woman writer, but one particularly known to transgress gender boundaries in scandalous ways. Once again, Elizabeth Barrett, boundary crosser, unsettles an established and gendered genre, one that gave her not only formal but also cultural expectations to challenge and remake.

BALLADRY AND SUBVERSION

Barrett's ballads have until the last two decades been dismissed by critics as sentimental and inconsequential, produced quickly in order to respond to a demand from a primarily female readership (Hayter, 1962, Leighton, 1986). But in 1989 Dorothy Mermin reinterpreted them as providing 'a covert but thorough-going reassessment, often a total repudiation, of the Victorian ideas about womanliness to which they ostensibly speak' (Mermin, 1989: 71). Mermin claimed, however, that the poet was unaware of the subversiveness of her own poems: 'Elizabeth Barrett told the stories in a style and tone that gave no hint of revisionary intention, and she discarded the ballad form without discovering how to use it effectively against itself' (Mermin, 1989: 95). However, in her book on Barrett Browning published in 1995, Marjorie Stone argued that not only were the poems revisionary but that Barrett consciously 'transforms the ballad form into a cultural palimpsest by intensifying its intertextuality' (Stone, 1995: 133). Barrett, Stone reasons, uses the ballad form against itself.

Barrett was writing in an age characterised by the revival of the ballad. Wordsworth and Coleridge's *Lyrical Ballads* of 1798 and Sir Walter Scott's ballads and narrative poems had been superseded by the ballads of Tennyson which dominate his 1842 collection, *Poems*. By the mid-Victorian period definitions of the ballad form were relatively amorphous; Victorian reviewers frequently blurred the edges between romances, romantic verse narrative and ballads. Barrett herself uses the terms 'ballad', 'lay', 'romance', 'romaunt' and 'rhyme' in the titles of her narrative poems. For this reason, Stone chooses to apply the term ballad to all of Barrett's narrative poems with clear affinities to the conventions of the ballad which she defines as 'the ballad stanza, the use of dialogue and the refrain, tragic and/or topical subject matter, narrative compression and intensity' (Stone, 1995: 102). The ballad genre for Barrett Browning and for mid-Victorian readers would have been widely recognised as a popular form of romance writing associated with folk traditions, jaunty and catchy poems with strong emotions and a fast-moving plot about tragic love, murder, jealousy, magic, romantic passion, unrequited love or the supernatural. Like the related romance genres of the gothic novel and the fairy tale, the ballad often features flattened characters who are clearly defined as heroes, victims or villains. As Alan Bold writes, balladry is 'an art of the contrast and counterpoint, the black balancing the milk-white' (Bold, 1979: 36).

Barrett was drawn to the ballad for its expressive qualities: 'all the passion of the heart will go into a ballad, & feel at home', she claimed (cited Mermin, 1989: 90) but she also used its powerful emotions to challenge and critique the workings, hierarchies and abuses of power. In her ballads of the 1830s and 40s, 'A Romance of the Ganges', 'The Romaunt of Margret' and 'The Romaunt of the Page', she uses a series of strong, assertive and angry heroines. In 'The Romaunt of the Page', for example, a woman disguises herself as a page in order to follow her new husband to the battlefield. The knight and his page discuss the nature of women and the knight reveals an idealised chivalric attitude to womanly virtue, preferring women to be separated from the world. Any woman who defied her womanhood to dress as a man and go into battle, he claims, would be 'unwomaned' in the act and would therefore no longer be fit to be a wife. The page/ wife, disillusioned by earthly love, dies bravely in battle having saved her husband from a similar fate. In this ballad, marriage to the knight is not the end-stop of the poem, but its problem. The knight's chivalric code and idealised notion of womanhood makes any love between them impossible, and while the page's death in battle might be seen as the conventional sacrificial death of unrequited love, it can also be seen either as a refusal to conform to his ideals or as revenge. The poem offers a critique of any marriage built upon chivalrous ideals as well as a critique of a medieval and 'heroic' version of masculinity.

Barrett manipulated the traditional ballad plots and motifs ironically, using, as Stone argues, 'narrative reversals and doublings' in order to investigate the 'female plots' which shape women's lives, 'the gender plots of encompassing ideologies' (Stone, 1995: 131). The later ballads show her using the genre in even more inventive ways and, in line with her increasing commitment to writing poetry about the contemporary world, she introduced greater realism into the plots as well as a greater degree of narrative complexity. One of the later ballads, 'Lord Walter's Wife', shows a sophistication of both subject matter and form. It is a dramatic dialogue between a would-be seducer and the woman who resists his manipulations. It begins in the middle of a conversation in which Lord Walter's wife (she is never named) has asked her husband's friend why he is leaving their house, to which he replies provocatively: 'Because I fear you . . . because you are far too fair' (l.3). Their badinage becomes progressively both more witty and more aggressive as she seeks to beat him at his own game, pushing him to his limits,

implying that she agrees to the affair he seems to be proposing. The more
enthusiastically she flirts, the more defensive he becomes, producing a string
of reasons against their liaison, to each of which she replies: 'Oh that is no
reason' (l.5). When he objects to an affair on the grounds that she has an
innocent daughter, for instance, she replies that the daughter is too young to
notice anything. He is wrong-footed. Finally he breaks, shocked by her sexual
compliance, exclaiming:

> 'Why, now, you no longer are fair!
> Why, now, you no longer are fatal, but ugly and hateful, I swear!'

> (ll.19–20)

At this she 'laugh[s] out in her scorn' (l.21) at men who bring their 'vices so
near / That we smell them' (ll.23–4) but then presume to comment on the
beauty of respectable women in suggestive ways:

> 'Too fair?— not unless you misuse us! and surely if, once in a while,
> You attain to it, straightway you call us no longer too fair, but too vile.'

> (ll.31–2)

Barrett Browning explores the moral dilemma in which the wife, and other
propositioned women like her, find themselves. If she reveals the man's
improper behaviour to her husband she risks destroying an important
friendship, but she cannot leave the situation unchecked if she is to protect
herself. At the last moment she gains the upper hand by pretending that the
conversation had been a game and that she had merely been inviting him to
dinner:

> 'Have I hurt you indeed? We are quits then. Nay, friend of my Walter, be mine!
> Come, Dora, my darling, my angel, and help me to ask him to dine.'

> (ll.53–4)

There is no further comment from the author to point the moral – the reader
must judge. By omitting narrative comment and by compressing the drama
into a ballad form based entirely on a tightly wrought dialogue between
two people inflected with metaphor to intensify and confuse interpretation,
Barrett Browning had encapsulated the moral ambiguity of a commonplace sexual drama played out '[b]etwixt the mirrors of its drawing-rooms'
(*AL* 5:206), a drama held up for us to observe and judge. Whereas the

didactism of *Aurora Leigh* is always embedded in dialogue and truth shown to be multi-sided, here Barrett Browning has removed the didactism entirely, leaving the conversation to speak for itself. It was a drama which the novelist William Makepeace Thackeray felt was too morally ambiguous to be included in the journal for which he had commissioned it. Margaret Forster argues that Thackeray rejected 'Lord Walter's Wife' because he thought that his readership could not tolerate a poem which 'was an attack on the "double standard" by which men could flirt and were thought amusing, and women flirt only to be condemned as wanton' (Preface 298). Barrett Browning replied to Thackeray:

> I am deeply convinced that the corruption of our society requires not shut doors and windows, but light and air: and that it is exactly because pure and prosperous women choose to ignore vice, that miserable women suffer wrong by it everywhere.

(Cited Cooper, 1988: 77)

DRAMATIC MONOLOGUE

I have argued throughout this chapter that Barrett Browning's experiment with poetic form was driven by her need to find ways of incorporating conversation, dialogue and debate into established poetic forms. This was not an end in itself but an important means of establishing and exploring the multi-sidedness of truth. I have also argued that she was concerned to reproduce *transformative* conversation. For these reasons she was especially drawn to the dramatic monologue, a genre which was, Cornelia Pearsall argues, 'in large measure a Victorian invention' (Pearsall, 2000: 68). Critics disagree over its definition, its origins and the degree to which it was indeed 'invented' by the Victorians (particularly by Felicia Hemans in the 1820s and Tennyson and Browning in the 1830s), but generally the dramatic monologue is defined as a poem in which a dramatised fictionalised speaker utters the poem in a particular place and at a critical moment in such a way as to gradually unfold character and situation. Tennyson was credited by Arthur Henry Hallam with its invention in 1831, though Felicia Hemans had used a version of the monologue in her 1828 collection, *Records of Women*. Hallam defined the form as 'a new species of poetry, a graft of the lyric on the dramatic' (cited Pearsall, 2000: 69). It was to become a genre particularly suited to exploring aberrant or disturbed mental states. Robert Browning, for example, used it to write poems about murderers and madmen, 'the utterances of so many imaginary persons, not mine', he claimed in the Preface to his volume *Men and Women*.

By the time Barrett used the dramatic monologue to its fullest extent in the late 1840s to write 'The Runaway Slave at Pilgrim's Point', she had already experimented with dramatised multiple voices in a number of forms including the dramatic lyric in *Prometheus Bound* (1833), *The Seraphim* (1838) and *A Drama of Exile* (1844). 'The Runaway Slave at Pilgrim's Point' shows features typical of her writing of the later 1840s: it is a poem which both engages with contemporary issues reflecting Barrett's conviction in the 1840s that she must write poetry of the here and now, and shows a particular interest in the spoken voice, characteristic of other poems like the *Sonnets from the Portuguese*, which she wrote in the late 1840s, perhaps stimulated in part by the correspondence and conversations with Robert Browning as detailed above. 'The Runaway Slave' is an important poem in its own right but is also important as a forerunner of the experiment with conversational, dramatised speech she developed in *Aurora Leigh*, which was itself, of course, conceived before she began writing 'The Runaway Slave'.

Although the form was already a 'new species', a hybrid of both lyric and dramatic forms, Barrett Browning regrafted on to it aspects of the ballad form, in particular balladic rhyme schemes, repetitions and rhythms. The features of the ballad which we have discussed above lend the poem a fast pace, a jaunty metre and a powerful emotional register underscored by the use of refrains. 'The Runaway Slave' is a dramatic monologue in that it is spoken by a dramatised speaker (a black, female slave) in a particular place (Pilgrim's Point, the landing place of the Pilgrim fathers) and at a particular critical moment (the point at which she has been captured) to a particular imagined audience (her captors). Gradually the story unfolds as the slave explains her situation and denounces her captors and the system that enslaved her. The grafting of ballad on to dramatic monologue results in one of the most powerful features of the poem, the giddy oscillations of mood captured in the swings from regular ballad metre to the guttural, twisted metre allowed by the freer form of the monologue. So the poem begins like this:

> I stand on the mark beside the shore
>   Of the first white pilgrim's bended knee,
> Where exile turned to ancestor,
>   And God was thanked for liberty.
> I have run through the night, my skin is as dark,
> I bend my knee down on this mark:
>   I look on the sky and the sea.

(ll.1–7)

But when the speaker reaches the most tragic point of her tale, when she wrestles with her anger and despair to tell how she murdered her own baby, the offspring of a brutal rape by her white master, Barrett abandons the regularity and fluency of the ballad for this wrenching and fragmentation of speech and meaning:

> Yet when it was all done aright, —
>   Earth, 'twixt me and my baby, strewed, —
> All, changed to black earth, — nothing white, —
>   A dark child in the dark!— ensued
> Some comfort, and my heart grew young;
> I sate down smiling there and sung
>   The song I learnt in my maidenhood.

(ll.183–9)

The poem does, however, remain a monologue throughout for the slave addresses her audience but does not engage in conversation with them. There is no answer to her invective. It is an address not a conversation.

Although the dramatic monologue was one of the most flexible of forms possible at this time and allowed Barrett Browning to experiment with speech as a means of expressing powerful emotions, essentially it was the philosophically ruminative, multi-sided quality of dialogue she craved. And for this she had to move beyond the confines of even the most adapted form of dramatic monologue she had yet discovered, to the 'new class of poem' represented by the experiment of *Aurora Leigh*, a poem in which Aurora's words and being are answered by the words of others, a poem in which spoken words *are answered*. When Romney claims that poetry is of no use, for example, Aurora responds, and between them, in duet, Aurora and Romney meditate upon the function of art and poetry, disagreeing yet in harmony, feeling their way together around the question, in conversation:

> 'Of use!' I softly echoed, 'there's the point,
> We sweep about forever in argument,
> Like swallows which the exasperate, dying year
> Sets spinning in black circles, round and round,
> Preparing for far flights o'er unknown seas.
> And we, where tend we?'
>   'Where?' he said, and sighed.
> 'The whole creation, from the hour we are born,
> Perplexes us with questions. Not a stone
> But cries behind us, every weary step,
> "Where, where?" I leave stones to reply to stones.
> Enough for me and for my fleshly heart
> To hearken the invocations of my kind,

When men catch hold upon my shuddering nerves
And shriek, "What help? What hope? What bread i' the house,
What fire i' the frost?" There must be some response,
Though mine fail utterly.

(*AL* 4:1168–84)

They are both right, of course, about the problems of 'usefulness', though they have found different ways of responding to the perplexing questions of the age.

Barrett Browning's poetry, then, is often, at its best, a poetry of ruminative conversation. In a lecture written in 1990, the Anglo-Indian writer Salman Rushdie compared society to a large and rambling house. Imagine you wake up in such a house, he wrote, and as you find your way around you come across a room in which people you know and people you don't know are all talking about the house in every possible way, talking 'about what is happening, and has happened and should happen'. Literature provides just this voice-room:

> Literature is the one place in any society where, within the secrecy of our own heads, we can hear voices talking about everything in every possible way . . . Wherever in the world this little room of literature has been closed, sooner or later the walls have come tumbling down.

(Rushdie, 1990: 15–16)

This metaphor is immensely resonant for the work of Barrett Browning, a poet concerned to talk about everything in her world in every possible way. Her poetry is almost always dialogic in form because it has conversation at its heart, *transformative* conversation.

6

'HOW DO I LOVE THEE?':
LOVE AND MARRIAGE

REBECCA STOTT

On January 10, 1845, Robert Browning wrote to Elizabeth Barrett for the first time, after reading her volume of poetry, *Poems*. He was a little-known thirty-two-year-old poet and playwright, she was an internationally renowned poet, an invalid, and a thirty-nine-year-old spinster. 'I love your verses with all my heart, dear Miss Barrett — I do, as I say, love these verses with all my heart,' the letter said. Over the course of the next twenty months, they would write each other close to six hundred letters — one of the greatest literary correspondences of all time. The pair's last letter was exchanged on September 18, 1846, the night before the two left for a trip to Italy, and two weeks after their secret marriage. Their romance, which she would eventually credit with saving her life, lasted for fifteen years and spawned some of the world's most beautiful poetry.

(www.historychannel.com/exhibits/valentine/brownings.html)

This extract comes from an internet site dedicated to the history of Valentine's Day. The story of the Brownings' marriage and Barrett Browning's *Sonnets from the Portuguese* have a powerful presence on wedding and romance internet sites, pages usually studded or embossed with cupids, roses and flowers, for the *Sonnets from the Portuguese* rank highly in the early twenty-first-century canon of poems-to-be-read-at-weddings. The Brownings' union has become memorialised as one of the nineteenth century's greatest love stories (see Lootens, 1996a: 116–57) and their poetry has become 'exhibit A in almost any discussion of nineteenth-century romance' (Pinch, 1998: 7). Yet both Robert and Elizabeth Barrett Browning were fascinated as poets not only by the beauty, transcendence and pleasure of love itself, but also by the problems of its expression, by its institutionalisation in marriage, by its relationship to 'darker' emotions such as hate, obsession and possession, and by its relationship to power.

In this chapter I will examine Barrett Browning's love poetry, her attempt to express her thoughts about love and her struggle with what we might call the 'epistemology of love' (how do we *know* the loved person; how do we *know* love; how do we feel except through an already mediated set of literary tropes?). I will also explore Barrett Browning's treatment of the ethics of love (what is the role of thinking in love; what conditions justify giving up the self to another?), and the sociology of love (what happens to men and women when their love becomes institutionalised in marriage?). And I will show that, for a woman who has become an icon of romance and of idealised marriage, Barrett Browning was often fiercely critical and political in her analysis of marriage as an institution.

LOVE AS HEAVEN

In a letter written to her sister soon after the publication of *Aurora Leigh*, Barrett Browning mused on the fact that people were talking about the poem as her 'gospel' and explained that the spiritual truths were not her own but were based on the teaching of the eighteenth-century Swedish philosopher and mystic Emmanuel Swedenborg:

> I was helped to it – did not originate it – & was tempted much (by a natural feeling of honesty) to say so in the poem, & was withheld by nothing except a conviction that the naming of the name of Swedenborg, that great seer into the two worlds, would have utterly destroyed any hope of general acceptance & consequent utility . . . most humbly I have used [Swedenborg's 'sublime truths'] as I could. My desire is, that the weakness in me, may not hinder that influence.

(Letter to Arabella Barrett, Dec 10–18, 1856; cited in Reynolds, 1996: 339)

Emmanuel Swedenborg (1688–1772) was the son of a professor of theology at Upsala who was driven to seek a scientific explanation of the universe and of the relation of the soul to the body and the finite to the infinite. He experienced a series of visions in the 1740s upon which he based a series of theosophical and visionary writings. Followers of Swedenborg's theosophical interpretations of the Bible formed the 'New Church' in London in 1778. Swedenborg influenced the works of many nineteenth-century writers, including the poets William Blake and Samuel Taylor Coleridge, the American philosopher and poet Ralph Waldo Emerson and the American feminist Margaret Fuller. His writings would also leave a mark on the writings of Honore Balzac, Charles Baudelaire, William Butler Yeats, August Strindberg and the philosopher William James.

Elizabeth Barrett, always hungry for philosophical and spiritual ideas but also temperamentally wary of dogma, approached Swedenborg's ideas from the earliest reading with some scepticism, as she wrote to Mary Mitford in 1842:

> Do you know anything of Swedenborgianism? Swedenborg was a mad genius —there are beautiful things in his writings, but manifold absurdities,—and more darkness I do assure you though you may scarcely find it creditable, than in mine. Anthropomorphism, universal in application, is the principal doctrine. God is man in form & spirit,—incarnate essentially in Christ, a manifestation of God as He is—only one Person being recognized. Moreover all the angels are men in form & spirit,—and Heaven itself is in the shape of a man— that being the perfect form. The text insisted on is of course 'Let us make man in our image'—and then Scripture is preached away, dreamed away, fancied away into thin air—only, you know, Swedenbourg [sic] was inspired himself, & when a man says that's he's inspired, what can anybody else say?

> (*BC* 6:128)

Yet she was right to identify the 'gospel' of *Aurora Leigh* as having its origins in Swedenborg's writings, for Swedenborg's central claim that 'The joys of heaven and eternal happiness are from love and wisdom and the conjunction of these in usefulness' (Swedenborg, 1995: 10) is the vision expressed by both Aurora and Romney at the end of the verse-novel:

> The world waits
> For help. Beloved, let us love so well,
> Our work shall still be better for our love,
> And still our love be sweeter for our work,
> And both commended, for the sake of each,
> By all true workers and true lovers born.

> (*AL* 9:923–8)

Swedenborg taught that God was infinite love and infinite wisdom and that from the Godhead emanated both the material and the spiritual world. Because the two worlds had a common origin in God, they were connected through a series of 'correspondences'. Spiritual truths are therefore embodied in the material world. He also believed that the original divine order had been perverted by human beings who, using their free will, had gradually severed the connection between the spiritual and material worlds. The intervention of Christ had therefore restored order to the universe by creating a new external pathway through which humans could approach God, and the Second Coming would be accomplished, not in the flesh, but rather through an intellectual and spiritual revolution, which Swedenborg saw as being achieved through his own writings and through his revelation of the hidden truths of the Bible.

In *Aurora Leigh*, Aurora comes to a Swedenborgian understanding that love, rather than art, is what 'makes heaven' (*AL* 9:659). The poem moves towards a full revelation of Swedenborgian principles as Romney and Aurora reconcile their differences in a passionate declaration of the three central Swedenborgian ideas of love, wisdom and use, couched in the vision of a New Jerusalem and in language that borrows heavily from Swedenborg's writings. Thus Barrett Browning casts Romney and Aurora as workers in an intellectual and emotional revolution which will transform society by opening the roads between the material and spiritual worlds. Within Swedenborgian teaching love and wisdom become manifest in *use*; indeed, 'Love and wisdom without use are not anything; they are only ideal entities; nor do they become real until they are in use' (Swedenborg, 1971: 875). 'Use is the doing of good from love by means of wisdom. Use is goodness itself' (Swedenborg, 1995: 183). So Aurora, always dedicated to her art, comes to understand the superior power of love in Book 9, at the point that she declares her love for Romney:

> Art symbolises heaven, but Love is God
> And makes heaven.

> (*AL* 9:658–9)

When she and Romney do embrace finally in Book 9, their embrace, though described in erotically physical terms, is also a spiritual one. Love and wisdom unite. The persistent crossing and bridging of the material and spiritual worlds is both the subject and the mission of the poem for, in Aurora's words, the role of the poet is expressed in Swedenborgian terms: 'to keep up open roads/ Betwixt the seen and the unseen, – bursting through/ The best of your conventions with his best' (2:468–70). In this scene of union the material and spiritual worlds are fused through their bodies and souls:

> Could I see his face,
> I wept so? Did I drop against his breast,
> Or did his arms constrain me? were my cheeks
> Hot, overflooded, with my tears, or his?
> And which of our two large explosive hearts
> So shook me? That I know not. There were words
> That broke in utterance .. melted, in the fire, –
> Embrace, that was convulsion, .. then a kiss

As long and silent as the ecstatic night,
And deep, deep, shuddering breaths, which meant beyond
Whatever could be told by word or kiss.

(*AL* 9:714–24)

While the communion between Aurora and Romney is said to be beyond understanding and beyond words, communion there is nonetheless:

The intimate presence carrying in itself
Complete communication, as with souls
Who, having put the body off, perceive
Through simply being. Thus, 'twas granted me
To know he loved me to the depth and height
Of such large natures . . .

(*AL* 9:749–54)

This is a description of physical and spiritual union much influenced by Swedenborg's ideas on conjugal love:

The Lord's Divine providence is most specific and most universal in connection with marriages and in its operation in marriages, because all delights of heaven flow from the delights of conjugial love, like sweet waters from a gushing spring. It is therefore provided that conjugial pairs be born, and they are raised and continually prepared for their marriages under the Lord's guidance, neither the boy nor the girl being aware of it. Then, after a period of time, the girl – now a marriageable young woman – and the boy – now a young man ready to marry – meet somewhere, as though by fate, and notice each other. And they immediately recognise, as if by a kind of instinct, that they are a match, thinking to themselves as from a kind of inner dictate, the young man, 'she is mine,' and the young woman, 'he is mine.' Later, after this thought has for some time become settled in the minds of each, they deliberately talk about it together and pledge themselves to each other in marriage. We say as though by fate, by instinct and as from a kind of dictate, when we mean by Divine providence, because when one is unaware that it is Divine providence, that is how it appears. For the Lord unveils their inner similarities so that they notice each other.

(Swedenborg, 1995: 20)

The portrayal of the love of Romney and Aurora as a love which is inevitable (preordained) yet postponed until both are spiritually ready for union, is one aspect of the poem that may have had its origin in the ideas of Swedenborg.

But while Swedenborg symbolises conjugal union as the sweet waters of a gushing spring, Barrett Browning's metaphor is characteristically more violent. She describes Aurora and Romney's embrace as an overflowing, but it is also a convulsion, a melting and an explosion. The metaphors of sexual desire and spiritual union are geological: it is like an earthquake, a volcano and a flood all at once, part of the geological violence and transformation of the old that will result in the New Jerusalem and new landscape envisaged at the end of the book.

Yet, characteristically for Barrett Browning, the poem also challenges Swedenborgian teachings at the same time as asserting them. Aurora begins to wonder about the implication of believing that love makes heaven – the implication for women in particular. After all, she has loved Romney for some time. Should she have refused him as she did when he proposed all those years ago? In particular, she worries that denying him then meant that she has been in a fallen state since, fallen from the heaven that she might have made:

> Art symbolises heaven, but Love is God
> And makes heaven. I, Aurora, fell from mine.
> I would not be a woman like the rest,
> A simple woman who believes in love
> And owns the right of love because she loves,
> And, hearing she's beloved, is satisfied
> With what contents God: I must analyse,
> Confront, and question; just as if a fly
> Refused to warm itself in any sun
> Till such was *in leone* [a constellation of the stars which signifies late summer]

> (*AL* 9:658–67)

As Sandra Gilbert and Susan Gubar point out (1979: 577), the imagery of this passage reveals significant contradictions in Aurora's attitude to love. Aurora claims that her options as a woman are either to make heaven (to love) or to fall from heaven (not to love), yet being in love is also like being a fly basking in sunshine – satisfied, contented, unthinking, drunk with warmth and pleasure. Aurora claims that, in declining Romney's offer of love, she had refused to be 'a woman like the rest,/ A simple woman' because instead of just accepting the gift of love at that point, she had insisted on analysing, confronting, questioning it. This refusal had resulted in her fall from heaven but had also ensured that she did not become a fly basking in the sunshine. The implication hangs for a moment that perhaps if she had been less proud when Romney had first proposed, more honest in her own feelings, the two lovers would not have had to suffer. Yet at the same time, the drama of the poem is created by that refusal and by the period of their joint exile from the 'heaven' of requited love, a period in which Aurora fulfils her vocation as a poet. It is also a period in which Romney is transformed; blinded, he comes to see Aurora not as a help-meet on a joint mission of reform, but as a woman and poet with a soul. Aurora's acceptance of love at the end of the poem is made possible precisely because they have both entered this struggle to understand, analyse and confront their feelings about each other.

THINKING LOVE

Love is idealised in the poem as what makes heaven, but *unthinking* love is disparaged. Earlier in the poem, at the point at which Aurora refuses to marry Romney in Book 2, for instance, she offers an analysis of women who are prepared to settle for any kind of love, unquestioningly:

> Women of a softer mood,
> Surprised by men when scarcely awake to life,
> Will sometimes only hear the first word, love,
> And catch up with it any kind of work,
> Indifferent, so that dear love go with it.
> I do not blame such women, though, for love,
> They pick much oakum . . .

(*AL* 2:443–9)

Picking oakum refers to the practice of untwisting and unpicking old rope to be mixed with tar and used for ship's caulking. It was tedious and backbreaking work which made the fingers bleed, work often given to convicts and the inmates of workhouses. Barrett Browning claims therefore that where love is acted upon by women in unthinking ways, a life of enforced servitude will often follow. Although the poem endorses the work ethic, it does not endorse the domestic slavery which so often accompanied marriage. Aurora is, after all, refusing not Romney's love, but Romney's offer of marriage as *work*; Romney was, she tells him scornfully, looking for a fellow-worker, not a lover. So Aurora's claims that she had been wrong not to yield to love earlier are undermined by such alternative reflections and knowledge. As she describes the proposal scene, Aurora suddenly assumes a retrospective view of Romney's proposal and her refusal, wondering for a moment what would have happened if she had accepted his offer of love:

> If he had loved,
> Ah, loved me, with that retributive face, . .
> I might have been a common woman now
> And happier, less known and less left alone,
> Perhaps a better woman after all,
> With chubby children hanging on my neck
> To keep me low and wise.

> (AL 2:511–17)

These tensions between love represented as an entry into servitude and/or unthinking complacency, and love as a Swedenborgian 'heaven' are shown to be tensions between being a 'common woman' and a dissenting independent-minded, *thinking* one, as Aurora is. For love is both a divine condition to be aspired to, as she discovers, and also one that at least potentially represents an obstacle to her own dissenting selfhood and to her ambitions to write. Had she said 'yes' when Romney first proposed, her life plot would have been a different one.

So while Barrett Browning endorses, even preaches, Swedenborgian principles about love as that which 'makes heaven' in *Aurora Leigh*, she constantly casts these 'truths' within the social and political contexts that bear on women's lives. Sonnet 22 of *Sonnets from the Portuguese* also shows her questioning Swedenborgian doctrines, exploring the relative benefits of the earthly/material and the divine/spiritual worlds as a place 'to love in'. In this poem male and female lovers, perfectly unified in love, transcend the material plane and turn into eroticised angels, their wings on fire. Barrett describes this process of angelic transformation and transcendence and then stops it abruptly with her injunction to the lover to 'think'. This monosyllabic imperative in the middle of the poem forms a 'volta' or turning point (interestingly a volta which arrives half a line earlier than it would be expected within a Petrarchan sonnet and so takes us by surprise – see Chapter Five on genre). At this point, having raised these two soul/angels in erotic rapture, she brings them sharply down to earth again. At least on earth they will be left alone, she says, and not be pressed upon by other angels, for the 'contrarious moods of men' recoil from pure spirits. At least on earth there will be a secluded place to 'love in' even though (and perhaps *because*) that space is rounded by 'darkness and the death-hour'.

> When our two souls stand up erect and strong,
> Face to face, silent, drawing nigh and nigher,
> Until the lengthening wings break into fire
> At either curvèd point, — what bitter wrong
> Can the earth do to us, that we should not long

Be here contented? Think. In mounting higher,
The angels would press on us and aspire
To drop some golden orb of perfect song
Into our deep, dear silence. Let us stay
Rather on earth, Belovèd, — where the unfit
Contrarious moods of men recoil away
And isolate pure spirits, and permit
A place to stand and love in for a day,
With darkness and the death-hour rounding it.

(Sonnet 22)

Angels, so often disembodied and androgynous in Western art, are given
tangible, heavy, erotic bodies here. Barrett describes souls as bodies, seraphic
bodies which have their feet on the earth: 'When our two souls *stand up*
erect and strong' (emphasis mine). Instead of casting souls as ineffable,
insubstantial, shadowy presences, Barrett Browning fully embodies them,
beautifully describing, for instance, the delicate curve and lengthening of the
angels' wings. By doing so she challenges established binaries between the
body and soul and sets up a 'correspondence' between the spiritual and
material worlds. So while on the one hand the poem questions the Swedenborgian privileging of the spiritual plane over the material one by reasserting
the worth of earthly love, it reconciles that tension by bringing the material
and spiritual into correspondence. The romantic sentiments of mutually
enjoined bodies and souls, of love as heaven and as a revelation of divine
truth may sound clichéd to a contemporary reader, but for Barrett Browning
it was part of a philosophical and theological system of considerable rigour
and complexity.

THE EPISTEMOLOGY OF LOVE

Dorothy Mermin and Angela Leighton have both attended to the problem
of reading the *Sonnets from the Portuguese* too reductively as direct autobiographical expressions of sincerity (Leighton, 1986; Mermin, 1986).
Mermin instead emphasises the sonnet sequence's 'emotional and intellectual complexity, the richness of reference, the elaborate and ingenious
conceits, and the subtle ways in which images are used both for their emotional power and to carry an argument' (145). It is this intertwining of emotional and intellectual enquiry, a quest to *understand* as well as *feel* love, that
characterises these poems. In this respect the *Sonnets* reveal a philosophical

concern with the 'epistemology of love' – the relationship between love and knowledge, and the ethics of love – what is the role of thinking and reflection in romantic love: is it inimical to feeling or an integral part of it?

I have already claimed that Barrett Browning in *Aurora Leigh* idealises love but not unthinking love. Her love poetry is driven by the same concerns as Aurora's: 'I must analyse,/ Confront and question' and the *Sonnets* are full of this concern to know, measure and define love. The most famous line, of course, is 'How do I love thee? Let me count the ways'. As Adela Pinch points out (Pinch, 1998: 7), the first verb of Sonnet 1 and therefore of the whole set of poems is 'thought': 'I thought,' the speaker begins, 'once how Theocritus had sung'. The poet/speaker mocks herself here as the contemplative musing poet who while thinking about love, becomes aware of a mystic shape moving behind her who draws her backward by the hair:

> And a voice said in mastery, while I strove, –
> 'Guess now who holds thee?' – 'Death,' I said. But there,
> The silver answer rang, – 'Not Death, but Love'.

> (Sonnet 1, ll.12–14)

This concern with the role of thinking in love echoes Aurora's musings in *Aurora Leigh* about whether she was right to have refused Romney's love. Barrett seems to be suggesting in this opening sonnet that the overcontemplative poet can risk losing heaven (love), yet the *unthinking* lover risks being turned into the 'common woman' who settles unquestioningly for the first declaration of love. The project of the sequence of sonnets is to work at that paradox – to integrate thinking and feeling.

Secondly, as Pinch points out, the sequence as a whole is obsessed with:

> spatial relations, with questions of scale and size, with measuring which of the two lovers is greater, smaller, higher, lower, nearer, or further than the other [and that this is] a symptom of the poem's meditation, on a more phenomenological level, on what it might mean to have a person, literally, in one's mind. What, Barrett Browning wants to know, does it mean to turn a person into a thought?

> (Pinch, 1998: 8)

Pinch argues that the poems question the ethics of such meditations by dramatising the conflicts between thinking, knowing and loving, with these conflicts coming to a head in Sonnet 29, where the poet is once again struck by self-consciousness about her own thinking:

I think of thee! — my thoughts do twine and bud
About thee, as will vines, about a tree,
Put out broad leaves, and soon there's nought to see
Except the straggling green which hides the wood.
Yet, O my palm-tree, be it understood
I will not have my thoughts instead of thee
Who art dearer, better! Rather, instantly
Renew thy presence; as a strong tree should,
Rustle thy boughs and set thy trunk all bare,
And let these bands of greenery which insphere thee
Drop heavily down — burst, shattered, everywhere!
Because, in this deep joy to see and hear thee
And breathe within thy shadow a new air,
I do not think of thee — I am too near thee.

(Sonnet 29)

In this extended metaphor, the speaker's thoughts are cast as the vines about the tree that, by an excess of budding and growth, soon conceal the tree itself and threaten to strangle it (there is also an implication that the vines are like restrictive clothes which conceal the true shape of the loved one – for when they are cast off the tree becomes 'all bare'). The kind of thoughts represented here, produced by a dangerous proximity, are cast as destructive and inimical to true knowing. The tree can only renew itself by casting off the insphering thoughts/vines, bursting and shattering them. Again these metaphors of explosion and bursting are part of the violence of love and knowledge, suggesting that, through such epiphanic moments of throwing off, new knowledge is gained. Finally, it is important to note that for Barrett Browning it is the degree of *proximity* in which these thoughts have been produced that is the problem, not thinking in itself: 'I do not think of thee – I am too near thee'. In Sonnet 15, for instance, which seems to pair with this one, an alternative kind of sight is represented, a vision of love which exceeds the object of love and travels into future time and space and ultimately to oblivion:

But I look on thee — on thee —
Beholding, besides love, the end of love,
Hearing oblivion beyond memory;
As one who sits and gazes from above,
Over the rivers to the bitter sea.

(Sonnet 15, ll.10–14)

And it is also thought and feeling enshrined or forced *into words* which is persistently problematised in these poems, not because Barrett necessarily believes that thought and feeling are possible without words, but rather that the words, phrases, conceits and metaphors that have been used to describe love in literature inhibit freshness of expression because they have been overused. After all, the first words of the sonnet sequence begin 'I thought once how Theocritus had sung'. She is thinking through the words of another as the poem begins, musing on a written text. Barrett persistently draws our attention to the way in which speech and writing, particularly literary writing, not only fashions experience, but also traps it in tropes, conceits and metaphors. She draws our attention to those habits and conventions of thought and representation that falsely or inadequately shape experience. Language – the attempt to fashion feeling into speech – is the paradox of these poems. Putting love into words must be done, particularly by lovers who are also poets, and yet the full expression of love is elusive. Literature and the conventions of writing can 'insphere' (contain, imprison, suffocate) established knowledge or can throw off the 'vines' of old knowledge, allowing us to see the tree as if for the first time. Barrett does not reject thinking about love but she does question our adherence to the old ways of knowing it, ways of knowing that have been controlled by writers and poets.

NOTHING LIKE THE SUN: THE LITERARINESS OF LOVE

In the chapter on genre I showed how Barrett reused the sonnet form, pushing it to its limits, spilling over its confines in a way that mimicked the cut and thrust of charged, enquiring conversation, demonstrating how closely related these poems are to the love letters written by herself and Robert. The poems both utilise the conventions of courtly love and challenge them so that Barrett, for instance, in speaking as a woman, troubles the long-established gender conventions of the sonnet form of the male speaking-thinking lover-poet and the female silent-listening or absent object of desire. Here in the *Sonnets from the Portuguese*, as I said earlier, the poems become a duet or at least the reported half of an on-going conversation.

But there are other important ways in which Barrett recasts the conventions of courtly love in the *Sonnets*. They question, for instance, the established epithets and conceits of love established by the Petrarchan form in particular. Barrett was acutely aware in her letters and poetry of the literariness of romantic love, made all the more intense because she and Robert as poets were engaged in a shared quest to define their love for each other and experiencing the weight of literary tradition in doing so. Shakespeare had also wittily rejected established conceits ('false compare') in his famous Sonnet 130, struggling instead to find new ways of expressing feeling:

> My mistress' eyes are nothing like the sun;
> Coral is far more red than her lips' red;
> If snow be white, why then her breasts are dun;
> If hairs be wires, black wires grow on her head.
> I have seen roses damasked, red and white,
> But no such roses see I in her cheeks;
> And in some perfumes is there more delight
> Than in the breath that from my mistress reeks.
> I love to hear her speak, yet well know
> That music hath a far more pleasing sound;
> I grant I never saw a goddess go;
> My mistress, when she walks, treads on the ground.
>   And yet, by heaven, I think my love as rare
>   As any she belied with false compare.

Several sonnets in *Sonnets from the Portuguese* address this problem of 'false compare'. Sonnet 13, for instance, begins:

> And wilt thou have me fashion into speech
> The love I bear thee, finding words enough,
> And hold the torch out, while the winds are rough,
> Between our faces, to cast light on each?

> (Sonnet 13, ll.1–4)

Instead, in this sonnet, the speaker opts for silence as the best form of sincerity:

> Nay, let the silence of my womanhood
> Commend my woman-love to thy belief,–
> Seeing that I stand unwon, however wooed,
> And rend the garment of my life, in brief,
> By a most dauntless, voiceless fortitude,
> Lest one touch of this heart convey its grief.

> (Sonnet 13 ll.9–14)

This conflict between potentially hollow speech and sincere silence is repeated elsewhere in the sequence. The speaker reminds her lover in Sonnet

21, for instance, that although she needs him to reiterate his love like the cuckoo he must 'love [her] also in silence with thy soul' (l.14). In the following sonnet in the sequence, Barrett continues to engage with the problems of language and silence explored in Sonnet 13 as the speaker addresses her lover as a *writer*, commanding him to find new ways of expressing his love and not to pre-script and define their love in ways that will not accommodate change:

> If thou must love me, let it be for nought
> Except for love's sake only. Do not say
> 'I love her for her smile – her look – her way
> Of speaking gently, – for a trick of thought
> That falls in well with mine, and certes brought
> A sense of pleasant ease on such a day' –
> For these things in themselves, Belovèd, may
> Be changed, or change for thee, – and love, so wrought,
> May be unwrought so. Neither love me for
> Thine own dear pity's wiping my cheeks dry, –
> A creature might forget to weep, who bore
> Thy comfort long, and lose thy love thereby!
> But love me for love's sake, that evermore
> Thou mayst love on, through love's eternity.

(Sonnet 14)

But all the soul-searching about the impossibility of original expression of romantic love is not all in earnest. As Mary Rose Sullivan has shown, the Brownings' habit of echoing each other's words and of 'adapting, reforming, and returning them ever more freighted with meaning' began early in their correspondence and 'inevitably spilled over into their composition of poetry' (Sullivan, 1987: 57). There is much that is self-parodic and witty in Barrett Browning's *Sonnets*. In Sonnet 37, for instance, the speaker laments the difficulty of originality and representation – writing about love, she laments, can be at worst a 'worthless counterfeit':

> Pardon, oh, pardon, that my soul should make,
> Of all that strong divineness which I know
> For thine and thee, an image only so
> Formed of the sand, and fit to shift and break.

(Sonnet 37, ll.1–4)

But while the poem strives for originality of expression, it culminates ironically with an image borrowed from one of Robert Browning's most well-known poems, *My Last Duchess*, in which the Duke draws the envoy's attention to a sculpture of 'Neptune . . . /Taming a sea-horse, thought a rarity,/ Which Claus of Innsbruck cast in bronze for me' (ll.54–6). In Barrett's sonnet, she ends by claiming that art is sometimes as hopelessly inadequate as commemorating salvation from shipwreck in the form of a sculptured porpoise, repeating Robert's image:

> As if a shipwrecked Pagan, safe in port,
> His guardian sea-god to commemorate,
> Should set a sculptured porpoise, gills a-snort
> And vibrant tail, within the temple-gate.

> (ll.11–14)

But while literature and the literary expression of love is often a hindrance to direct expression, the sonnets show how useful literary or artistic representation can be in providing tropes to think through. For instance, Barrett alludes to Tennyson's *Mariana in the Moated Grange* in one letter to Robert: 'I am like Mariana in the moated grange & sit listening too often to the mouse in the wainscot' (*BC* 10:254). But in a later letter she clarifies the analogy when she writes 'For have I not felt twenty times the desolate advantage of being insulated here and of not minding anybody when I made my poems? . . . and caring less for suppositious criticism than for the black fly buzzing in the pane?' (*BC* 10:271). The analogy is actually a difference, for unlike Mariana who suffers from an excess of feeling, Barrett's insulation has resulted not in emotional excess but in indifference to criticism. Throughout the sonnet sequences the burdensome legacy of Romantic poetry is used both as the material for new poetry and its adversary.

LOVE IN TEXT; LOVE IN CONTEXT

In *Victorian Women Poets: Writing Against the Heart*, Angela Leighton argues that Elizabeth Barrett Browning 'learned early to distrust the iconic postures of romance in favour of a socialised and contextualised account of desire' (Leighton, 1992: 87). This claim is everywhere confirmed by Barrett Browning's love poetry which relentlessly places love under a sociological microscope. Love does not exist in the abstract – it is always felt and acted upon by people shaped and determined by the ideas of their time, people in the world. For many women in the nineteenth century, love, however pleasurable or transcendent, was especially deterministic, for love was so often the entry point into a much more circumscribed world within the institution of marriage or outside it as a result of betrayal or a fall from respectability:

> It is this sceptical awareness of the sexual politics of sensibility which marks out Barrett Browning's poetry from that of her predecessors. Love, in her work, is not a sacred ideal, removed from the contingencies of the world, but is dragged in the dust of that reality which was itself so hard-won an experience and a theme for her.

> (Leighton, 1992: 544)

Barrett's ballads in particular address the danger of untempered feeling, of women who, like the 'women of a softer mood' evoked in *Aurora Leigh* (2:443), are consigned to a life of picking oakum because they love too much or too quickly or unwisely. In 'Bertha in the Lane' and 'A Year's Spinning,' the two heroines have been betrayed by absent lovers who do not even appear in the poem. In the first poem, the heroine, on her deathbed, confesses to her sister Bertha that she is dying of a broken heart. She had overheard, she says, her lover, Robert, declaring his love to her more beautiful sister in the lane. Still in love with Robert, still listening out for the sound of his footstep at the door like Mariana in Tennyson's poem, she dies self-consumed, yet refusing to blame either Bertha or Robert for their feelings. Instead it is the weakness of her own womanhood that has killed her:

> Do not weep so – Dear, – heart-warm!
>   All was best as it befell.
> If I say he did me harm,
>   I speak wild, – I am not well.
> All his words were kind and good –
> *He esteemed me*! Only, blood
> Runs so faint in womanhood.

> (ll.155–61)

In 'A Year's Spinning' the betrayed woman, a spinner, has borne her lover's child which has since died. Her lament, like that of the dying sister in 'Bertha in the Lane', is not a call of revenge but rather one of despair about the weakness and vulnerability of women raised on a diet of false ideals and romantic love. These are the fragile 'women of a softer mood' resigned to picking oakum or death. Now that 'her spinning is all done' (l.5), her life and hope are extinguished. In 'The Romance of the Swan's Nest' the danger of self-deluding, self-consuming love is all the more sharply drawn as Barrett tells the story of 'Little Ellie' who sits beside a river imagining an idealised lover for herself in the language and imagery of romantic and chivalric love, straight out of a formulaic romance. In this fantasy, she imagines herself taking him to see the swan's nest among the reeds. In reality, while she has been dreaming, the swan's nest has been deserted and the eggs gnawed by rats. The dream has been violated.

The act of betrayal always happens offstage in these ballads for it is the consequences of the betrayal on women's lives that interest Barrett. So often the damage affects other women and children in the story: the spinner's shamed mother, the dead baby, Bertha who loses her sister because her beauty stimulated the act of betrayal. In 'A Romance of the Ganges', Luti, betrayed by her lover, reveals that betrayal to her rival Nuleeni and demands that Nuleeni become her accomplice in revenge. She demands that Luti whisper Nuleeni's name to her husband on their wedding day and again to their child when he asks about his father's deeds. These ballads show that untempered love is dangerous and often the result of the socialisation of women to expect to fulfil their lives only in a love plot (what we might call the imposition of a 'false consciousness'), a subject also addressed by other women writers of the nineteenth century from Mary Wollstonecraft to Harriet Taylor. In the ballads, Barrett persistently shows love as taking its place within an economy of power and sexual exchange. Indeed as Stone argues:

> In her ballads of the 1830s and 40s, [Barrett] employs the starker power structures of medieval society to foreground the status of women in a male economy of social exchange, and to unmask the subtler preservation of gender inequities in contemporary Victorian ideology.

> (Stone, 1995: 108–9)

THE POLITICS OF MARRIAGE

Throughout her life Barrett Browning, icon of Victorian marriage and romance, was outspokenly critical of the institution of marriage and of many of the marriages she saw around her. '*Marriage in the abstract* has always seemed to me the most profoundly indecent of all ideas,' she wrote to Mary Mitford during Robert's courtship (*BC* 12:63), continuing:

> & I never could make out how women, mothers & daughters, could talk of it as of setting up in trade, . . as of a thing to be done. That life may go on smoothly upon a marriage of convenience, simply proves to my mind that there is a defect in the sensibility & the delicacy, & an incapacity to the higher happiness of God's sanctifying. Now think & see if this is not near the truth. I have always been called romantic for this way of seeing, but never repented that it was *my* way, nor shall.

> (*BC* 12:62–3)

While Barrett Browning valued love as transcendent, even divine, she was no romantic as far as marriage was concerned – she had always been critical of women who believed marriage to be the only fulfilment for a woman; even during her often lonely and reclusive life, she was no 'Little Ellie' conjuring an imaginary lover out of thin air. A dream recorded in her diary when she was twenty-five shows that here at least marriage was experienced as a nightmare of further incarceration not a release from her present circumstances: 'I dreamt last night that I was married, just married; & in an agony to procure a dissolution of the engagement' (D: 111). Even when Robert insisted that she consider marriage as the only way they could live together abroad, she procrastinated and deferred committing herself to a final decision (see Forster, 1988: 164–77); the love letters written in the six months before they married show Barrett wrangling and tormented about marriage and its relation to power and money. She shows herself uncertain about how to judge the materialism of wedding preparation (the trousseau) in a letter to Miss Mitford, 'A year for marriages, is it? Well – it seems so – and some marry unfortunately (or fortunately) *without* trousseaus' (BC 13:213). Watching the preparations for her cousin Arabella Hedley's wedding, Barrett commented: 'there does enter into the motives of most marriages a good deal of that hankering after the temporary distinction, emotion and pleasure of being for a while a chief person . . .' (BC 13:213). The expense of Arabella's wedding seemed grotesque to her: 'six dress pocket handkerchiefs, at four guineas each [. . .] forty guineas of lace trimming on the bridal dress' (BC 13:185). She was haunted by her experience and memory of repressive or unhappy marriages, she wrote to Robert:

> To see marriages which are made everyday! Worse than solitudes & more desolate! In the case of the two happiest I ever knew, one of the husbands said in confidence to a brother of mine . . . that he had 'ruined his prospects by marrying,' – & the other said to myself at the very moment of professing an extraordinary happiness, . . . 'But I should have done as well if I had not married her.'

> (BC 12:259)

And again only a few months before she agreed to marry him, she wrote:

> When I was a child I heard two married women talking. One said to the other 'The most painful part of marriage is the first year, when the lover changes into the husband by slow degrees.' The other woman agreed, as a matter of fact is agreed to. I listened with my eyes & ears, & never forgot it . . . as you observe – It seemed to me, child as I was, a dreadful thing to have a husband by such a process.

> (BC 13:126)

Barrett was supremely conscious of how divided their experiences were and would be – marriage would establish very different rights and conventions of behaviour for them as men and women. Would they be able to resist the stereotypical male and female behaviour so visible in all the marriages around them?

> Did you ever observe a lord of creation knit his brows together because the cutlets were underdone, shooting enough fire from his eyes to overdo them to cinders[. . .] Did you ever hear of the litany which some women say through the first course . . low to themselves . . Perhaps not! it does not enter into your imagination to conceive of things, which nevertheless *are*.
>
> Not that I ever thought of YOU with reference to SUCH – oh, no, no!
>
> (*BC* 12:221)

The answer was to dissent, of course, to determine not to be a 'common woman' or a 'common man' in life and marriage (a determination which would be given to Aurora Leigh later), but the abuse of power, she felt, seemed to be enshrined in marriage – almost produced by it. She wrote the following letter on the anniversary of American Independence (at a time when she had already significantly begun to write 'A Runaway Slave at Pilgrim's Point' which so powerfully attacks the institutionalisation of slavery and the abuse of power):

> Oh, I understand perfectly, how as soon as ever a common man is sure of a woman's affections, he takes up the tone of right & might . . & he *will* have it so . . & he *wont* have it so! –I have heard of the bitterest tears being shed by the victim as soon as ever, by one word of hers, she had placed herself in his power. Of such are 'Lover's quarrels' for the most part. The growth of power on one side . . & the struggle against it, by means legal & illegal, on the other.
>
> (*BC* 13:116)

Her critique of marriage at this point is powerfully and astutely political. One wonders how, with this view of marriage, she could ever agree to marry, but at the same time one wonders how in the 1840s the Brownings might have lived together abroad *without* being married. Barrett Browning's critique of marriage did not decline after her marriage either; indeed she continued to write ever more politically about marriage and the abuse of women's rights. As Margaret Forster points out, 'the happier Elizabeth became with her man, the more furious she became at how men abused women' (Forster, 1998: 204).

The politics of marriage were most powerfully explored in *Aurora Leigh*. Romney in the course of the poem makes four proposals – two to Aurora and two to Marian. Three of these proposals are made, Barrett Browning shows us, for the wrong reasons, for Romney is driven by motives which are bound up with money, duty and inheritance. As Angela Leighton points out (1986), Aurora's answer to Romney's first proposal and Marian's answer to his second provide a critique of the system of values that underpin his dubious good intentions: 'Here's a hand shall keep/ For ever clean without a marriage-ring', Marian replies to his offer of marriage. She is, she claims, already clean – she does not need his marriage ring to cleanse her. Aurora's rejection of his first proposal is based upon her understanding of what he has actually said which in her words amounts to the following statement:

> 'Come, sweep my barns and keep my hospitals,
> And I will pay these with a current coin
> Which men give women'

> (*AL* 2:539–41)

In paraphrasing Romney's proposal this way, Aurora shows her understanding of marriage as a transaction based upon law and money – marriage is the 'current coin' which men pay women in exchange for their labour. This analysis is also extended by Marian when she angrily asserts her rights as a mother:

> 'Mine, mine,' she said. 'I have as sure a right
> As any glad proud mother in the world,
> Who sets her darling down to cut his teeth
> Upon her church-ring. If she talks of law,
> I talk of law! I claim by mother-dues
> By law, – the law which now is paramount,–
> The common law, by which the poor and weak
> Are trodden underfoot by vicious me,
> And loathed for ever after by the good'

> (*AL* 6:661–9)

Barrett Browning, dissenter, is audible here in Marian's words, in this fierce analysis of the conflicts between common law and natural law. What is common is not always right. Instead, common law enshrines the rights of men against 'the poor and weak'. In this analysis she places herself in the tradition of Mary Wollstonecraft, Margaret Fuller, George Sand, and Barbara Bodichon who wrote in *A Brief Summary, In Plain Language, Of The Most Important Laws Concerning Women; Together With A Few Observations Thereon* in 1854: 'Women, more than any other members of the community, suffer from over legislation' (Bodichon, 1854: 13).

Marriage was a political issue in 1856 when this poem was published. The Matrimonial Causes Bill was making its way through Parliament and would become an Act in 1857. The Act would allow wives who could prove extreme cruelty or desertion to obtain a divorce and empower courts to force estranged husbands to pay maintenance to their former wives. It would deny the husband rights to the earnings of a wife he had deserted, and returned to a woman divorced or legally separated the property rights of a single woman. Behind this Act was the much-publicised marriage of the poet and novelist Caroline Norton which drew public attention to the severe economic penalties which women suffered when they separated from their husbands. After leaving her abusive husband in 1836, Norton had been prevented from seeing their three sons and had been cut off financially for by law all she had once owned including her inheritance, was her husband's by marriage. After her husband's unsuccessful attempt to prove her guilty of an adulterous affair, Norton filed for divorce on the grounds of cruelty. Her claim was rejected, however, as English law did not recognise cruelty as just cause for divorce. By this point Norton was earning money from her writing, but by law all her earnings belonged to her husband. Determined to use her personal misfortune to gather support for legal reform, she drew attention and support for her cause through the publication of pamphlets and the influence of her friends in Parliament, and in 1855, she published her most important pamphlet, *A Letter to the Queen on Lord Chancellor Cranworth's Marriage and Divorce Bill*, in which she reviewed the position of married women under English law:

1. a married woman has no legal existence whether or not she is living with her husband;
2. her property is his property;
3. she cannot make a will, the law gives what she has to her husband despite her wishes or his behaviour;
4. she may not keep her earnings;
5. he may sue for restitution of conjugal rights and thus force her, as if a slave to return to his home;
6. she is not allowed to defend herself in divorce;
7. she cannot divorce him since the House of Lords in effect will not grant a divorce to her;
8. she cannot sue for libel;
9. she cannot sign a lease or transact business;
10. she cannot claim support from her husband, his only obligation is to make sure she doesn't land in the parish poorhouse if he has means;
11. she cannot bind her husband to any agreement.
In short, as her husband, he has the right to all that is hers; as his wife she has no right to anything that is his.

(33)

Marriage, and women's rights and ownership of property within it, was the subject of much conversation and writing in the mid-1850s; it preoccupied social reformers, legislators, churchmen, poets and novelists. The Act secured some property rights to wives who were separated from their husbands but it maintained men's legal rights to all marital property. Barrett Browning's commitment to examining the legal injustice of marriage was part of that series of conversations and part of her commitment to exploring the concerns of 'this live, throbbing age' (*AL* 5:203). 'No longer,' writes Angela Leighton, 'a poetry of "love of love", hers is a poetry which constantly asks about the conventions of power which lie behind love, and which affect the improvised expression of the heart ... those systems of socialisation represented by sex, class and money, for instance, and the systems of literary meaning, represented by historical and political reference, for instance, everywhere make themselves felt' (Leighton, 1992: 80).

In *The Ring and the Book* published after Elizabeth Barrett Browning's death, Robert Browning memorialised his wife's language and understanding of love and marriage. The passage reads as a homage to her ideas (Swedenborg taught that marriage as a pure union existed in heaven among angels) and part of the on-going conversation between them about marriage as a flawed human institution, a 'conversation' that continued beyond Barrett Browning's death:

> Marriage on earth seems such a counterfeit,
> Mere imitation of the inimitable:
> In heaven we have the real and true and sure.
> 'Tis there they neither marry nor are given in
> Marriage but are as angels: right,
> Oh how right that is, how like Jesus Christ
> To say that! Marriage-making for the earth,
> With gold so much, – birth, power, repute so much,
> Or beauty, youth so much, in lack of these!
> Be as the angels rather, who, apart,
> Know themselves into one, are found at length
> Married, but marry never, no, nor give
> In marriage; they are man and wife at once
> When the true time is: here we have to wait
> Not so long neither!

(*The Ring and the Book*, 7:1821–38)

7

''TWIXT CHURCH AND PALACE OF A FLORENCE STREET': ELIZABETH BARRETT BROWNING AND ITALY

SIMON AVERY

On 19 September 1846, a week after they were secretly married, Elizabeth Barrett Browning and her new husband left England to begin the journey which would eventually lead them to health, happiness and a new personal and professional relationship in Tuscany. Joined in Paris by their mutual friend, the art historian and campaigner for women's rights Anna Jameson, they travelled down through Europe, negotiating transport difficulties, Elizabeth's frailty, and Edward Barrett's inevitable disowning of his daughter for daring to marry the man she loved, until they eventually reached Pisa in mid-October. After an initial period of excitement while adjusting to living in a foreign country, the couple started to find Pisa increasingly dull and so, after five months, they moved to Florence, the city of Dante and Michelangelo which would become their home for the next fourteen years, until Barrett Browning's death in 1861. A strong Anglo-American community was already established there when the Brownings arrived and although the city was not as fashionable as it once had been, its relative inexpensiveness, coupled with its immense beauty and intriguing history, meant that it was extremely attractive for two poets with a limited income. Florence was, as Barrett Browning wrote enthusiastically to Mary Russell Mitford soon after their arrival, 'unspeakably beautiful, by grace both of nature & art,—& the wheels of life slide upon the grass (according to continental ways) with little trouble & less expense' (*MRM* 3:216).

There had never been much doubt in the Brownings' minds that when they finally married they would live in Italy. Certainly, for two poets so steeped in Romanticism, the country possessed a wide range of associations since, as Jacob Korg has noted, during the early decades of the nineteenth century Italy had almost become 'the second native land of English poetry' (1983: 9), with Keats, Shelley and Byron all living and working there for substantial periods of time. Many works by these poets, as well as a number of key Romantic novels such as Ann Radcliffe's *The Mysteries of Udolpho* and

Germaine de Staël's *Corinne*, celebrated Italy as one of the wombs of Western civilisation, a country of liberty and passion, warmth and fertility, of beautiful Tuscan landscape and the sublime Alps, the glories of Italian Renaissance art and architecture, and the fascinating cruelty and tyranny of the Borgias, the Medicis and Machiavelli. Before his marriage, Robert had travelled round the peninsula twice, drawn by the artistic heritage and his reading of Giorgio Vasari's *Lives of the Painters* (1550), and used it as the setting for several early works, including *Sordello* (1840) and *Pippa Passes* (1841). Elizabeth had similarly developed a keen interest in the country, reading a number of histories and guides, including Hans Christian Andersen's *The Improvisatrice; or Life in Italy* (1835) and Mary Shelley's *Rambles in Germany and Italy* (1844), and repeatedly writing to Mitford of her dreams of being able to travel there. As she wrote in 1845, she wished she could be 'out of doors every day in an Italian sun' (*MRM* 3:140). It is little wonder, then, that the married couple should be drawn to the country, both as lovers and as poets, when they made their plans to leave England.

Many of the myths and associations which Italy held for Barrett Browning and her contemporaries are reflected in her long poem *Aurora Leigh*, which was written after she had been living in Florence for nearly a decade and which is structured around a series of contrasts between Italy and England. The daughter of a beautiful Florentine woman, a 'white-veiled rose-crowned maiden' (*AL* 1:81), who dies soon after her birth, Aurora is brought up by her English father who loses his previous austerity and learns to be loving and compassionate, the text suggests, by his living in the beautiful Tuscan landscape '[a]mong the mountains above Pelago' (1:111). On her father's death, however, Aurora is transported to England, a land of 'frosty cliffs' (1:251) and '[a] nature tamed' (1:634), where her aunt threatens to eradicate her natural Italian warmth and spontaneity by subjecting her to a 'cage-bird life' (1:305). As Aurora states, contrasting the vibrancy of her homeland and the repression of this new world, 'Italy/ Is one thing, England one' (1:626–7).

Indeed, as the narrative develops, England becomes increasingly associated with prejudice, betrayal and exploitation as Aurora fights to be recognised as a working woman dedicated to her art in 'close London life' (3:40) and the seamstress Marian is raped and then sold into a brothel. For both women, true freedom only comes in a final move to Italy, the country depicted throughout the poem as a feminised motherland in contrast to the patriarchal England. As Aurora says on her return:

> And now I come, my Italy,
> My own hills! Are you 'ware of me, my hills,
> How I lean towards you? do you feel to-night

The urgency and yearning of my soul,
As sleeping mothers feel the sucking babe
And smile?

(*AL* 5:1266–71)

Italy is thus figured as a nurturing life force which allows Aurora, now a successful poet, to offer support to Marian and the child which is the outcome of her rape. Establishing themselves in a house on the hill of Belloguardo overlooking Florence and the river Arno, they reconfigure their positions as outsiders and exiles from the social structures of the 'chill north' (6:307) into a supportive sisterhood, freed from previously imposed identities and able to achieve new emotional attachments. Marian is transformed from 'fallen woman' into pastoral heroine, while for Aurora this return to the motherland both consolidates her power as an independent woman and precipitates a new understanding with her previously spurned lover, Romney. She consequently becomes, as Romney states, the 'Italy of women' (8:358), embodying the liberties, vitality and naturalness of the country which, the logic of the text argues, are simply impossible to sustain in England.

Barrett Browning's own move to Italy, as Anna Jameson told her, had not only '*improved*' her well-being but had positively '*transformed*' her (Markus, 1995: 90). Certainly her letters to Mary Russell Mitford and her sisters are crammed with depictions of her new world, its natural and artistic beauties, its customs and ways of life, but possibly even more important for her future poetry was her increasing fascination with Italy's political situation and particularly the call for national unification.

Since the Vienna Congress at the end of the Napoleonic Wars in 1815, much of Italy had been under the controlling forces of the Austrians. Parts of northern Italy were under the direct rule of the Austrian Emperor in Vienna, while members of the Habsburgs, the Austrian Imperial family, had been made sovereigns of most of the other Italian states – including the Tuscan Grand Duke Leopold II who ruled from 1824 to 1859 and who was a cousin of the Emperor. As a consequence of the reactionary stance of the Austrian Chancellor Metternich and the repressive constitutions of many of the individual states, a number of secret societies such as the revolutionary Giuseppe Mazzini's 'La Giovane Italia' ('Young Italy') movement began to emerge as part of a wider commitment to what became known as the Italian *Risorgimento*, meaning 'rebirth' or 'resurgence'. Such societies were concerned with galvanising support for more liberal constitutions and ultimately for total unification of the Italian states. Although the revolutionary activities of 'Young Italy', like the series of earlier revolutions in 1820 and 1831, achieved little lasting change on Italy's political front, most being defeated by the intervention of Austrian or constitutional forces, they nevertheless increased awareness across Europe of Italy's plight and provided a basis for the subsequent revolutionary actions which would finally bring unification to fruition by the end of the 1860s.

Barrett Browning's support for the Italian cause was unwavering, a fact that should not surprise us given her youthful commitment to the cause of Greek unification in the 1820s (see Chapter Two). Once again, here was a body of people fighting for liberty from tyranny, attempting to claim independence and a right to govern themselves as they saw fit – all concerns which naturally won Barrett Browning's empathy and fitted with her general Whiggish concerns. Indeed, as Alison Milbank argues, 'Italy for the Whigs was the source (with Greece) of their aesthetic and political inheritance' (Milbank, 1998: 11). Moreover, as we saw in Chapter Four, Barrett Browning's work of the 1840s as it was reflected in the two-volume *Poems* (1844; 1850) marked a growing commitment to contemporary political and social concerns in texts such as 'The Cry of the Children', 'The Cry of the Human', 'Lady Geraldine's Courtship' and 'The Runaway Slave at Pilgrim's Point'. It therefore seems almost inevitable that Barrett Browning should turn overtly to concerns of Italian politics in much of her later poetry – particularly when a number of key events in the progress towards unification were occurring directly outside her apartment window on Florence's Casa Guidi. In the following sections, then, I will explore how Barrett Browning represented a number of the debates around unification in her long poem *Casa Guidi Windows* (1851) and selected shorter poems from her later collection *Poems Before Congress* (1860). How might unification be achieved? What was the role of secular and spiritual leaders? How might the populous be motivated into action? And how are political and personal concerns to be reconciled, if indeed they can be?

THROUGH CASA GUIDI WINDOWS

Casa Guidi Windows is a two-part work written over the period 1847–51 which reflects the changing political events in both Tuscany and Italy as a whole during that time. Part One of the poem, completed by March 1848, focuses on the new hopes of a more liberated Italy raised by concessions to the Florentine people by Grand Duke Leopold II of Tuscany. Part Two, however, completed by 1851, reflects upon the despair felt by many supporting unification when these hopes were defeated through the re-establishment of reactionary constitutions after the revolutions of 1848–49. The two parts of the poem mirror one another in a number of respects, using similar images and scenes to reflect upon the political situation. In particular, the poem is constructed around two processions which take place outside the windows of Barrett Browning's home: the first celebrating the Duke's concessions and the second occurring as he is escorted back through Florence by the Austrian guards to the Pitti Palace which was situated across the street from where the Brownings lived.

As well as being part of the solid reality of Barrett Browning's daily life, therefore, the window in this poem functions as an important structuring device since it provides a means of framing the political events occurring outside. As the speaker (whom we can align with Barrett Browning herself) watches the external events unfolding, she occupies one of those threshold positions which Barrett Browning constantly utilises in her poetry (see Chapter Three), situating herself just within the 'feminised' domestic space but also on the edge of the 'masculinised' public/political space. A number of critics have suggested that these spatial dynamics point both to the inability of women to engage overtly with political events and their subsequent naïvity about how to interpret the political events they see. Deborah Phelps, for example, argues that the poet-speaker resembles Tennyson's Lady of Shalott, 'always sequestered from direct relation to the world of action outside her window' and that while she attempts to 'bridge the distance between herself and the world by declaring a public stance', she only succeeds in 'affecting her immediate surroundings: the home, the child' (Phelps, 1990: 227). Interestingly, these were ideas which Barrett Browning herself had suggested in the 'Advertisement' which was affixed to the first edition of the poem in 1851:

> This poem contains the impressions of the writer upon events in Tuscany of which she was a witness. 'From a window', the critic may demur. She bows to the objection in the very title of her work. No continuous narrative nor exposition of political philosophy is attempted by her. It is a simple story of personal impressions, whose only value is in the intensity with which they were received, as proving her warm affection for a beautiful and unfortunate country, and the sincerity with which they are related, as indicating her own good faith and freedom from partisanship.

(CW 3:249)

As I argued in Chapter Two, however, Barrett Browning often used these introductions, prefaces and advertisements as ways of offsetting potential criticism from the reading public and the literary establishment. For as she might have seen it, if she openly admits her limitations as she thinks others might see them, then how can she be held to account for the more subversive views which may be presented?

Unfortunately, however, the parameters which Barrett Browning sets up in the Advertisement – that *Casa Guidi Windows* is limited, subjective, politically naïve – have been rehearsed by critics almost ever since, a situation summed up by Julia Markus in her 1977 edition of the poem where she argues that it has too often been dismissed as a 'long, random, impressionistic work' written by an 'unknowledgeable and hysterical female' (Markus, 1977: xix). In the past two decades, the poem has fared little better in feminist studies of Barrett Browning's works, despite the fact that issues of gender and women's place within the political sphere are clearly central to it. One of the most frequently cited essays, Sandra Gilbert's 'From *Patria to Matria*: Elizabeth Barrett Browning's Risorgimento' (1984), for example, offers some extremely interesting psychoanalytic readings of Italy as a metaphor for the poet's 'own personal and artistic struggle for identity' but avoids dealing explicitly with the actual *politics* which Barrett Browning addresses, rather transforming 'Italy from a political state to a female state of mind, from a problematic country in Europe to the problem condition of femaleness' (Gilbert, 1984: 134; 136). Markus (1977; 1995), Cooper (1988) and Mermin (1989) have offered more detailed and politically aware analyses of the poem but overall there still remains a tendency to overlook *Casa Guidi Windows* and the other Italian poems in comparison with the attention paid to *Aurora Leigh* or *Poems* (1844). As Cooper notes, Barrett Browning's involvement in political affairs 'had to be amateur' because of her gender (Cooper, 1988: 128), but this does not mean that she was uninformed for she read widely in the local and national newspapers and learnt much about the issues at stake from contacts in Florence. And as I aim to demonstrate in the following sections, rather than being 'a simple story of personal impressions', *Casa Guidi Windows* is a powerfully argued and astutely observed commentary on the achievements and problems of the *Risorgimento*. The windows of Casa Guidi permitted Barrett Browning to look more deeply and more perceptively than she has often been given credit for.

SEARCHING FOR A NEW VOICE

Throughout this study we have demonstrated how Barrett Browning constantly negotiated inherited literary traditions and reconfigured established genres into new forms more suitable for the issues she sought to address. Such negotiation is also central to *Casa Guidi Windows* as a critic in *Literary World* highlighted in 1851 when he described the poem as being 'bathed in the old light of new tradition' (Donaldson, 1993: 45), a phrase which suggests Barrett Browning's fundamental concerns here (as elsewhere) with the relations between past and present. How far should the past be allowed to impinge upon the present? How should we negotiate the past? Should traditions and history be venerated or challenged and questioned? Given the agenda of *Casa Guidi Windows*, to attempt to mobilise support for Italian unification, it is hardly surprising that these questions are highly political ones.

Part One of the poem opens with Barrett Browning seeking to find a place for her own writings within an established tradition of literature on Italy. Reflecting in the opening verse paragraphs upon the 'innumerous/ Sweet songs' (Part 1:14–15) lamenting the fate of Italy which has been created by patriotic singer-poets such as Vincenzo da Filica, she concludes that their work – the work of 'Bewailers' (1:21) – is essentially ineffectual as political discourse. Not only are their words so 'sheathed in music' that the pity expressed in them 'scarcely pain[s]' (1:18–19), but she claims that they also depict Italy using a range of disabling literary and mythological images of womanhood as 'childless among mothers' (1:22), 'Widow of empires' (1:21), a 'shamed sister' whose beauty is responsible for her downfall ('Had she been less fair/ She were less wretched', 1:25–6), 'corpse-like on a bier' for all the world to weep over (1:33), and the 'Juliet of Nations' (1:36) whose crown of violets has slipped and blinded her sight. As Markus notes (1977: 73–4), all these images were used by Barrett's immediate male Romantic predecessors, and particularly by Byron in Canto IV of *Childe Harold's Pilgrimage*. In her own poem, however, Barrett Browning argues that such over-familiar images, functioning merely as empty signifiers, allow the listener/ reader to avoid having to face the truth of the actual social and political situation directly, 'since 'tis easier to gaze long/ On mournful masks, and sad effigies/ Than on real, live, weak creatures crushed by strong' (1:46–8).

Writing to Mary Russell Mitford from Pisa in December 1846, Barrett Browning had already expressed the disappointment she and Robert found in modern Italian literature, which they saw as 'purely dull & conventional' with 'not breath nor pulse' (*MRM* 3:198). As the opening pages of *Casa Guidi Windows* imply, many of her fellow poets were equally 'conventional' in their depictions of Barrett Browning's newly adopted homeland. What is therefore required, she suggests, is a new song which, rather than continually rehearsing Italy's elegy, will bring back 'breath' and 'pulse' by dealing specifically with the present and inspiring the thought and action required for unification to be achieved. She thus advocates a modern poem for those 'who stand in Italy to-day' (1:49) and implies that her own *Casa Guidi Windows* is just such a poem.

But in order to write a new, modern work, Barrett Browning had to reject the muse figures of her predecessors – the array of grotesque images of Italy as bound, despoiled and mutilated women – and to look instead to a new source of inspiration which she embodies in a small boy singing '*O bella libertà, O bella!*' beneath her apartment window (1:3). Functioning as something akin to Wordsworth's trope of the innocent child who can re-educate his elders – 'The Child is father of the Man' as Wordsworth defines it ('My Heart Leaps Up', l.17) – the boy comes to represent both freedom and the legitimacy of the Italian cause. And as Barrett Browning states in the first of many body images deployed in this poem, 'the heart of Italy must beat,/ While such a voice had leave to rise serene' (1:8–9). Moreover, his singing ''Twixt church and palace of a Florence street' (1:10), as well as recording the location of the Brownings' apartment near both the San Felice church and the Pitti Palace, articulates a hope for future unity between religious and political structures in Italy's new Jerusalem, which Barrett Browning models, in a similar manner to the close of *Aurora Leigh*, as the 'great Hereafter in this Now' (1:299).

It is this song which therefore becomes the progenitor for Barrett's own as she embraces her role as new singer of the *Risorgimento* through her explicit identification with the child:

> The hopeful child, with leaps to catch his growth,
> Sings open-eyed for liberty's sweet sake:
>   And I, a singer also from my youth,
> Prefer to sing with these who are awake,
>   With birds, with babes, with men who will not fear
> The baptism of the holy morning dew. . . .
>
> Than join those old thin voices with my new,
>   And sigh for Italy with some safe sigh
> Cooped up in music 'twixt an oh and ah,—
>   Nay, hand in hand with that young child, will I
> Go singing rather, '*Bella libertà*,'
>   Than, with those poets, croon the dead . . .
>
> (1:153–8; 162–7)

There is also, however, another, older Florentine tradition to which Barrett Browning appears to relate her own poetry, for in an extended discussion of the foremost Renaissance painter, sculptor and poet Michelangelo, she clearly points to the political underpinning of art. Barrett Browning recounts how 'divinest Angelo' (1:98) was asked by Pietro de' Medici, 'the unworthy successor of Lorenzo the Magnificent' as she calls him in her notes to the poem (*CW* 3:403), to build a statue out of snow outside the Palazzo and how the prince subsequently stood at his window and laughed when, despite the artist's labour, it '[d]issolved beneath the sun's Italian glow' (1:102). Barrett

Browning uses this narrative to highlight both the ruler's degradation of art and the way in which leaders of authoritarian systems believe they have control over all aspects of culture. For as Pietro asserts,

> this genius needs for exaltation,
> When all's said, and howe'er the proud may wince,
> A little marble from our princely mines!

(1:107–9)

Pietro argues here that no one can work without the support of the state but Michelangelo subsequently transforms the prince's laughter of scorn into his own laughter of triumph as he creates his great statues of Night and Day, Dawn and Twilight for the New Sancristy of the Medici church of San Lorenzo. As Barrett Browning defines them, these huge statues are waiting 'in marble scorn' for the 'freeing of the unborn' (1:74; 78). They therefore symbolise a call for liberty from the abuse of power represented by Pietro and, more widely, from all tyrannical systems (in this respect they can be compared with Barrett Browning's earlier treatment of Hiram Powers' statue of the Greek Slave – see Chapter Four). And it is within this tradition of art having a political basis that Barrett Browning then sets her own work, for as she aligns herself with the young boy singing 'O bella libertà', she is able to answer Michelangelo and tell him that after three hundred years of waiting the day of liberation he had envisaged is 'at hand' (1:145). As Milbank argues, despite the Florentines' failure to understand the message embodied in Michelangelo's statues, this woman poet will act as his interpreter and 'call the nation to action by her poetry' (Milbank, 1998: 6).

CASA GUIDI WINDOWS PART ONE: CELEBRATING THE CIVIC GUARD

The first political procession which the Brownings witnessed from their apartment windows was the celebration to mark Duke Leopold II's granting the Florentines the right to form their own civic guard, the 'Guarda Civica', in order to protect their property (Markus, 1977: 83). Coincidentally, this event, which was seen by many as a first step towards wider liberation and ultimately unification ('The first torch of Italian freedom' as Barrett Browning describes it in the poem, 1:465), took place on the Brownings' first wedding anniversary on 12 September 1847, a connection which was not lost on Barrett Browning, as she wrote to Mary Russell Mitford:

our Florentines kept the anniversary of our wedding day (& the establishment of the civic guard) most gloriously a day or two or three ago, forty thousand persons flocking out of the neighbourhood to help the expression of public sympathy & overflowing the city. The procession passed under our eyes into the piazza Pitti, where the Grand Duke & all his family stood at the Palace window melting into tears, to receive the thanks of his people [. . . .] I am glad to have seen that sight . . and to be in Italy at this moment, when such sights are to be seen.

(MRM 2:221)

In the poem, the civic guard processions are depicted with equal optimism. As the speaker watches with tears in her eyes, a stream of Florentines 'flood' the city streets in 'tumult and desire' (1:452–3) before being joined by representatives from other Tuscan cities who 'streamed up to the source/ Of this new good at Florence' (1:462–3). In contrast to much of the Condition of England literature being produced in the 1840s and 1850s where the flood of crowds represents revolutionary threat (see Chapter Eight and Stott 1999), water imagery in *Casa Guidi Windows* functions as an important signifier of the health of the political state, the return to 'the source' here suggesting a return to a purer, more legitimate system. Significantly, therefore, the populace are depicted as achieving a new unity, their faces turned 'all one way' as previous antagonistic feelings are dissolved ('Friends kissed each other's cheeks, and foes long vowed/ More warmly did it', 1:527–8). Certainly, the procession reflects something of the carnival spirit as it was theorised by the Russian critic Mikhail Bakhtin, where established social hierarchies of power, class, discipline and dependency are broken down (see Selden, 1997: 193). For here all tiers of society – lawyers, priests, monks, artists, traders – merge together with a new celebration of 'Il popolo' ('the people', 1:499), a phrase which recalls, as Markus notes (1977: 84), the revolutionary mottos of Mazzini. That Barrett Browning sees this mingling of different classes under a common purpose to be essential to the future hopes of the *Risorgimento* is further emphasised by the new image of the Italian people forming a healthy body rather than the distorted and grotesque bodies by which the older poet-singers imaged the country:

> The first pulse of an even flow of blood
>> To prove the level of Italian veins
> Towards rights perceived and granted.

(1:468–70)

And yet alongside these exuberant images of Tuscany's new unity and hope for the future lies an urgent warning to the people of the necessity of continued action rather than a mere display of pageantry and political rhetoric. 'Those lappets on your shoulders, citizens', Barrett Browning argues, 'are not intelligence,/ Nor courage even' (1:747; 751–2), and she calls for the development of a 'civic spirit, living and awake' as well as a civic guard (1:746). For their rendezvous point, the potential revolutionaries use 'the holier ground' of Dante's stone (1:598) where one of the city's most original and liberal thinkers of the late thirteenth and early fourteenth centuries sat 'pour[ing] alone/ The lava of his spirit when it burned' (1:605–6), an image which is an interesting precursor of Aurora Leigh's (in)famous description of her own radically modern poetry as 'the burning lava of a song' (AL 5:215). During the nineteenth century there was a resurgence of interest in Dante as a challenging commentator on politics, social structures and aesthetics – Ruskin called him 'the central man of all the world' in Stones of Venice, for example (Milbank, 1998: 61), and the Pre-Raphaelites used him as a key influence on their work – and there is certainly a sense in Barrett Browning's poem that his spirit is one of the driving forces behind the push for Italian unification. And yet, as Barrett Browning emphasises, for the revolutionaries to meet there merely to talk is not enough: 'For Dante sits in heaven, and ye stand here,/ And more remains for doing, all must feel,/ Than trysting on his stone from year to year' (1:649–51).

Behind these warnings seems to lie a deep distrust on Barrett Browning's part of the abilities of the populace to organise themselves effectively enough to bring about political change. Certainly, the potential apathy of the masses is evidenced in her depiction of them as almost sub-human:

> Can she [Italy] count
> These oil-eaters with large live mobile mouths
>   Agape for macaroni, in the amount
> Of consecrated heroes of her south's
>   Bright rosary?

(1:199–203)

As we have noted elsewhere, Barrett Browning's depiction of the populace was often negative (see, for example, the arguments concerning the representations of the working classes in Aurora Leigh in Chapter Eight), and the grotesqueness of the imagery here serves only to suggest that the majority are driven by basic primal instincts. And yet this demeaning depiction is an essential part of Barrett Browning's political agenda in her attempt to stir the Italians into meaningful transformative action. As she says in Part Two of the poem when she more overtly criticises them, 'if your hearts should burn, why, hearts *must* burn' (2:283). Certainly, as the above quotation indicates, it was not with the masses that she saw future hope to lie, but with an individual hero, a line of thinking which, as we have shown at various points throughout this study, was at the heart of Barrett Browning's political philosophy and which, following Carlyle in particular, is crucial to the arguments of *Casa Guidi Windows*.

OF DUKES, POPES AND HEROES

Casa Guidi Windows repeatedly emphasises the need to revere the past, to 'cast . . . violets' of respect where necessary (1:262) but not to be stultified by history or the achievements of predecessors and thereby prevented from moving forward. The best honour that can be granted to great men of the past (the gender is clear in her poem) is to perform 'actions, to prove theirs not vain' (1.414). Indeed, as Barrett Browning emphatically states early on in Part One, 'We do not serve the dead—the past is past' (1:217).

In line with this thinking, then, Barrett Browning argues that 'Heroic ashes' of the past can only be of limited use (1:189) and that despite a vintage tradition of Italian heroes, including Virgil, Cicero, Catullus, Caesar, Boccaccio, Dante, Petrarch and Raffael, a *new* hero-leader must be found for the present in order to organise the 'simple, blind and rough' proto-revolutionaries (1:599). In 1847 Barrett Browning evidently had no doubt that Italy *could* bring about unification and that Metternich could 'fix no yoke unless the neck agree' (1:663), but she clearly believed that a move forward could only be achieved through a strong leader who would 'Teach, lead [and] strike fire into the masses', thereby binding them 'into a unity of will,/ And make of Italy a nation' (1:837–40).

As Markus has noted (1977: 90), Barrett Browning's thinking about the ideal leader in this poem seems to have been particularly indebted to Carlyle's 1840 lecture 'The Hero as King' where he defines the king as:

> the most important of Great Men. . . . practically the summary . . . of *all* the various figures of Heroism; Priest, Teacher, whatsoever of earthly or of spiritual dignity we can fancy to reside in a man, embodies itself here, to *command* over us, to furnish us with constant practical teaching, to tell us for the day and how what we are to *do*. He is called *Rex*, Regulator, *Roi*: our own name is still better; King, *Könning*, which means *Can*-ning, Able-man.

> (Carlyle, 1993: 169)

As Carlyle continues, the finding of the 'Able-man', as he terms this superior leader, has to be the business 'of all social procedure whatsoever in this world' (Carlyle, 1993: 169), an argument which Barrett Browning endorses in Part One of *Casa Guidi Windows* as she explores the potential of either the secular Duke Leopold II or the spiritual Pope Pius IX ('Pio Nono') being transformed into the required Able-man. Certainly Leopold's granting a Civic Guard to the Florentine people offers promise 'When multitudes approach their kings with prayers/ And kings concede their people's right to pray/ Both in one sunshine' (1:548–50). Indeed, these concessions are viewed as a means of bringing morality and systems of justice together into a unity which is a crucial component of Barrett Browning's ideal political system:

> O heaven, I think that day had noble use
> Among God's days! So near stood Right and Law,
> > Both mutually forborne! Law would not bruise
> Nor Right deny, and each in reverent awe
> > Honoured the other.

(1:537–41)

Furthermore, the Duke's bringing his children to the Palazzo Pitti window 'to suggest/ *They* too should govern as the people willed' (1:559–60) re-inforces this sense of hope both by drawing an implicit connection with the young boy-muse singing '*O bella libertà*' and by emphasising the Duke's seemingly more feminised qualities of love and empathy rather than the brutal confrontation which the proto-revolutionaries advocate as the means of bringing about change (1:675). And yet as Markus notes (1977: xxvii), despite Barrett Browning's obvious support for Leopold, her depiction of him as mild, sad and having '*perhaps*/ Sufficient comprehension' (1:565–6; italics added) suggests that he is far from the Carlylean 'Able-man' she seeks.

The depiction of Pope Pius IX is even more problematic, however. Elected in 1846, Pius IX was seen by many as exacting a radical break with a tradi-tion of oppression and corruption as he rapidly initiated a series of liberal measures which resulted, for example, in amnesty being granted to all political prisoners, reforms in administration, education and the law, and the ending of press censorship in the Papal States. As Andrina Stiles points out (Stiles, 1989: 19), his election came just three years after the publication of Vincenzo Gioberti's influential political text, *Of the Moral and Civil Primacy of the Italians* (1843), one of the key propositions of which was that the Pope and the Catholic Church should be central to any nationalist revival. In a letter of September 1847, Barrett Browning wrote to Mary Russell Mitford of the Pope as 'a great man', arguing that 'For liberty to spring from a throne is wonderful, . . but from a papal throne is miraculous' (*MRM* 3:222). By the time of writing *Casa Guidi Windows*, however, her view was much more tem-pered, for as she suggests, the past actions of the papacy, 'history's bell/ So heavy round the neck' (1:865–6), indicate that the idea of a Pope as heroic unifier is at best improbable. Certainly, her condemnation of the history of the papacy is strident as she represents it causing despair in 'free men, good men, wise men', revelling in 'dread shows' of women being burnt by 'a licensed mob', and producing 'priests, trained to rob' (1:901–7). Barrett Browning, the firm believer in religious tolerance and what she termed a 'Universal Church of Christ' (*BC* 8:149) where no one is persecuted for their beliefs, thus draws attention to the horrific violence upon which the papal system is based, refusing, as Cooper notes (1988: 136), 'to be awed by the trappings of papal power'.

Certainly, Pius IX could never be a suitable hero-leader for Italy since he could never achieve that state of disinterestedness which Barrett Browning had argued from *The Battle of Marathon* onwards was crucial for a strong leader (see Chapter Two). Rather, he must 'prefer/ "The interests of the Church"' (1:999–1000) and therefore, in a parody of the earlier depiction of Michelangelo's St Lorenzo sculptures, Barrett Browning configures the Pope as half-man, half-statue, an embodiment of the rigidity of established religion:

> At best and hopefullest,
> He's pope—we want a man! his heart beats warm,
> But [. . .] enchanted to the waist,
> He sits in stone and hardens by a charm
> Into the marble of his throne high-placed.
> Mild benediction waves his saintly arm—
> So, good! but what we want's a perfect man,
> Complete and all alive: half travertine
> Half suits our need, and ill subserves our plan.

> (1:1034–42)

There are echoes here of Robert Browning's dramatic monologue 'A Bishop Orders His Tomb at Saint Praxed's Church', published a few years earlier in 1845, where again the marble the Bishop desires for his tomb suggests a greater concern with power and material corruption than with the soul and fundamental Christian values. Certainly, the Pope's hardened solidity here is in sharp contrast to the need to 'Open wide the house' of Christ which Barrett Browning calls for as a key step in expanding '[t]he inner souls of men' and creating 'civic heroes' (1:781; 793–4).

There is clearly a sense, therefore, that neither ducal nor papal powers will suffice to provide an heroic Able-man and as Part One closes there is a renewed sense of urgency concerning the absence of a 'new/ Teacher and leader' who will take Italy forward (1:1028–9). Cooper has argued that the ending of this Part is 'buoyant and confident' (1988: 138), and yet I would suggest that it is rather riven with tension and ambiguity since the final verse paragraph, which records the beginning of revolutionary activity in Naples and Palermo in January 1848, highlights the 'shrieks' and '[r]ows of shot corpses' in an 'apocalypse of death' (1:1204–5; 1209). As Barrett Browning appears to suggest, however, this bloodshed and sacrifice is a necessary part of the ritual of nationalistic overthrow. Franz Fanon has argued concerning the nationalist uprisings in Africa in the twentieth century that violence can function as a means of cleansing or even re-birthing, in that it firstly liberates consciousness and then destroys the social and political institutions of the colonial society which act as the instruments of oppression (Hansen, 1977: 115). Consequently, the colonised person is 'freed . . . from his feelings of inferiority and humiliation and restor[ed] to the fullness of himself as a man' (sic, 121). While Barrett Browning is clearly against brute force for its own sake in this poem, calling instead for force to be combined with reasoned thinking, she certainly recognises that violence against the oppressive coloniser is necessary for liberation and purification to take place. As she would re-emphasise in Part Two, rather than a peace which is founded on colonial oppression she would prefer 'the struggle in the slippery fosse/ Of dying men and horses, and the wave/ Blood-bubbling' (2:403–5). At the end of Part One, however, her overly emphatic 'Behold, they shall not fail' (1203) seems to imply that she fears that Charles Albert of Savoy's men might well do just that – and in the event, as Part Two of the poem documents, fail they did.

In March 1848 Barrett Browning sent what would become Part One of *Casa Guidi Windows* to *Blackwood's Magazine*, calling it 'A Meditation in Tuscany', a title which itself belies the 'simple story' nomenclature she later used in the Advertisement (*CW* 3:249). Six months later, however, *Blackwood's* returned the manuscript, arguing that it was both too obscure (a charge which has often been thrown at the poem) and already out of date in the fast-moving European revolutionary scene of that year. Nevertheless, not to be deterred Barrett Browning began work on what would become Part Two of the poem, which allowed her to bring her reflections on the movement towards unification up to date and thus rework a number of the political analyses and ideas of Part One. The resulting dual time scheme of the poem can be compared with that earlier, more influential account of revolution in Wordsworth's *The Prelude*, where Wordsworth, 'poet-hero of a movement essential to the better being of poetry' as Barrett called him in her *Book of the Poets* (1843, *CW* 6:304), initially celebrated the hopes embodied in the early stages of the French Revolution before recording his despair when it failed to meet utopian political expectations. Like Wordsworth, Barrett Browning's own explorations of experiences both during and after revolution in *Casa Guidi Windows* record both hope and despair and allow her to reflect more widely on the nature and process of history and political change.

CASA GUIDI WINDOWS PART TWO:
THE VOICE OF DEFEAT

1848 was, of course, a major year of revolutions across Europe as country after country rose up against repressive regimes, seeking greater freedom. The uprisings in Sicily and Naples in January 1848 which close Part One of *Casa Guidi Windows* were the first of such revolutions and the insurrectionary fervour quickly spread to many of the other Italian states. In Barrett Browning's Tuscany, Duke Leopold, like a number of other rulers, was forced to grant a constitution to the people by the end of February but within a year, fearing that Tuscany was about to become a republic, he fled to Siena and then on to Naples where he joined Pope Pius IX who had also fled there following the murder of his chief minister.

In the Duke's absence, a predominantly democratic provincial government was formed in Florence, but the following month a decisive victory was won by the Austrian powers at the Battle of Novara, where Charles Albert of Savoy was leading Italian troops in support of revolts in Lombardy and Venitia. Austria's victory marked the beginning of a much wider defeat of the Italian liberal movement, in the wake of which many moderate Florentines called for the return of Leopold. As Markus notes, however, rather than coming back at his people's bidding, Leopold came back escorted by Italy's hated oppressors (Markus, 1995: 129). His commitment to Austria's agenda was then clearly evident a few nights later by his appearance at the opera wearing Austrian uniform. 'Leopoldo Secondo' no more, he had clearly sold out to become 'Leopold d'Austria'.

The promise of unification which had seemed certain in 1848 had all but evaporated by mid-1849, therefore, and the new sense of despair felt by Barrett Browning and many of her contemporaries is explored throughout the shorter Part Two of *Casa Guidi Windows*. Indeed, as Matthew Reynolds has argued in his discussion of the metre of the poem, this bleakness is caught even within the poetic rhythms with the shift from the uplifting metre representing the 'throb of life' in Part One to a 'more depressed' and 'weary'-sounding metre in Part Two (Reynolds, 2001: 95). Certainly there is a reworking of many of the ideas, tropes and images of Part One in a far more sombre hue.

Looking back on her previous writing about Italy, the poet-speaker reflects that she 'wrote a mediation and a dream' (2:1) and that the young boy-muse she used as inspiration could not possibly survive in the wake of such eventual defeat: 'I leant upon his music as a theme,/ Till it gave way beneath my heart's full beat' (2:3–4). Similarly, the earlier carnival-like procession of Part One is replaced here by a procession representing the betrayal of Tuscany by the Duke and the reassertion of Austrian control:

> From Casa Guidi windows, gazing, then,
> I saw and witness how the Duke came back.
>   The regular tramp of horse and tread of men
>   Did smite the silence like an anvil black
>   And sparkless. . . .
>   . . . sword and bayonet,
>   Horse, foot, artillery,—cannons rolling on
> Like blind slow storm-cloud gestant with the heat
>   Of undeveloped lightnings, each bestrode
> By a single man, dust-white from head to heel,
>   Indifferent as the dreadful thing he rode,
> Like a sculptured Fate serene and terrible.

> (2:286–90; 301–7)

Here the Austrians appear ghost-like, each of them compared to 'a sculptured Fate', a phrase which both suggests a mythic scene as Mermin points out (1989: 168) and picks up on the rigidity of oppression associated earlier with the statuesque Pope. In contrast to the previous celebration, the Florentines have now 'learnt silence' (2:358), sold out by a leader who is depicted as both a false father to the people and an 'illegitimate Caesar' (2:86). The Florentines may have tried to look favourably on Leopold's faults and make them into virtues ('It was understood/ God made thee not too vigorous or too bold', 2:43–4) and yet underneath the surface appearance, as Barrett Browning wrote to her sister in May 1849, 'He is made of the stuff of princes—faithless and ignoble' (quoted in Hayter, 1962: 131).

On a more personal level, however, Barrett Browning connects her earlier failure to see through the Duke with a tendency to judge emotionally because of her gender, arguing that it was 'my woman's fault/ That ever I believed the man was true!' (2:64–5). Indeed, she returns to this argument when she recalls seeing the Duke with his children while she herself was pregnant:

> And I, because I am a woman—I,
>   Who felt my own child's coming life before
> The prescience of my soul, and held faith high,—
>   I could not bear to think, whoever bore,
> That lips, so warmed, could shape so cold a lie.

> (2:95–9)

Such admissions of emotional response have done irrevocable damage to Barrett Browning's reputation as a commentator upon Italian affairs, reinforcing the idea of a woman dabbling in politics with little wider understanding.

Hayter, for example, argues that 'As usual, she believed too easily in the Grand Duke Leopold's single-minded good intentions' (1862: 131), and Barrett Browning herself writes in the Advertisement that she took 'shame upon herself that she believed, like a woman, some royal oaths, and lost sight of the probable consequences of some obvious popular defects' (*CW* 3:249). However, there is an honesty and openness about Barrett Browning's shift in position in the two parts of this poem, particularly in her refusal to separate public politics from private emotion, and, as Markus notes, if she was taken in by the Duke's conduct, then so was much of Europe (Markus, 1995: 133). Certainly as the poet herself makes clear, such 'discrepancies' as those between her earlier and her present stances are 'painful' but must be accepted since they indicate 'the interval between aspiration and performance, between faith and disillusion, between hope and fact' (*CW* 3:249).

Not willing to represent herself as completely misguided, however, Barrett Browning also points out in the Advertisement that she 'certainly escaped the epidemic "falling sickness" of enthusiasm' for the Pope which emerged with his liberal reforms (*CW* 3:249). Markus has demonstrated in her discussion of poems and articles about the Pope submitted to *The Tuscan Athenaeum* during this period that this 'falling sickness' was indeed rife (1995: 134), but as we have already seen, Barrett Browning is highly critical of the papacy throughout the poem. The Pope had fled Rome for Naples in November 1848 and by March 1849 Mazzini was in charge of the Roman Republic, one of the great triumphs of the *Risorgimento*. Three months later, however, the Pope persuaded the French Republic to send in troops to dissolve the Republic and to reinstate reactionary papal control. These actions resulted, Barrett Browning argues, in 'Peter's chair' being 'shamed' (2:445) and reveal that the church he represents, rather than being open, 'cramp[s] the souls of men' (2:508). As she repeatedly stresses, whatever valiant actions may arise in the future, 'Pope Pius will be glorified in none' (2:441).

Barrett Browning's analysis of the failure of the 1848 revolutions, however, extends much further than isolating the Duke and the Pope. Returning to her arguments of Part One, she overtly condemns the Italian people for a lack of action when they had the opportunity to form a republican government, satirising them for their ineffectual playing at politics (the imagery of theatrical performance is strong throughout this section):

> How down they pulled the Duke's arm's everywhere!
> How up they set new café-signs, to show
>   Where patriots might sip ices in pure air—
> (The fresh paint smelling somewhat)!

(2:124–6)

Similarly the guard are shown to be more concerned with representing '[t]he true republic in the form of hats' (2:151) and chalking walls 'with bloody caveats' (2:153) than with fighting for their cause, having 'no knowledge, no concept, nought' (2:202) without a strong leader. Barrett Browning's earlier fears of apathy and mere theatrical show have therefore been fulfilled, but if the Florentine people have no real commitment to the cause and a lack of 'soul conviction' (2:258), this is only a symptom of a wider international malaise. For despite Europe's cultural indebtedness to Italy which Barrett Browning describes in Part One as the plundering of 'this earth's darling' (1:1187), most European countries appear more concerned, as we saw at the beginning of Chapter Four, with the show of prosperity and 'civilisation' embodied in the Great Exhibition than with assisting Italy achieve unification. As Deirdre David argues (1987: 130), 'Europe after the events of 1848 is painted by Barrett Browning as a "Fair-going world", bent upon exhibiting glories of trade and trophies of imperialism, and deaf to the cries of people suffering under domestic and foreign tyranny.' 'Great nations have great shames', Barrett Browning writes (2:648). Indeed, in the preface to *Poems Before Congress*, she would stridently condemn non-intervention by foreign powers in such extreme cases as Italy's:

> non-intervention in the affairs of neighbouring states is a high political virtue; but non-intervention does not mean, passing by on the other side when your neighbour falls among thieves,—or Phariseeism would recover it from Christianity.

> (*CW* 3:315)

In the wake of such non-intervention in the events described in *Casa Guidi Windows*, however, Barrett Browning turns to solutions to the Italian question nearer home.

RE-OPENING THE WINDOWS

About halfway through Part Two of *Casa Guidi Windows*, Barrett Browning both literally and symbolically shuts the windows of her apartment: 'I have grown too weary of these windows', she states (2:430). And yet despite the seeming failure of plans for unification articulated throughout, a new sense of hope appears to emerge by the end of the poem in a combination of public and personal elements. In an address to the Austrian troops Barrett Browning had already defiantly depicted a time when the Italians would rise up again:

Ye stamp no nation out, though day and night
   Ye tread them with that absolute heel which grates
And grinds them flat from all attempted height.
   You kill worms sooner with a garden-spade
Than you kill peoples: peoples will not die;
   The tail curls stronger when you lop the head:
They writhe at every wound and multiply,
   And shudder into a heap of life that's made
Thus vital from God's own vitality.

                    (2:337–45)

Despite the grotesqueness of the imagery here which again compares the populous to a subhuman species, there is a strong sense of regenerative power which appears to have its source in God as if God himself, rather than religion as mediated through the Pope, is endorsing the movement for unification. By the close of the poem, Barrett Browning also locates this regenerative power in a new reverence for Italy's recent dead, the soldiers who died in battle, Charles Albert who 'Shaking Austria's yoke/ . . . shattered his own hand and heart' (2:711–12), and for the first time a woman, Garibaldi's wife, who fought alongside her husband while six months pregnant and died horrifically, feeling 'her little babe unborn/ Recoil, within her, from the violent staves/ And bloodhounds of the world' (2:680–2).

   The final and most dominant image of hope in the poem, however, is located in Barrett Browning's own son Penini who, born during the 1849 revolutionary activity, is depicted standing at the open apartment window, the sun streaming onto his curls in an image of the classical epic hero. Replacing the earlier young boy singing beneath Casa Guidi windows, it is this boy who now becomes the embodiment of liberal ideas for the future and the representative of all 'young Florentine[s]' (2:743) who, supported by female nurturing and guidance, will become the new source of political energy and lead the oppressed motherland into unification and freedom. With a final return to the water imagery pervading this work in the 'New springs of life . . . gushing everywhere/ To cleanse the water-courses' (2:762–3), the political future now seems more assured.

FURTHER REFLECTIONS:
POEMS BEFORE CONGRESS

Casa Guidi Windows is a powerful and confident work, shifting deftly between political debate, historical analysis and philosophical enquiry, all carefully controlled by regularly rhyming stanzas of iambic pentameter. Distinguished from Barrett Browning's early works, as Cooper notes (1988: 124), by the new assertive use of the subjective 'I' throughout, the result, as Porter and Clarke define it, is nothing less than 'a condensed lyric epic of a modern nation's birth' (*CW* 4:xv). And yet Barrett recognised that this was a poem 'which numbers of people will be sure to dislike profoundly, & angrily, perhaps' (*MRM* 3:323). Indeed, when the poem was published in 1851, reviews were considerably mixed. While the *United States Magazine* viewed the poem as 'perhaps the finest' of Barrett Browning's works and Charles Kingsley, writing in *Fraser's Magazine*, called her 'one of the greatest poets— of modern Europe', the *Guardian* called *Casa Guidi Windows* a 'complete failure' which only showed that the poet was 'really not at home in politics and social philanthropy' (Donaldson, 1993: 50; 47; 45). Significantly, however, her status as poet of the *Risorgimento* was confirmed in Italy when both Francesco Guerazzi, dictator of the Roman Republic, and the revolutionary republican Giuseppe Mazzini contacted her on the publication of *Casa Guidi Windows* to praise her support for unification – despite the fact that neither of them is depicted very positively in the poem. And she would continue to write on the Italian cause for the rest of her life, declaring to Mrs Ogilvy concerning the country of her birth that 'I dont [*sic*] pretend to understand (much less to excuse) this alleged indifference of the English people towards the Italians. And who can?' (*MDO* 48).

Barrett Browning's next volume after *Casa Guidi Windows*, the epic *Aurora Leigh*, draws, as I suggested above, on many of the nineteenth century's (often paradoxical) associations of Italy as a land of liberty from English repression, of beauty, warmth and culture. However, except for one reference to 'the Austrian boar/ . . . / . . . raking up our grape/ And olive gardens with his tyrannous tusk,/ And rolling on our maize with all his swine' (*AL* 8:100–7), overt concerns with Austria's oppression of Italy are all but erased from *Aurora Leigh*, although, of course, the whole poem stands as a testament to the country's greatness. But in the final volume Barrett Browning herself saw to press, *Poems Before Congress* (1860), she returned to the issue of Italian unification with a power and stridency which is sometimes even more forceful than in her previous works.

Near the end of *Casa Guidi Windows*, Barrett Browning states that 'Life throbs in noble Piedmont' (2:731), by which she suggested that hopes of a united Italy lay not in Rome as Mazzini had seen it in the formation of the 1849 Roman Republic, but in Turin with the House of Savoy, King Victor Emmanuel II and his minister Camillo Benso Cavour. Again, Barrett Browning was proved right, for these figures were to be central to the *Risorgimento*'s work towards unification over the next decade. Cavour, a key architect of Italian unification, quickly developed into one of Barrett Browning's new heroes ('A hundred Garibaldis for such a man', she once wrote, *CW* 6:378), and was matched only by her overwhelming admiration for Napoleon III of France, who she viewed, despite his authoritarianism and much to Robert's despair, as the potential saviour of Italy. In April 1859, when Austria declared war on Piedmont, it seemed as if a final battle was being fought as Napoleon III joined forces with Victor Emmanuel, achieving victories at Magenta and Solferino while Garibaldi won battles at Varese and Como. But then Napoleon turned tail and, under the Treaty of Villafranca, agreed with Emperor Franz Joseph of Austria to leave Venice in Austrian control and restore the central states to their previous rulers. Barrett Browning was devastated at what she saw as an ultimate betrayal and in her collection *Poems Before Congress*, the title of which refers to a planned International Congress on Italian unification which eventually failed to take place, she recorded in eight poems her changing reactions towards Napoleon and the political situation in Italy in the 1850s.

The longest poem of the collection, and the one which most disturbed English reviewers, was the celebratory 'Napoleon III in Italy' which records the leader's martial prowess with great admiration and attacks those leaders who criticised his policies. Napoleon is constructed by Barrett Browning here as the 'Sublime Deliverer!' (l.94) who will revenge the abuse of the Italians by the Austrians who 'wound them/ In iron, tortured and flogged them', 'Taxed them and then bayoneted them' and 'Us[ed] their daughters and wives' (ll.207–12). He is, as Barrett Browning sees him, the necessary Carlylean Able-man whose autocracy is carefully defended:

> Autocrat? let them scoff,
>   Who fails to comprehend
> That a ruler incarnate of
>   The people, must transcend
> All common king-born kings.

(293–7)

As the poem's martial rhetoric and repeated refrain 'Emperor/ Evermore' indicate, her devotion at the time of writing this poem is uncompromised. Indeed, as she wrote in her correspondence in 1859, Napoleon was for her

> The only great-hearted politician in Europe—but chivalry always came from France. The emotion here is profound—and the terror, among the priests. Always I expected this from Napoleon, and, if he will carry out his desire, Peni[ni] and I are agreed to kneel down and kiss his feet.'

(Kenyon 1897 2:307)

In 'A Tale of Villafranca', however, Barrett Browning tackled her dismay at Napoleon's making peace with Austria after fighting alongside Italy. The poem takes many of the traditional postures of a fairy tale addressed to her son Penini: 'My little son, My Florentine/ Sit down beside my knee' (ll.1–2). In sharp contrast to the measured iambic pentameter of *Casa Guidi Windows*, the rhythms and language of 'A Tale of Villafranca' are more suited to a nursery rhyme than political rhetoric as Barrett Browning sets out to explain 'why the sign/ Of joy which flushed our Italy/ Has faded since but yesternight' (ll.3–5). She tells how 'A great man (who was crowned one day)' began to 'shape' a 'great Deed' (ll.8–9) which would eventually become the unification of Italy. But when he shows this germ of the 'Deed' to 'sovereigns, statesmen, north and south' (l.22), it is seen as a threat to be destroyed at all costs: 'all cried "Crush it, maim it, gag it!/ Set dog-toothed lies to tear it ragged,/ Truncated and traduced' (ll.61–3). The poem concludes with Napoleon lamenting the slowness of the growth of men's souls and the fact that his plans were conceived before their time: 'God's fruit of justice ripens slow' (l.68). Even here, therefore, Barrett Browning attempts to defend Napoleon's actions but in a poem published after her death, 'First News from Villafranca', she records her reactions more damningly:

> Peace, peace, peace, do you say?
>   What!—with the enemy's guns in our ears?
>   With the country' wrong not rendered back?
> What!—while Austria stands at bay
>   In Mantua, and our Venice bears
>   The cursed flag of yellow and black? . . .
>
> No, not Napoleon!—he who mused
>   At Paris, and at Milan spake,
>   And at Solferino led the fight:
> Not he we trusted, honoured, used
>   Our hopes and hearts for . . . till they break,
>   Even so, you tell us . . . in his sight.

(ll.1–6; 19–24)

Other works in *Poems Before Congress* revisit some of the ideas explored earlier in *Casa Guidi Windows*. 'An August Voice' is a sharp critique, presumably in the voice of Napoleon, of those who betrayed the Italian cause by seeking to reinstate Duke Leopold. 'Christmas Gifts' returns to the vehement attack on Pope Pius IX who leaves his people in a spiritual wasteland ('Our souls are sick and forlorn,/ And who will show us where/ Is the stable where Christ was born?', ll.4–6), and 'Italy and the World' suggests that despite past failures, the oppressed country will arise one day in a pseudo-apocalyptic resurrection:

> . . . Arise with a shout
> Nation of Italy, slain and buried!
>
> Hill to hill and turret to turret
>   Flashing the tricolor,—newly created
> Beautiful Italy, calm, unhurried,
>   Rise heroic and renovated
> Rise to the final restitution.

(ll.29–35)

Poems Before Congress was written, Barrett Browning notes in the Preface, 'under the pressures of the events they indicate' and 'because I love truth and justice' (*CW* 3:314). Yet if *Casa Guidi Windows* had received negative reviews, *Poems Before Congress* suffered far worse as commentators reacted harshly against Barrett Browning's condemnation of the apathy of other European powers and her seeming support of a figure such as Napoleon. The poems are 'a perfect shriek', wrote *London Quarterly Review*, while *The Spectator* called them a 'species of insanity' and *John Bull* argued they were 'blind to historic truth' (Donaldson, 1993: 88; 83–4). While it *is* true that the poems in this collection generally lack the sustained force of *Casa Guidi Windows* and certainly of Barrett Browning's preceding volume, *Aurora Leigh*, they nevertheless re-emphasise the role as political commentator on Italian affairs which Barrett Browning made her own in the last decade of her life.

By March 1861, all the Italian states except Rome and Venice had voted to join with Piedmont in a new unified Italy under the leadership of Victor Emmanuel, 'King of us all', as Barrett Browning would call him in her poem 'King Victor Emmanuel Entering Florence' (l.8, *Last Poems*). Barrett Browning thus saw her desire for unification and freedom of her adopted homeland almost completed, but within three months of the establishment of the new Italian parliament she was to die from the severe worsening of her diseased lungs. Following her death, Florence formally recognised the great contribution Barrett Browning had made to the Italian cause when the shops near her home closed on the day of her funeral and when the council subsequently erected a tablet on Casa Guidi commemorating the woman who had brought together the learning of a scholar and the inspiration of a poet, and whose verse was 'a golden ring wedding Italy and England'. As Oscar Wilde was later to write of her:

To Greek Literature she owed her scholarly culture, but modern Italy created her human passion for liberty. When she crossed the Alps she became filled with a new ardour . . . It is pleasant to think that an English poetess was to a certain extent a real factor in bringing about the unity of Italy that was Dante's dream, and if Florence drove her great singer into exile, she at least welcomed within her walls the later singer that England had sent her.

(Wilde, 1908: 112–13)

Throughout her life, Barrett Browning's political philosophies had remained remarkably consistent. Initially grounded in the political ideas promoted by the Whig party, she would constantly champion the rights of the individual in social, political and religious contexts and likewise support all countries who were attempting to break free from systems of external oppression. 'I am simply a DEMOCRAT,' she wrote to Mary Russell Mitford in 1852 (*MRM* 3:345), although, as we have seen, that commitment to democracy could be complicated by a distrust both of the masses and of large-scale social philosophies such as socialism (satirised in *Aurora Leigh*) and communism. Instead, Barrett Browning consistently turned to the ideas of a great political hero figure in true Carlylean fashion, whether that was the liberal poet-hero Byron in her early years or, later and more problematically, Napoleon III. Essentially, however, it was her commitment to democracy and the means of bringing about the widest freedom for the widest number of people which was the fundamental drive behind her writing.

As Barrett Browning herself demonstrated throughout her life, politics was clearly an arena in which she felt the educated nineteenth-century woman had an important role to play, not least because politics and the oppressions of power so often began in that smallest of societal units, the family. Indeed, her political vision was often strikingly modern in its understanding of the ubiquity and multivalence of systems of power and cycles of oppression, an understanding perhaps most clearly exemplified by her defence of her father's tyrannies: the 'evil' is so often to be found not in isolated individuals but 'in the system' (*BC* 11:43). It was such systems of oppression that Barrett sought to challenge, critique and deconstruct throughout her life in a body of political poetry which might be called a poetics of power.

8
'WHERE ANGELS FEAR TO TREAD':
AURORA LEIGH

REBECCA STOTT

Mrs Browning's *Aurora Leigh* is, as far as I know, the greatest poem which the century has produced in any language.

(John Ruskin, *Things to be Studied*, 1856; cited David, 1987: 95)

THE POEM

The idea for a long experimental verse-poem came to Elizabeth Barrett in 1844 in London; a decade later, married and living in Italy with her husband and young son between 1853 and 1856, she wrote the poem in short bursts at the rate sometimes of thirty to forty lines a day; *Aurora Leigh* was finally finished in 1856 and published in London and Boston in 1857. It is a masterpiece: passionate, inventive and experimental, with a fast-moving plot and full of ideas and conflicts of opinion. It is a white-hot piece of writing and because so much of it is written as dialogue or conversation, it expands and breathes when it is read aloud. Aurora is fiercely independent and a clever and original thinker who refuses to accept dogma and convention. Her personality drives the poem, her thoughts and reflections and conversations glitter on every page. As Cora Kaplan argues, it is 'the fullest and most violent exposition of the "woman question" in mid-Victorian literature . . . a collage of Romantic and Victorian texts reworked from a woman's perspective . . . the longest poem of the decade . . . a vast quilt, made up of other garments, the pattern dazzling because, not in spite of, its irregularities' (Kaplan, 1978: 5).

PLOT STRUCTURE

Aurora Leigh is a verse-poem which tells an epic adventure story about the growth to maturity of a woman poet. Large-scale philosophical rumination is balanced throughout by the rigorous attention paid to the small-scale details of place, character and time. With its combination of characteristics from both the realist novel and the epic poem, it is an unusual piece of writing both for its own time and for today.

However, although verse-novels of this scope were unusual in the mid-nineteenth century, verse narratives of a shorter duration were not. Two had been published to critical acclaim in 1848: Tennyson's *The Princess* and Arthur Hugh Clough's *The Bothie of Tober-Na-Vuolich*. Though Tennyson's poem was a kind of comic medieval fairy tale and Clough's told the story of a group of undergraduates on holiday in contemporary Scotland, both poems deal with, as Kaplan has shown, the issues at the heart of *Aurora Leigh*: women's role in the world, women's education, socialism and the role of the poet. (Kaplan, 1978: 27–9). They are poems of and about mid-Victorian Britain. Both *The Princess* and *The Bothie of Tober-na-Vuolich* are therefore shadow poems in *Aurora Leigh*; their presence and influence come in and out of focus continually and, in many ways, *Aurora Leigh* is written in dialogue with them both. Kaplan concludes that this 'conversation' is a critical one, for in it Barrett Browning refuses to accept the male versions of female experience offered by Clough and Tennyson and offers her own woman-centred version (Kaplan, 1978: 29).

The plot structure of *Aurora Leigh* is a relatively simple one, comparable to many of the *Bildungsroman* novels (narratives of development and 'education') so popular in the nineteenth century. Like *Oliver Twist* or *Jane Eyre*, *Aurora Leigh* tells the story of a child's development into adulthood as a series of character-shaping spiritual and physical ordeals. By the end of the *Bildungsroman*, conflicts have usually been resolved, the turbulent soul of the protagonist has calmed and marriage or success is achieved or imminent. Rags have been replaced by literal or spiritual or romantic riches – sometimes all three. As Romney puts it in *Aurora Leigh*: 'Through bitter experience, compensation sweet' (*AL* 9:593). But *Aurora Leigh* was a much rarer version of the *Bildungsroman* form for it was also a *Kunstlerroman*, a story plotting the maturation of an *artist/writer*, a form that traditionally told of the protagonist's struggle to find not just a settled adult *identity* but also an *art*. And in one last respect *Aurora Leigh* was a very rare species of *Kunstlerroman* indeed for its artist/writer was a *woman*.

However, in other important ways, as critics have shown (DuPlessis, 1985; Cooper, 1988; Case, 1991), it reworks the plot structures of the *Bildungsroman* from a woman's perspective. Aurora is a woman in love but she is also a poet pursuing her art, two paths which take her in different directions. Alison Case has shown how there are essentially two different kinds of story in the verse-novel, and these two stories are told in different ways. Book 5 is the turning point, the book in which Aurora sets out her (and Barrett

Browning's) poetic manifesto and produces her long-awaited masterpiece. In this respect this Book is the culmination of the *Kunstlerroman* plot but Aurora is not yet complete and the book sets Aurora out on a new quest, this time for emotional fulfilment, which leads her first to the sisterly rescue and love of Marian and then to Romney. The remaining four books, then, read like a journal written day by day as Aurora travels from Paris to Florence where she settles with Marian. As Case argues:

> The mixed narration of *Aurora Leigh* allowed [Barrett Browning] to create a kind of double teleology for the novel, in which the struggle toward artistic in-dependence and success, the plot of poetic 'ambition', could be kept relatively isolated from the undermining influence of the traditional love story, with its emphasis on female passivity and lack of emotion or sexual self-knowledge, its insistence on loving self-abnegation as the proper 'end' of female existence.

> (Case, 1991: 32)

We can see this tightly structured plot pattern and sequence more clearly in a summary provided by Helen Cooper:

Written in England:
1. Aurora's parents' marriage, her childhood in Italy, adolescence in England, birth as a poet.
2. Romney's proposal on Aurora's twentieth birthday.
3. Aurora as a writer in London, introduction of Lady Waldemar, Marian Erle's story.
4. Marian's story continued, the abortive wedding.
5. A pivotal book: Aurora's meditation on Art, Lord Howe's party, Aurora's decision to leave England for Italy.

Written in Paris and Italy:
6. Aurora's discovery of Marian in Paris, Marian's explanation of the abortive wedding, Marian's second story.
7. Marian's story continued, the journey to Italy, letters to Lord Howe and Lady Waldemar.
8. Romney's arrival in Florence, his and Aurora's reassessment of the discussion that took place on her twentieth birthday.
9. Marian's refusal to marry Romney, Aurora's union with Romney, her rebirth as a poet.

(Cooper, 1988: 53–4)

Cooper sets out the story in this way in order to show that Aurora repeats, in the last four books, the experiences of the first four but in reverse order so the whole plot forms something of a circle with the book beginning and ending with a marriage union (Books 1 and 9) and weaving together the three life stories of Romney, Marian and Aurora. But while the plot may be tightly structured in this way, it serves to hold together a poem of great elasticity of thought and potentially explosive polemic about class and gender conflicts, marriage and prostitution, the relation of art to politics and the Condition of England.

THE POLEMICAL NATURE OF THE POEM

One of the striking features of the correspondence which Elizabeth Barrett Browning wrote to friends from Italy to England in the wake of the publication of her novel-poem *Aurora Leigh* is her declared surprise that her poem had not given *more* offence. She repeats this over and over again in the letters she wrote that winter:

> To Arabella Barrett: 'I agree with you in wondering at the manner in which, generally speaking, I have escaped the charge of impropriety; it's quite beyond my own expectation.'

> (10–18 December 1856; Reynolds, 1996: 339)

> To Anna Jameson: 'the kind of reception given to the book has much surprised me, as I was prepared for an outcry of quite another kind, and extravagances in a quite opposite sense'.

> (26 December 1856; Reynolds, 1996: 340)

> To Henrietta Surtees Cook: 'I can scarcely understand how more offence has not been given and taken in certain quarters . . . Robert says I am longing to be abused a little – mind, I don't say so.'

> (10 January 1857; Reynolds, 1996: 341)

> To Anna Jameson: 'I am entirely astonished at the amount of reception I have met with – I who expected to be put in the stocks and pelted with the eggs of the last twenty years' 'singing birds' as a disorderly woman and freethinking poet! People have been so kind that, in the first place, I really come to modify my opinions somewhat upon their conventionality, to see the progress made in freedom of thought.'

> (2 February 1857; Reynolds, 1996: 342)

What does all this mean? *Why* had she expected to be put in the stocks and pelted with eggs for writing this book? What had she intended *Aurora Leigh* to be and do? From the letters she wrote during the reviewing period, it is clear that she had expected the book to be damned for its impropriety – after all she had told the story of a raped woman who bears a child and she had told that story as not simply a *poem* but an *epic poem* which would have been regarded by some people as a scandalous misuse of a sacred and ancient form. But she had also written a book that stood out against conventionality of thought and judgement of all kinds and the measure of its success in this respect was the degree of disturbance the poem stirred. She hoped it would make waves. What were the features of the poem that were likely to make waves among her English literary audience? What were the contexts in which this ambitious, innovative and original poem was both written and read?

THE CONDITION OF WOMEN: PROSTITUTION

In 1888 Thomas Hardy wrote a dissenting and taboo-breaking story about sexual exploitation in serial form, *Tess of the D'Urbervilles*, which, like *Aurora Leigh*, offered an unsentimental 'case-study' of the life of a fallen woman who is provocatively represented as a wronged but still pure woman. Indeed, Hardy used the subtitle 'A Pure Woman' knowing that it would shock and offend certain sensibilities, provoke discussion and hopefully change minds. He explained in his 1892 Preface to the novel version of the story that he saw 'offence' as part of the work of the novel:

> So densely is the world populated that any shifting of positions, even the best warranted advance, galls somebody's kibe. Such shiftings often begin in sentiment, and such sentiment often begins in the novel.

> (Preface July 1892; Hardy, 1982: 39)

In his Preface to the earlier 1891 edition, Hardy wrote in words that echo the moral compulsion to testimony that is so much a part of the dissenting voice of *Aurora Leigh*:

> I would ask the genteel reader, who cannot endure to have said nowadays what everyone thinks and feels, to remember the well-worn sentence of St Jerome's: if an offence come out of the truth, better it is that the offence come than that the truth be concealed.

> (Preface 1891; Hardy, 1982: 35)

Like Hardy, Elizabeth Barrett Browning had intended to use dissent to cause offence so that she might provoke the kinds of conversations in drawing rooms that would be needed for attitudes to change concerning prostitution and sexual purity. Both worked. Hardy, for example, wrote with delight:

> The Duchess of Abercorn tells me that the novel has saved her all the future trouble in the assortment of her friends. They have been almost fighting over her dinner-table over Tess's character. What she now says to them is 'Do you support her or not?' If they say 'No indeed. She deserved hanging: a little harlot!' she puts them into one group. If they say 'Poor wronged innocent!' and pity her, she puts them in the other group where she is herself.

> (Hardy, 1994: 258)

Elizabeth Barrett Browning wrote similarly delightedly to Mrs Jameson in February 1857:

> What has given most offence in the book, more than the story of Marian—far more!—has been the reference to the condition of women in our cities. Which a woman oughtn't to refer to, by any manner of means, says the conventional tradition. Now I have thought deeply otherwise. If a woman ignores these wrongs, then may woman as a sex continue to suffer them; there is no help for any of us – let us be dumb and die.

> (Kenyon, 1897, II:254)

However, as Angela Leighton points out, Barrett Browning treats the subject of the fallen woman significantly differently from her immediate predecessors who had represented the fallen woman in fiction: Nathaniel Hawthorne in *The Scarlet Letter* (1851) and Mrs Gaskell in *Ruth* (1853). For unlike Gaskell and Hawthorne she was less interested in the restoration of purity (the poem powerfully argues, like Hardy does in *Tess*, that Marian has not lost her purity) than she was in 'the codes of verbal propriety enforced on women' (Leighton, 1986: 145). She argues that 'it is time women used their eyes, conscience and voice against the corrupt guardians of decency and delicacy' (Leighton, 1986: 145). Like Harriet Beecher Stowe, Barrett Browning was concerned to show how it is not just corrupt men who are responsible for maintaining the suffering inherent in the complex and unjust systems of slavery and prostitution and the systems of prejudice that kept women from education, work and financial autonomy. In *Aurora Leigh*, for instance, Aurora suffers at the hands of her aunt, who, having lived a repressive 'cage-bird life' (*AL* 1:305), believes that all other women should be raised the same way. When Barrett Browning tells the story of Marian's tragedy of sexual exploitation, the brutal, sexually abusive men are kept offstage but the exploitative women are given centre-stage parts: Marian's mother tries to sell her for sex, Lady Waldemar in her lust for Romney is responsible for Marian being raped in a brothel and after Marian is raped, it is her female employer who dismisses her, outraged that she is pregnant and unmarried. It is not that Barrett Browning blames women for these systems of injustice – far from it – but rather that she insists few people are not complicit in subtle ways in the maintenance and continuation of such systems.

However, Marian is a problem to many critics precisely because Barrett Browning chose to make her absolutely free of sexual desire and so fully a victim. Kaplan argues, for instance, that 'in order for the author to absolve her, she must be denied the self-generated sexuality which is permitted to upper-class women in *Aurora Leigh* . . . through the trauma of her rape Marian becomes a virtuous untouchable, at once transformed from a good child into a self-determining woman . . . but an unmarriageable one' (Kaplan, 1978: 25). Indeed, Marian is so desexualised after the rape, that when Romney comes to claim her as his wife, Barrett Browning describes her as a saint, provocatively drawing upon the iconography of Pre-Raphaelite painting and the idealisation of women typical of Coventry Patmore's *The Angel in the House* (1854):

> She stood there, still and pallid as a saint,
> Dilated, like a saint in ecstasy,
> As if the floating moonshine interposed
> Betwixt her foot and the earth

> (*AL* 9:187–91)

But it is also true to say that Marian has an important part to play as an agent of the plot and not just its victim. She comes to be increasingly outspoken in her condemnation of the systems of social justice she experiences and in her claim to selfhood and autonomy. She plays an important part in Aurora's development, not just as the saved one, but also as the saviour/ sister who shares a utopian and pastoralised home with Aurora back in Aurora's homeland – indeed, motherland – Italy. In some ways Marian comes to fulfil Aurora's 'mother-want' (*AL* 1:40), a want of mothering due to her mother's early death and substitution by a repressive, unfeeling aunt. Marian becomes the object of Aurora's hunger, 'Whom still I've hungered after more than bread' (6:454). Dorothy Mermin calls Aurora's quest for Marian 'The daughter's quest for the mother. Here women are both subject and object, men little more than distractions' (Mermin, 1989: 190). It is an extraordinary role to give a fallen woman within an epic poem: certainly, Marian is desexualised and even idealised but her idealisation casts her powerfully and transgressively against the iconography of the fallen woman: she is proud, outspoken, she is Mary, mother of the hungry Aurora, saint and redeemer.

DEHUMANISATION, THE CONDITION OF ENGLAND AND SOCIAL REFORM

A fragment of a surviving notebook written by Elizabeth Barrett as she planned the poem in the late 1840s indicates that Marian's story of sexual exploitation was meant to play only a small part in the larger vision of the poem, which concerns the various ways in which the 'Condition of England' has become dehumanised. Barrett began the poem as a series of binaries which framed the drama of the poem:

[Italy & [against] England]
1. Education against development
   System against instinct
   Love & philanthropy
2. The Ideal against the practical –
3. The Ideal works itself out

(Cited in Reynolds, 1996: 346)

This early formulation (even formula) is visible in the final poem: Aurora (Italy, development, instinct, love, the Ideal) and Romney (education, system, philanthropy, the practical) embody the majority of these oppositions and their conflict and eventual resolution is worked out through a love plot and through an unfolding series of conversations which are also in part a courtship (see Chapter Five on genre). But it is also clear from this early fragment that Barrett is not setting herself against socialism per se but against systems and abstracts, and therefore against the dogmatism of a certain kind of socialism, singled out in the poem as the theories of the philosopher and social reformer Charles Fourier, who proposed that the problems of society would be solved by the establishment of communes or phalanges.

But while Barrett Browning begins by describing rigid oppositions and conflict, the poem in its choreographed and staged debates of great elegance and passion enacts a rhetorical dance which involves negotiation and partnership, not warfare. By setting the binaries of the poem within a love plot Elizabeth Barrett Browning allows for a much greater intellectual subtlety in her exploration of different ideological positions. The poem may start out as a conflict between two people who are absolutely opposed to each other, with Aurora striking out for poetry and Romney for social theory, but as it progresses the conversations themselves in all their subtlety undermine that absolute opposition. As Stone observes: 'that the distinction between bread [Romney's socialism] and verse [Aurora's use of art as a way to move souls] is a false one is something *Aurora Leigh* in its entirety demonstrates' (Stone, 1995: 150). A poet can play a part in reform by opening people's eyes to the reality of injustices such as prostitution, Aurora argues to Romney:

> It takes a soul,
> To move a body: it takes a high-souled man,
> To move the masses, even to a cleaner stye:
> It takes the ideal, to blow a hair's-breadth off
> The dust of the actual.

(*AL* 2:479–83)

Stone argues that it is Marian who reconciles the positions of 'these two high-minded, idealistic cousins' by revealing that the 'projects of both are excessively abstract and intellectual . . . In part through Marian, Aurora and Romney eventually learn that neither the ideal nor the practical can suffice in itself' (Stone, 1995: 151) They come to learn that together body and soul are combined; that they are stronger agents for social reform unified in love than they are apart.

But there is a further dimension to the reconciliation of these opposites in the poem since Barrett Browning claimed that her poem was inspired by the work of Swedish philosopher and mystic Emmanuel Swedenborg whom Barrett Browning called 'that great Seer into the two worlds' (Kenyon, 1987 2:243). Swedenborg argued that the universe consists of two worlds, one of spirit and one of nature, and that all aspects of the material world correspond to their counterparts in the spiritual world (see Chapter Six on Love and Marriage). Furthermore, the material world is made up of signs and symbols that mark these correspondences between the Actual (the material world) and the Ideal (the spiritual world). Barrett Browning claimed in a letter to her sister Arabella that she had used Swedenborg's 'sublime truths' in her poem extensively; the conflict embodied in the Aurora (art/spirit) versus Romney (socialism/body) binary is revealed to be a false one as spirit and body come to 'correspond', working together towards reform in the name of love.

Many critics have drawn attention to the problem of Elizabeth Barrett Browning's critique of Christian socialism and her representation of the working classes. Both Cora Kaplan and Deirdre David, for instance, have identified the poem's politics as conservative for different reasons. Cora Kaplan praises the poem's brave and courageous feminism but argues that a glance at the poem's 'vicious picture of the rural and urban poor' reveals that there are 'painful contradictions in a liberal feminist position on art or politics' (Kaplan, 1978: 11). The poem fails to make 'any adequate attempt at analysing the intersecting oppressions of capitalism and patriarchy' and gives 'no answer to the misery of the poor except her own brand of Christian love – and poetry' (11). The point of observing these contradictions, she claims, is that:

> works of art should not be attacked because they do not conform to notions of political correctness, but they must be understood in relation to the seductive ideologies and political possibilities both of the times in which they were written and the times in which they are to be read.

(Kaplan, 1978: 12)

The passage Kaplan refers to here in particular is the description of Romney's marriage in which Barrett Browning describes the working-class guests in the language of the grotesque:

> They clogged the streets, they oozed into the church
> In a dark slow stream, like blood [. . .]
> While all the aisles, alive and black with heads,
> Crawled slowly toward the altar from the street,
> As bruised snakes crawl and hiss out of a hole
> With shuddering involution, swaying slow
> From right to left, and then from left to right,
> In pants and pauses. What an ugly crest
> Of faces rose upon you everywhere
> From the crammed mass! you did not usually
> See faces like them in the open day:
> They hide in cellars, not to make you mad
> As Romney Leigh is.

(*AL* 4:553–74)

Kaplan, as I have said, describes this scene as 'vicious'. It is a picture replicated elsewhere in the poem when Barrett Browning describes Marian's mother's attempt to sell her daughter and in the women Aurora sees when she visits Marian. What is offensive to Kaplan and to other readers is not just that the poor are shown to be dehumanised by their working conditions and daily lives but are also shown to be physically revolting and corrupt: they are likened to the ooze of blood, like animals they crawl, hiss, sway and pant up out of a hole 'with shuddering involution'. The use of the word 'crest' is interesting because it clearly alludes to the crest of a 'snake' but also to the 'crest' of a rising wave, one of the dominant metaphors used to describe dangerous crowds in nineteenth-century novels (see Stott, 1999). They are also undifferentiated from each other and from the revulsions of the city itself, rising as they do apparently from a hole, and disappearing back into it.

It is, however, important to remember that Barrett Browning also damns the aristocratic guests at this wedding by reporting their 'vicious' and superficial conversations and gossip in the church and that Barrett Browning's use of the grotesque is most intensely deployed in the poem as a whole in her description of Lady Waldemar. Lady Waldemar may be physically beautiful but she is shown to be spiritually and morally grotesque. Aurora recoils in moral horror in all her encounters with Waldemar's predatory sexuality, her dishonesty and manipulation and her condescension. She is described as being, like the urban poor, 'out of nature' (*AL* 3:358) and importantly even describes herself as one of a kind – typical of other lustful aristocratic women:

> We fine ladies, who park out our lives
> From common sheep-paths, cannot help the crows
> From flying over, – we're as natural still
> As Blowsalinda. Drape us perfectly
> In Lyon's velvet, – we are not, for that,
> Lay-figures, look you: we have hearts within,
> Warm, live, improvident, indecent hearts,
> As ready for outrageous ends and acts
> As any distressed seamstress of them all
> That Romney groans and toils for.

> (*AL* 3:456–65)

Like the urban poor and even Aurora's aunt who 'lives a cage-bird life' and represses Aurora because she knows of no other way of living, Lady Waldemar has become dehumanised by a society that is 'out of nature'. In all such descriptions the judgement of women's malice, sexual greed and cruelty is no less absolute but it is almost always framed by an often tender understanding of why and how they have come to be this way: 'the evil is in the system' as Barrett claimed about her father's tyrannous behaviour (*BC* 11:43).

CARLYLE'S OOZE

However, there are other ways of contextualising the passage described by Kaplan as 'vicious'. It was written sometime early in 1856, in the middle of the decade most concerned with political, social and *sanitary* reform. It was a point in history where the discourses of sanitary and social reform became inextricably interlinked. The nightmare vision of the urban poor expressed in these passages should be seen in the context of the aftermath of the European revolutions of 1848 and the fear of the British middle class that revolution would spread to the British Isles – like a kind of contagion. Contagion discourse was further heightened by the cholera epidemics of the late 1840s and the famines in Ireland which forced many starving Irish labourers and their families to migrate to the already overcrowded industrial cities of Britain.

The Condition of England was parlous, Carlyle, Kingsley and Gaskell argued in their writings of the 1840s. Industrialisation had dehumanised the urban poor who were now living against nature in slum conditions like slaves to the machines which were making factory owners and financial speculators rich. The discourse of reform was motivated by genuine compassion but also by horror and fear that if something were not done soon, the urban poor would rise up in revolution as they did across Europe in 1848. Carlyle's prose had become increasingly apocalyptic by the beginning of the 1850s, and the vision of the state of England which he penned in 1850 in the *Latter-Day Pamphlets* clearly influenced the images of the poor in *Aurora Leigh*. The Condition of England was comparable only to a shipwrecked people clinging to a rotten corpse of a pig in high sewage-laden seas. The rhetoric he uses is full of images of apocalyptic and scatological horror; contagion, waste and moral putrefaction become the dominant keywords of his vision of England choked and rotting in its own excrement, particularly when he describes the 'ooze' of prostitution:

Thirty thousand wretched women, sunk in that putrefying well of abominations; they have oozed in upon London, from the universal Stygian quagmire of British industrial life; are accumulated in the *well* of the concern, to that extent. British charity is smitten to the heart, at the laying bare of such a scene; passionately undertakes, by enormous subscription of money, or by other enormous effort, to redress that individual horror; as I and all men hope it may. But, alas, what next? This general well and cesspool once baled clean out to-day, will begin before night to fill itself anew. The universal Stygian quagmire is still there; opulent in women ready to be ruined, and in men ready. Towards the same sad cesspool will these waste currents of human ruin ooze and gravitate as heretofore; except in draining the universal quagmire itself there is no remedy. 'And for that, what is the method?' cry many in an angry manner. To whom, for the present, I answer only, 'Not emancipation, it would seem, my friends; not the cutting loose of human ties, something far the reverse of that!'

(Carlyle, 1850: 33)

Instead, Carlyle claims, the answer is strong moral and heroic leadership and a nation united in its commitment to working for reform: 'To work, then, one and all; hands to work!', the first essay concludes. Carlyle's grotesque and simultaneously visionary language influenced many descriptions of the urban poor in the fiction and rhetoric of the 1850s: the language of the Condition of England is so often the metaphor of the rotten tide, of people who have been polluted like the water of the Thames by urbanisation and industrialisation.

Both Carlyle and Barrett Browning use this grotesque imagery to embody the moral pollution they see as choking the heart of the nation. The dominant words used to describe the urban poor in this scene from *Aurora Leigh* are drawn from the world of the grotesque: they petrify, they are dissolute, they are physically repulsive, the creatures of nightmare:

> Those, faces? 'twas as if you had stirred up hell
> To heave its lowest dreg-fiends uppermost
> In fiery swirls of slime, – such strangled fronts,
> Such obdurate jaws were thrown up constantly
> To twit you with your race, corrupt your blood,
> And grind to devilish colours all your dreams
> Henceforth, – though, haply, you should drop asleep
> By clink of silver waters [. . .]

(*AL* 4:587–94)

Carlyle's influence on the imagery, ideas and philosophy of *Aurora Leigh* is widespread. When Barrett Browning describes, for instance, the rioting of the crowd (they suspect a class conspiracy after the marriage is cancelled in Marian's absence), she again uses Carlylean metaphors, this time drawn from Carlyle's seminal *History of the French Revolution* (1837). One of the most influential books of the mid-Victorian period, it came to dominate the ways in which people responded to and imagined revolution as a great natural force comparable to earthquakes, volcanoes and tidal waves. Carlyle's revolutionary crowds are thunderous, swelling and apocalyptic seas in the city: during the storming of the Bastille, 'the streets are a living foam-sea, chafed by all the winds' (1:186); at the storming of the Tuileries, Lafayette is described as a 'Sea-ruler' barely able to control the force of the tempest and,

Carlyle asks, what 'if . . . the *sub*marine Titanic Fire-powers came into play, the Ocean-bed from beneath being *burst*?' (1:441). By 1850, in an essay entitled 'The Present Time' in *Latter-Day Pamphlets*, he was still using oceanic metaphors even more powerfully to describe the state of European society in the wake of the revolutions of 1848:

> In such baleful oscillation, afloat as amid raging bottomless eddies and conflicting sea-currents, not steadfast as on fixed foundations, must European Society continue swaying, now disastrously tumbling, then painfully readjusting itself, at ever shorter intervals,—till once the new rock-basis does come to light, and the weltering deluges of mutiny, and of need to mutiny, abate again!

> (Carlyle, 1850: 10)

In *Aurora Leigh* the rioting crowds are described as a storm-sea and earthquake:

> From end to end, the church
> Rocked round us like a sea in storm, and then
> Broke up like the earth in earthquake.

> (*AL* 4:857–9)

Apocalypse and deluge imagery of a Carlylean kind are to be found everywhere in *Aurora Leigh*, part of its epic sweep and its concern with the Condition of England. Yet, it is also a pessimistic vision particularly associated with Romney who describes the present day in phrases drawn straight from Carlyle:

> The world, we're come to late, is swollen hard
> With perished generations and their sins:
> The civiliser's spade grinds horribly
> On dead men's bones, and cannot turn up soil
> That's otherwise than fetid.

> (*AL* 2:262–6)

But Barrett Browning was no uncritical borrower of pervasive Carlylean tropes; nor was her vision of the future an apocalyptic one. Her oozing crowd is not the ooze of putrefaction but the ooze of *blood*. She recasts Carlyle's ooze as social *wound*. The image is no less grotesque but it points in a different metaphorical direction for the blood is sacrificial and Christlike and indicates a wounded but still living body whereas the putrefaction of

Carlyle's world is beyond saving – the corpse is already rotting. However, Barrett Browning (and Aurora her mouthpiece – the dawning Aurora of a new age) is more optimistic than Carlyle. Her London is grotesque, dangerous, but also sublime at the same time. It is the place of the social wound, it is full of violence and conflict but it is also full of inspiration and hope for the poet who would use her poetry to redeem the world.

Barrett Browning's representations of the great cities of Paris, London and Florence in *Aurora Leigh* are quite rightly anthologised for they form set-pieces, word paintings of extraordinary poetic vision. Here is Aurora's description of London, for instance, as seen from her garret window which reveals not only Barrett Browning's use of Carlyle but also her familiarity with the deluge and apocalyptic painting of John Martin and John Danby:

Serene and unafraid of solitude
I worked the short days out, – and watched the sun
On lurid morns or monstrous afternoons
(Like some Druidic idol's fiery brass
With fixed unflickering outline of dead heat,
From which the blood of wretches pent inside
Seems oozing forth to incarnadine the air)
Push out through fog with his dilated disk,
And startle the slant roofs and chimney-pots
With splashes of fierce colour. Or I saw
Fog only, the great tawny weltering fog,
Involve the passive city, strangle it
Alive, and draw it off into the void,
Spires, bridges, streets, and squares, as if a spunge
Had wiped out London, – or as noon and night
Had clapped together and utterly struck out
The intermediate time, undoing themselves
In the act. Your city poets see such things
Not despicable [. . .]

[. . .] sit in London at the day's decline,
And view the city perish in the mist
Like Pharaoh's armaments in the deep Red Sea,
The chariots, horsemen, footmen, all the host,
Sucked down and choked to silence – then, surprised
By a sudden sense of vision and of tune,
You feel as conquerors though you did not fight,
And you and Israel's other singing girls,
Ay, Miriam with them, sing the song you choose.

(*AL* 3:169–203)

Again it is blood that oozes here from the wretches pent inside the 'Druidic idol' of the sun but the range of epic and apocalyptic images in this short passage is extraordinary. Elsewhere in the poem the imagery is violent and drawn both from the 'flows' and eruptions of the human body and the flows of geological landscape in a Swedenborgian series of 'correspondences'. Blood oozes like a sea, milk flows like lava: the 'Ideal' mirrors and corresponds with the 'Actual' in a series of symbols and signs. But Barrett Browning counters the 'red sea' of Carlyle (the apocalyptic sea of fire) with the 'Red Sea' of the epic story of Moses, in which the liberated slaves are allowed through divine intervention to cross to a new free land. Miriam is given especial significance in Barrett Browning's recasting of the flight from Egypt narrative, supplant-ing her brother Moses, for she is the truth-teller, the narrator/observer, and she is also both sister and mother, the redeemer who placed Moses in the bull-rushes, thereby saving him from death and thrusting him into a new role as the saviour and Carlylean hero of a lost, dehumanised and enslaved people. There is hope, miracle and divine intervention for those who are lost, Barrett Browning claims with her epic biblical allusions. All is not lost so long as there are heroes and truth-tellers such as Moses and Miriam to lead their people out of spiritual and physical slavery.

Redemption from the fallen Condition of England is the subject of this poem and redemption is so often figured in the metaphors of rescue from shipwreck or drowning and in divine intervention imagined as breast milk which comes like manna from a feminised heaven to those who are hungry or spiritually starved. A number of critics including Dorothy Mermin (Mermin, 1989) have pointed out the poem's constant eroticised references to suckling and breasts, but if seen within a Swedenborgian context, the milk flow between mother and child has a clearly transcendental significance, emblematising union and spiritual sustenance. For instance, in Book 1, Aurora claims that her soul survived intact through the tortures of a feminine education because:

I had relations in the Unseen, and drew
The elemental nutriment and heat
From nature, as earth feels the sun at nights
Or as a babe sucks surely in the dark.

(*AL* 1:472–6)

The ooze of the poem, the powerful red flow of the social wound, which so dominates the conversations of the characters in the poem (how do we treat such a wound?) is countered by the white and redemptive imagery of milk, which is itself compared to the spiritual power of poetry and of nature.

Carlyle's 'Present Day' must be redeemed and healed – but how to heal is part of the problem the poem presents and never entirely answers.

METAPHORS OF VIOLENCE

Deirdre David argues that 'knifing and bleeding are prominent symbols in the severe condemnation of female sentimentality which Romney . . . issues to Aurora' (David, 1987: 122). The world of women, so often sentimentalised and idealised by male nineteenth-century poets and writers such as John Ruskin and Coventry Patmore, is shown by this poet to be at least latently violent. When Barrett Browning uses epic to describe the dramas that take place 'betwixt the mirrors of [our] drawing-rooms' (*AL* 5:206), she reveals the passions and angers and physical and psychological violence which take place behind closed doors at the heart of the family, by adults to children, by men to women, and between women in particular. Because Aurora's aunt blamed Aurora's Italian mother for taking her brother (Aurora's father) away to Italy where he subsequently died, Aurora's aunt receives Aurora into her household with a sense of duty but also with a degree of hatred. The child senses the violence in her aunt's eyes immediately:

> [. . .] she wrung loose my hands
> Imperiously, and held me at arm's length,
> And with two grey-steel naked-bladed eyes
> Searched through my face,—ay, stabbed it through and through,
> Through brows and cheeks and chin, as if to find
> A wicked murderer in my innocent face

> (*AL* 1:325–30)

Aurora's education in this house, a woman's education, is like water torture 'flood succeeding flood/ To drench the incapable throat and split the veins' (Book 1, 468–9). Living in her aunt's house is like being 'smeared with honey, teased/ By insects, stared to torture by the noon' (2:890–1). Aurora makes no apology for the epic scale of her analogy for she follows it up by broadening the analogy to other women raised and educated as she has been: 'many patient souls 'neath English roofs/ Have died like Romans' (2:892–4). She describes 'woman's spite':

> A woman takes a housewife [packet of needles] from her breast
> And plucks the delicatest needle out
> As 'twere a rose, and pricks you carefully

> 'Neath nails, 'neath eyelids, in your nostrils, – say,
> A beast would roar so tortured, – but a man,
> A human creature, must not, shall not flinch,
> No, not for shame.

(AL 5:1045–51)

Stabbing and bleeding permeate every aspect of the poem. Violence is not just an experience that Aurora *suffers*, it also characterises her determined denial of those aspects of her femininity that keep her enslaved. When Romney compliments her on her hair, for instance, by saying: 'Your Florence fireflies live on in your hair . . . it gleams so', Aurora tells us:

> Well, I wrung them out,
> My fire-flies; made a knot as hard as life
> Of those loose, soft, impracticable curls

(AL 5:1132–4)

Similarly, Aurora's frustration with the bloodlessness of her early poetry is likened to infanticide:

> I ripped my verses up,
> And found no blood upon the rapier's point;
> The heart in them was just an embryo's heart
> Which never yet had beat, that it should die;

(AL 3:245–7)

And even her glimpse of Marian's face through the crowd in Paris, accompanied as it is by fear and desperation, is likened to the surfacing of a dead body in an idealised pastoral scene:

> It was as if a meditative man
> Were dreaming out a summer afternoon
> And watching gnats a-prick upon a pond,
> When something floats up suddenly, out there,
> Turns over a dead face, known once alive . .
> So old, so new!

(AL 6:235–40)

Aurora Leigh is full of violent eruptions and flows, bodies surfacing through water, lava erupting from mountain ranges, eyes that stab and gestures that wound, but while the poem shows us the violence of human interrelations, particularly within the family, it is also concerned with the redemption and healing achieved through human sympathy and tenderness.

RAINING THE SKY BLUE

The violence of the poem, the social wound of dehumanised people, is countered again and again by tenderness, compassion and touch. Even Romney, caught up in his social theories, is capable of great tenderness. At a crucial moment in Aurora's childhood, for instance, he reaches for her and his touch cancels her loneliness for a moment:

> Once, he stood so near
> He dropped a sudden hand upon my head
> Bent down on woman's work, as soft as rain –

> (*AL* 1:543–5)

Marian describes to Aurora Romney's tenderness, when he had sat by her hospital bedside where Marian lay recovering from her flight from her cruel and exploitative mother:

> She told me how he raised and rescued her
> With reverent pity, as, in touching grief,
> He touched the wounds of Christ . . .

> (*AL* 3:1224–6)

Aurora becomes a sister to Marian and through love redeems her suffering:

> Yet indeed,
> To see a wrong or suffering moves us all
> To undo it though we should undo ourselves [. . .]
>   So it clears,
> And so we rain our skies blue.

> (*AL* 7:214–16; 228–9)

Poetry, particularly, can work like spring rain, as Romney confesses finally in Book 8, when Aurora's touch extends to return Romney's touch, not physically but through her published book. He testifies to the power of her words:

> You have written poems, sweet,
> Which moved me in secret, as the sap is moved
> In still March-branches, signless as a stone:
> But this last book o'ercame me like soft rain
> Which falls at midnight, when the tightened bark
> Breaks out into hesitating buds
> And sudden protestations of the spring . . .
>
> You have shown me truths,
> O June-day friend, that help me now at night
> When June is over! truths not yours, indeed,
> But set within my reach by means of you,
> Presented by your voice and verse the way
> To make them clearest.

                                              (*AL* 8:592–8; 608–13)

In the violence of its imagery, in its use of blood and milk, red and white symbolism, in its portrayal of the violence done between women as well as to women by men, in its dissenting sensibilities and its passionate claim for women's experience to be heard and finally in its symbolic blinding of the hero, the poem is not unlike Charlotte Brontë's *Jane Eyre* (published in 1847). Jane also describes dreams of dead babies and her aunt is similarly violent and abusive in locking the young Jane in the Red Room as a young child. When a friend pointed out the similarities, Barrett Browning sent for a copy of *Jane Eyre* to check what she remembered and acknowledged the similarities between Romney's blinding and Rochester's, but, despite her protestations of the overall differences between the books, there are many other similarities.

The poem borrows elements of many mid-Victorian novels and long poems in its discussion of issues and problems of the day: the Condition of England, the role of women and the role of the poet. It is a kind of bricolage in this respect (see Reynolds, 1992) but it is also, as I have said elsewhere, a method by which Barrett Browning puts her voice into dialogue with other poets, artists and intellectuals of her day. The poem itself enacts a conversation; it is inherently dialogic in form. It is on one level an autobiography and a *Kunstlerroman* but it is also three *bildungsroman* narratives interwoven – those of Marian, Romney and Aurora. This is the source of its openness and its resistance to didacticism for these three voices converse and disagree throughout. In the end the three voices reach a consensus and agreement about the union of the body and soul and the need for individuals to work in different ways to cure the social wound and move to a more just society. Deirdre David argues:

Barrett Browning's enduring insistence on the cultural function of the poet-intellectual *in* the world originates in this imperative to work: the poet clears a symbolical path, unlocks a symbolic door, dissolves the encrustations of debasing materialism which cover man's soul. Carlyle's Gospel of Work is the good news elaborated by Aurora and Romney at the end of the poem.

(David, 1989: 156)

The final words of the poem, though, with their invocation of a New Jerusalem, provide a powerful counter-future to Carlyle's thunderous pessimism about the Present Age, offering a vision of a new world far beyond Carlyle's apocalypse, a world in which Swedenborgian principles reign with principles of love and renewal and 'correspondence' between the material and the spiritual worlds:

> The world's old,
> But the old world waits the time to be renewed,
> Toward which, new hearts in individual growth
> Must quicken, and increase to multitude
> In new dynasties of the race of men;
> Developed whence, shall grow spontaneously
> New churches, new economies, new laws
> Admitting freedom, new societies
> Excluding falsehood: HE shall make all new.

(*AL* 9:941–8)

POLEMICAL FORM:
THE RECEPTION OF THE POEM

Aurora Leigh is a poem about wide-ranging modern issues and preoccupations written by a woman not in lyric but in epic mode. As such its form as well as its content performs a transgressive act of *renewal* for generally speaking, although with some notable exceptions, epic poetry was not written by women, nor was it used to deal with commonplace or polemical issues – this was often regarded to be the work of the novel.

Although it is difficult to generalise about the sorts of expectations literary reviewers had of women poets in the mid-Victorian period, there are published statements that show that there were, in most quarters, differences of expectation placed upon poetry written by men and poetry written by women. One of these pieces of evidence is a book by Mary Ann Stodart, who

was an educational writer publishing books for women and girls in the 1830s
and 1840s, called *Female Writers: Thoughts on Their Proper Sphere and on
Their Powers of Usefulness* (1842). The advice she gives to her readers is to
write the kind of poetry that she believes women write best: that is poetry
which is 'beautiful in form, delicate in sentiment, graceful in action' (Stodart
in Reynolds, 1996: 388). For Stodart, the difference is expressed primarily in
terms of scale: men write epic, dramatic, heroic poetry well whereas women
excel at the delicate, the subtle and the small-scale:

> We [women] cannot range through heaven and hell with the fiery wind of our
> glorious poet Milton; we cannot ascend to the height of great argument, and
> justify the ways of God to man . . . It is not within our province to dive into the
> deep recesses of the human heart with that myriad-minded man, our own
> Shakespeare, and to drag into the open day-light the hidden secrets of the soul.

(Stodart in Reynolds, 1996: 389)

There is much to suggest that Stodart's distinction between male poets and
female poets was a widely held view until considerably later in the century. It
is a view suffered and resisted by Aurora Leigh herself from as early as Book 2
in which the twenty-year-old Aurora and her cousin Romney argue about
the limitations of female creativity. Romney's words about women's creative
and intellectual limitations are dreadful and damning:

> You play beside a death-bed like a child,
> Yet measure to yourself a prophet's place
> To teach the living. None of all these things,
> Can women understand. You generalise
> Oh, nothing, – not even grief! Your quick-breathed hearts,
> So sympathetic to the personal pang,
> Close on each separate knife-stroke, yielding up
> A whole life at each wound, incapable
> Of deepening, widening a large lap of life
> To hold the world-full woe. The human race
> To you means, such a child, or such a man,
> You saw one morning waiting in the cold,
> Beside that gate, perhaps. You gather up
> A few such cases, and when strong sometimes
> Will write of factories and of slaves, as if
> Your father were a negro, and your son
> A spinner in the mills. All's yours and you,
> All, coloured with your blood, or otherwise
> Just nothing to you [. . .]
>   [. . .] Therefore, this same world

Uncomprehended by you, must remain
Uninfluenced by you.

(*AL* 2:180–220)

The whole of the poem is written against this view in a way – the claim that women can't do epic, can't do large-scale, can't dive deep into the recesses of the human heart. Romney believes that women are limited as writers for the same reasons as Stodart: they are too passionate, too governed by the heart, the limitations of their experience of the world make them take one example and fabricate a generalised picture from it. Yet while Stodart argues that women should simply write with these limitations in mind, Romney believes they should not write poetry *at all*. More significantly, he believes poetry itself is impotent to make adequate changes in a fallen world. Romney's argument about women poets, based as it is on a conviction of women's lack of knowledge of the world, cannot be countered by Aurora at this stage in her sheltered life. It silences her. Yet she retorts eventually with a statement of determination:

> perhaps a woman's soul
> Aspires, and not creates: yet we aspire,
> And yet I'll try out your perhapses, sir,
> And if I fail . . why, burn me up my straw
> Like other false works – I'll not ask for grace.

(*AL* 2:487–90)

Throughout the poem, Aurora resists arguing with Romney on the grounds of his insult in Book 2; she does not say: women *can* write poetry, *can* write epic, *are* able to see the bigger picture. To do so would be to accept the premises on which Romney built his argument and to generalise: that women's souls and vision *are* essentially different from men. Throughout the poem, she asks simply to be judged as a *poet* and by the poetry she writes, not as a *woman* poet. And as a poet, she believes that epic is the form for her day:

> The critics say the epics have died out
> With Agamemnon and the goat-nursed gods;
> I'll not believe it. I could never deem [. . .]
> That Homer's heroes measured twelve feet high.
> They were but men: — his Helen's hair turned grey
> Like any plain Miss Smith's who wears a front;
> And Hector's infant whimpered at a plume
> As yours last Friday at a turkey-cock.

All actual heroes are essential men,
And all men possible heroes: every age,
Heroic in proportions, double-faced,
Looks backward and before, expects a morn
And claims an epos.

(*AL* 5:139–54)

The passage is a fascinating one, rich in allusion and imagery. Aurora begins by saying that epics have not died out with the Greeks as some of her contemporaries believe, nor does she believe that the age of the Greeks was any different essentially from her own: Homer's heroes were just men and Homer's women aged and Homer's children were frightened of the same things as Victorian children. All men and women are 'possible heroes' she claims, extending Carlyle's lament about the lack of heroes in the present age. But as is evident in this passage, in making all men and women 'possible heroes', in dramatising the heroism of everyday life and revealing the ideal at the heart of the real, she domesticates epic in writing of the heroic trials and tribulations of a woman poet making her way in the world and the tragedy and rebirth in motherhood of a 'fallen woman'.

The project of making an epic from the day-to-day life of a woman poet and from a story of prostitution and rape made waves and laid Barrett Browning open to charges not just of being a bad poet but also of betraying her own purity as a woman: H.F. Chorley, for instance, writing for *The Athenaeum*, criticised her mingling of 'what is precious with what is mean . . . Milton's organ is put by Mrs Browning to play polkas in May-Fair drawing-rooms . . . "Aurora Leigh" contains too many pages . . . perversely trivial'. But elsewhere in the same review he praised her for the epic scale and loftiness of tone of the poem, even though he used clearly feminised analogies to celebrate 'the high thoughts, the deep feelings, the fantastic images showered over the tale with the authority of a prophetess, the grace of a muse, the prodigality of a queen' (Chorley in Reynolds, 1996: 407). For other critics the mixing of high form (epic) with low subject matter (prostitution) was a problem, resulting in a kind of soiling. William Aytoun, a Scottish poet and critic, for instance, denounced the poem in *Blackwood's Edinburgh Magazine* because:

It is not the province of the poet to depict things as they are, but so to refine and purify as to purge out the grosser matter; and this he cannot do if he attempts to give a faithful picture of his own times, for in order to be faithful, he must necessarily include much with is abhorrent to art, and revolting to the taste, for which no exactness of delineation will be accepted as a proper excuse.

All poetical characters, all poetical situations, must be idealised. The language is not that of common life, which belongs essentially to the domain of prose. Therein lies the distinction between a novel and a poem.

(Aytoun in Reynolds, 1996: 416)

But the offence of using a high form for low subject matter is intensified for Aytoun by the fact that it has been committed by a woman poet; that 'a lady capable of producing so exquisite a picture, should condescend to fashion into verse what is essentially mean, gross and puerile' (Aytoun in Reynolds, 1996: 419). The implication of Aytoun's words is that the offence given by the poem is a double one: that it contains indecent material and that it is written by a woman who should know better and who has soiled her hands in writing so outspokenly, as if speaking 'out of turn' was not just vulgar but sexually improper. Barrett Browning had, of course, anticipated such a reception when she wrote in 1857 to Anna Jameson: 'I who expected to be put in the stocks and pelted with the eggs of the last years' "singing birds" as a disorderly woman and a freethinking poet' (Reynolds, 1996: 342). It was a charge that put her in the stocks in the company of her disorderly sisters, Marian and Aurora.

NON-CONFORMISM: SPEAKING THE TRUTH

Elizabeth Barrett's intentions in writing the poem were clearly subversive. In the much-quoted letter of 1845 written to Robert Browning, she described her ambition as:

the writing of a sort of novel-poem – a poem as completely modern as 'Geraldine's Courtship', running into the midst of our conventions, & rushing into drawing-rooms & the like, 'where angels fear to tread' & so, meeting face to face & without mask, the Humanity of the age & speaking the truth as I conceive of it out plainly.

(*BC* 10:102–3)

This statement of intention is a commitment to speaking the truth out plainly in order to challenge conformity where that conformity is regarded to be wrong or untrue. Marjorie Stone has astutely located *Aurora Leigh* in the tradition of Victorian sage discourse, identifying its characteristics as the following:

its representation of a prophetic speaker, its pronounced Biblical allusions and typological patterning, its polemical sermonizing on the times, its argumentative intertextuality, its exploitation of metaphor and definition as strategies of persuasion, its quest for a sustaining 'Life Philosophy', and its vision of a new social and spiritual order.

(Stone, 1995: 138)

However, the poem can be even more precisely located within Victorian *non-conformist* sage discourse, one shared by the intellectuals Harriet Martineau and Thomas Carlyle. Non-conformism was an umbrella term used to describe dissenting Protestants in the nineteenth century who worshipped outside the Anglican church. Non-conformists or dissenters included Congregationalists, Presbyterians, Quakers, Methodists, Unitarians and Baptists and their combined number in the religious census of 1851 was almost equal to that of the Anglican church. While each non-conformist religious group worshipped in different ways and put different emphases on religious doctrine, they did have much in common including an allegiance to liberal values, to the centrality of the individual conscience over the intercession or mediation of religious authorities such as priests, and a dedicated commitment to work and to social and political reform. In his book *The Rationale of Religious Enquiry* (1836), James Martineau, Harriet's brother, one of the leaders of the Unitarian movement and, from 1841, a professor of moral philosophy at Manchester New College, argued that 'reason is the ultimate appeal, the supreme tribunal, to the test of which even Scripture must be brought' (Hall, 1950: 61–2). Reason above dogma above all.

Barrett was raised in a Congregationalist household but her religious and spiritual ideas were drawn from many different sources including, as I have shown, the mysticism of Swedenborg. She described herself primarily as a freethinker and was drawn to the sage writing of non-conformists such as Harriet Martineau and Thomas Carlyle. Harriet Martineau was a freethinker of a Unitarian background and much of what she wrote about social and political matters was overlaid with non-conformist values, particularly a commitment to the individual conscience and to the right of the individual to develop his or her own religious belief and political opinion. Many non-conformists were united in their conviction that social evils were humanly created, not God inflicted, and could and should be remedied by human efforts but they often disagreed about *how* such remedies might be put in place. In the late-eighteenth and early nineteenth century, non-conformist groups were closely identified with the campaign for social and political reform. *Aurora Leigh* espouses non-conformist values such as the primacy of the individual conscience, commitment to social and political reform (though embodying dissent about how such reform is to be put in place) and to the importance of work.

Aurora Leigh can be viewed then as a dissenting poem in its emphasis on social and political reform, in its impassioned claim for a public role for poets (male and female) as moral truth-seekers, in its commitment to the testimony of the individual conscience over moral orthodoxy and in its impassioned challenge to orthodoxes of all kinds. It is also the work of a dissenting *feminist* poet. Because of the emphasis on the individual conscience, women (at least potentially) had much greater power within dissenting groups than elsewhere and a stronger social and public role if they chose to take it. Primitive Methodism even sanctioned women preachers (George Eliot used a Methodist woman preacher in *Adam Bede*). Like Margaret Fuller and Harriet Martineau, Barrett Browning stressed the importance of testifying as a woman in spaces 'where angels fear to tread'. Women must have a voice here and elsewhere. Harriet Martineau used similar phrases repeatedly in her writings and she, like Thomas Carlyle and Barrett Browning, had a wide and loyal readership. In the concluding pages of Martineau's *Eastern Life: Present and Past*, for instance, which was published in 1848 and contains within its title a reference to Carlyle's recently published work of sage discourse, *Past and Present*, she claims that the traveller 'must speak, and with fidelity' about the values that he or she sees in the new culture for:

> When all thinkers say freely what is to them true, we shall know more of abstract and absolute truth than we have ever known yet. – It is no concern of the thoughtful traveller's whether what he says is familiar or strange, agreeable or unacceptable to the prejudiced or to the wise. His only concern is to keep his fidelity to truth and man, to say simply and, if he can, fearlessly, what he has learned and concluded. If he be mistaken, his errors will be all the less pernicious for being laid open to correction. If he be right, there will be so much accession, be it little or much, to the wisdom of mankind.

> (Martineau, 1848: 334)

The original source of Barrett Browning's phrase 'where angels fear to tread' is from Alexander Pope's 'Essay on Criticism': 'For fools rush in where angels fear to tread' (Book 1, line 625). Barrett Browning's reuse of the phrase casts the fool within Shakespearean tradition as both outsider and truth-teller. This definition of the poet recalls a scene in the novel where Aurora, now an established poet living in London, attends a soirée at Lord Howe's and overhears a heated conversation between two men about free love. When Lord Howe rebukes them for speaking so unguardedly in her presence she retorts:

[. . .] 'my dear Lord Howe, you shall not speak
To a printing woman who has lost her place,
(The sweet safe corner of the household fire
Behind the heads of children) compliments,
As if she were a woman. We who have clipt
The curls before our eyes, may see at least
As plain as men do. Speak out, man to man;
No compliments, beseech you.'

(AL 5:805–12)

This is a complex passage, no less so for being full of irony and innuendo, and offers a masterly critique of the price to be paid by a woman in refusing to conform to gender norms. In this passage, Aurora claims a different place in the drawing room, one quite distinct from the 'sweet safe corner' usually held by women after dinner, segregated from men. This claim to a new space is premised on a *loss of the feminine* ('the sweet safe corner' and the feminine curls – 'we have clipt the curls from before our eyes') but also on *gain of sight* – now the curls have been 'clipt', she can see plainly like a man. And it is on these grounds of her 'clipt' femininity, made possible by her being a 'printing woman' or poet, that she asks to be spoken to as an equal and refuses compliments.

The energy of the poem, then, the passion of Aurora's voice, which, more than a fast-paced plot, drives the poem forward, is clearly shaped by Elizabeth Barrett Browning's conviction of not just 'the right to write' but of a moral duty to 'testify' and to dissent. As she wrote in an unsent letter to Napoleon III about Victor Hugo, 'It is a woman's voice, sire, which dares to utter what many yearn for in silence.' If poets are the only 'truth-tellers left to God', then all the more reason why she and Aurora and eventually Marian should speak, should 'rush into drawing-rooms and the like where angels fear to tread'. Their testimony, compelled as it is by moral directives, is outspoken and direct, 'without mask'. In Book 6, Marian also claims the right to direct speech as a prostitute, rejecting the hints and 'delicate reserves' expected of women:

Enough so! — it is plain enough so. True,
We wretches cannot tell out all our wrong
Without offence to decent happy folk.
I know that we must scrupulously hint
With half-words, delicate reserves, the thing
Which no one scrupled we should feel in full.

(AL 6:1219–24)

Interestingly Marian uses the phrase 'tell *out*' as Elizabeth Barrett Browning had used the phrase 'speaking the truth as I conceive of it *out* plainly' (emphasis mine) in relation to the testimony of her poem. It isn't just speaking that matters or telling that matters but speaking and telling *out*. Outspokenness then is presented as not just inevitable but central if the emotions caused by the (offensive) writing are going to be potentially transformative.

As Cora Kaplan points out, these were exciting times for women for the taboo 'against women's entry into public discourse as speakers or writers was in grave danger of being definitively broken in the mid-nineteenth century as more and more educated, literate women entered the area as imaginative writers, social critics and reformers' (Kaplan, 1978: 9). We need only think of the number of controversial books published in the late 1840s and early 1850s in Britain and America that were driving conversations about slavery, women and social issues further than they had perhaps yet been pushed: Margaret Fuller's polemical and visionary *Woman in the Nineteenth Century* published in Britain and America in 1845 had been released in Britain in 'Slater's shilling library for parlor table and railway carriage' in 1850, Harriet Beecher Stowe's *Uncle Tom's Cabin* was published in 1852, Elizabeth Gaskell's *Ruth* in 1853 and Anna Jameson's book about the condition of women, *The Communion of Labour*, in 1856. Harriet Beecher Stowe's anti-slavery novel played its part in leading to the changes in legislation which would precipitate the American Civil War. After the publication of *Aurora Leigh*, a woman reader wrote to Elizabeth Barrett Browning arguing that it wasn't a woman's place to speak on such political matters. Barrett Browning replied:

> Oh, and is it possible that you think a woman has no business with questions like the question of slavery? Then she had better use a pen no more. She had better subside into slavery and concubinage herself, I think, as in the times of old, shut herself up with the Penelopes in the 'women's apartment', and take no rank among thinkers and speakers.

> (Cited in Moers, 1977: 40)

In this outspoken and dissenting poem, Elizabeth Barrett Browning not only continued to refuse her place in the woman's apartment as a 'clipt' woman, but has also indeed claimed and confirmed her rank among not only great political thinkers and speakers, but also among political and epic poets.

CHRONOLOGY

SIMON AVERY

Given the emphasis throughout this study on placing Elizabeth Barrett Browning in a range of different contexts, the following chronology records the major events in the poet's life alongside concurrent political, social and cultural events occurring in Britain, Europe and America.

EBB = Elizabeth Barrett Browning; RB = Robert Browning

Year	Events in Elizabeth Barrett Browning's Life	Literary and cultural events	Events in social, political and economic history
1806	6 March: Elizabeth Barrett Moulton-Barrett born at Coxhoe Hall, County Durham. She is the eldest child of Edward Moulton-Barrett (1785–1857) and Mary Graham-Clarke (1781–1828).	John Stuart Mill born. Walter Scott, *Ballads and Lyrical Pieces*.	Pitt dies (January). Grenville (Tory) becomes Prime Minister and Fox (Whig) Foreign Secretary in the 'Ministry of All the Talents'. Fox dies in September. Ongoing Napoleonic Wars: French occupy Naples in February. Britain declares war on Prussia (April). Napoleon abolishes the Holy Roman Empire (August). Prussia declares war on France (October), but French beat them at the Battle of Iéna-Auerstadt. Russia and Turkey declare war.

Year	Events in Elizabeth Barrett Browning's Life	Literary and cultural events	Events in social, political and economic history
			Napoleon's 'Continental System' blocks British ships from entering European ports (November), causing great economic hardship for Britain. Napoleon invades Poland (December).
1807	26 June: Edward Moulton-Barrett, EBB's beloved brother ('Bro'), born.	Byron, *Hours of Idleness*. Hegel, *Phenomenology of the Spirit*. Thomas Moore, *Irish Melodies*. Germaine de Staël, *Corinne*. William Wilberforce, *A Letter on the Abolition of the Slave Trade*. Wordsworth, *Poems in Two Volumes*.	Tories win General Election (May). Portland becomes Prime Minister. Britain makes the slave trade illegal in the colonies (May) but slavery itself remains in place for another 27 years. Russia and Prussia form an alliance to rid the German states of the French. Russian-Prussian Alliance defeated at the Battle of Friedland (June). France and Spain make a pact to take over Portugal (October). Portuguese royal family flee to Brazil (November).
1808	Barrett family leave Coxhoe in the autumn, spending time in London and Surrey.	Felicia Browne (Hemans), *Poems, England and Spain*. Thomas Clarkson, *The History of the Abolition of the African Slave Trade by the British Parliament*.	United States bans the importing of slaves from Africa (January), although slave practices continue. France invades Spain (February). Spain rises against French occupation (May).

Year	Events in Elizabeth Barrett Browning's Life	Literary and cultural events	Events in social, political and economic history
		Goethe, *Faust, Part One.* Scott, *Marmion.*	Napoleon makes his brother, Joseph, King in June, initiating the Peninsular War. In August, a British army lands in Portugal. Joseph flees from Madrid. British forces under Wellesley defeat the French at Vimiero, near Lisbon.
1809	Barretts move to Hope End, Herefordshire, purchased for £27,000. 4 March: Henrietta, EBB's sister, born.	Charles Darwin, William Gladstone, Edgar Allen Poe and Alfred Tennyson born. Thomas Paine dies. Robert Bowyer (ed), *Poems on the Abolition of the Slave Trade.* Maria Edgeworth, *Tales of Fashionable Ladies.* Goethe, *Elective Affinities.* Schlegel, *On Dramatic Art and Literature.* Charlotte Smith, *Peacock at Home.* Tory *Quarterly Review* founded by John Murray.	French defeat the British in the Battle of Corunna in Spain (January). Austria declares war on France (February). British drive French out of Portugal (May). French capture Vienna and Napoleon annexes the Papal States (May). Pope Pius VII subsequently excommunicates Napoleon. French defeat the Austrians at the Battle of Wagram (July). Austria under Metternich makes peace with France (October). Perceval becomes Prime Minister (October).
1810		Elizabeth Stevenson (later Gaskell) born. De Staël, *L'Allemagne.* Scott, *The Lady of the Lake.* Southey, *The Curse of Kehama.* Wordsworth, *Guide to the Lakes.*	South American states start rebellion against French and Spanish rule (April). France annexes the Netherlands (July) and several north German states (December).

Year	Events in Elizabeth Barrett Browning's Life	Literary and cultural events	Events in social, political and economic history
1811		Thackeray born. Jane Austen, *Sense and Sensibility*. Mary Tighe, *Psyche, or the Legend of Love*.	Napoleon annexes the German Grand Duchy of Oldenburg (January). George III declared insane (February). Prince of Wales becomes Prince Regent. British forces defeat French in Spain (May). Luddite machine-breaking in Nottinghamshire.
1812	7 May: Robert Browning born in Camberwell, South London. He is the eldest son of Robert Browning and Sarah Anna Browning (neé Wiedemann).	Charles Dickens born. Byron, *Childe Harold's Pilgrimage* Cantos 1 & 2. Brothers Grimm, *Fairy Tales*. Felicia Browne (Hemans), *The Domestic Affections*.	Machine-breaking becomes a hanging offence after further rioting (March). British capture Badajoz, Spain (April). Perceval assassinated (May). Liverpool becomes Prime Minister. Napoleon invades Russia (June). USA declares war on Britain over trade disputes (June). British defeat French at Salamanca, Spain (July). Russians are defeated by French at Borodino and retreat from Moscow (September). Beaten by the Russian winter, Napoleon begins retreat (October).
1813	4 July: Arabella, EBB's sister, born.	Austen, *Pride and Prejudice*. Byron, *The Bride of Abydos*; *The Giaour*. Mary Russell Mitford, *Narrative*	Prussia declares war on France. Russia and Prussia occupy Dresden (March). Wellington defeats the French at Vittoria, Spain (June).

Year	Events in Elizabeth Barrett Browning's Life	Literary and cultural events	Events in social, political and economic history
		Poems on the Female Character. Amelia Opie, *Tales of Real Life.* Scott, *Rokeby* and *The Bridal of Triermain.* P.B. Shelley, *Queen Mab.* Southey, *Life of Nelson.* Southey made Poet Laureate.	Napoleon defeats Prussians at Battle of Dresden (August). Allies then defeat French at the Battle of Leipzig (October). Austrians defeat the French in Italy in the same month. Wellington invades southern France (November).
1814	7 January: Sariana, RB's sister, born.	Austen, *Mansfield Park.* Byron, *The Corsair*; *Lara.* Maria Edgeworth, *Patronage.* Scott, *Waverley.* Southey, *Roderick, the Last of the Goths.* Wordsworth, *The Excursion.* *New Monthly Magazine* begins publication.	France defeated (March). Napoleon abdicates and is exiled to the island of Elba. Louis XVIII returns to Paris (May) and in June assumes the throne 'by right'. Congress of Vienna begins to discuss the future of Europe (November). The Treaty of Ghent ends the war between Britain and America (December).
1815	October to November: EBB and her parents travel around France, including Calais, Boulogne, Rouen and Paris.	Anthony Trollope born. Byron, *Hebrew Melodies.* Scott, *The Lord of the Isles*; *Guy Mannering.* Wordsworth, *Poems*; *The White Doe of Rylstone.*	British Corn Laws introduced, limiting the importing of foreign grain. Start of industrial depression. Napoleon escapes from Elba (March) and returns to France, starting the Hundred Days War. Allies of Britain, Prussia, Russia and Austria sent to fight him.

Year	Events in Elizabeth Barrett Browning's Life	Literary and cultural events	Events in social, political and economic history
			Austria declares war on Jachim Murat, King of Naples (April) and defeat him in May. Congress of Vienna establishes new European frontiers (June). Battle of Waterloo (June) finally defeats Napoleon, who abdicates again. In August, Napoleon is exiled to St Helena.
1816	15 July: George, EBB's brother, born.	Charlotte Brontë born. Austen, *Emma*. Byron, *Childe Harold's Pilgrimage* Canto 3; *The Prisoner of Chillon*; *The Siege of Corinth*. William Cobbett, *Political Register*. Coleridge, *Christabel*; *Kubla Khan*. James Mill, *The History of British India*. Scott, *Old Mortality*. Shelley, *Alastor and Other Poems*. Elgin Marbles taken to London.	Severe economic depression. The 'Spa Fields Riot' – a march on the Tower of London (December).
1817	EBB begins learning Greek with Edward ('Bro') under the tutelage of Daniel McSwiney.	Jane Austen dies. Byron, *Manfred*; *The Lament of Tasso*. Edgeworth, *Ormond and Harrington*. Hazlitt, *The Characters of*	Fearing revolution, the British government suspends Habeas Corpus, the law preventing a person from being held without trial (March).

Year	Events in Elizabeth Barrett Browning's Life	Literary and cultural events	Events in social, political and economic history
		Shakespeare's Plays. Felicia Hemans, *Modern Greece.* Keats, *Poems.* Thomas Moore, *Lalla Rookh.* David Ricardo, *The Principles of Political Economy and Taxation.* Scott, *Harold the Dauntless.* Mary Shelley, *History of a Six Weeks Tour.* Southey, *Wat Tyler.* *Blackwood's Magazine* founded.	Princess Charlotte dies in childbirth (November).
1818	June: EBB writes a short autobiographical essay entitled 'My Own Character'.	Emily Brontë and Karl Marx born. Austen, *Northanger Abbey* and *Persuasion* (posthumous). Byron, *Childe Harold's Pilgrimage,* Canto 4; *Beppo.* Coleridge, *Biographia Literaria.* Hazlitt, *Lectures on the English Poets.* Hemans, *Translations from Camoens, and Other Poems.* Keats, *Endymion.* Thomas Love Peacock, *Phododaphne; Nightmare Abbey.* Scott, *Rob Roy; Heart of Midlothian.* Mary Shelley, *Frankenstein.* P.B.	Habeas Corpus reinstated (January). Tories win general election (June). Allies agree to end the occupation of France (October). Expansion of British rule in India.

Year	Events in Elizabeth Barrett Browning's Life	Literary and cultural events	Events in social, political and economic history
		Shelley, *Revolt of Islam*. Radical publisher Richard Carlile tried and imprisoned.	
1819	EBB finishes her first major poem, *The Battle of Marathon*, a four-book epic.	Victoria (future Queen), John Ruskin, Mary Anne Evans (later George Eliot), Arthur Hugh Clough born. Byron, *Mazeppa*; 'Ode to Venice'; *Don Juan* Cantos 1 & 2. Crabbe, *Tales of the Hall*. Hazlitt, *Lectures on the English Comic Writers*. Hemans, *Tales and Historic Scenes in Verse*. John Polidori, *The Vampyre*. Scott, *Bride of Lammermoor*, *Ivanhoe*. P.B. Shelley, *The Cenci*. Wordsworth, *Peter Bell*; *The Waggoner*.	Peterloo Massacre in Manchester (August). Troops charge a crowd of peaceful demonstrators calling for parliamentary reform. Eleven people are killed. Subsequent introduction of the repressive Six Acts forbidding public demonstrations and imposing press censorship.
1820	Fifty copies of EBB's *The Battle of Marathon* are privately printed as a present from her father for her fourteenth birthday. Edward ('Bro') leaves for Charterhouse and EBB's tutoring in the classics ceases.	Anne Brontë born. Byron, *Don Juan* Cantos 3 & 4. John Clare, *Poems Descriptive of Rural Life and Scenery*. Hazlitt, *Lectures on the Dramatic Art of the Age of Elizabeth*. Washington Irving, *The Sketchbook*.	George III dies (January) and George IV accedes to the throne. Revolution breaks out in Spain (January). The Duc de Berry, heir to the French throne, is assassinated (February). Cato Street Conspiracy (February).

Year	Events in Elizabeth Barrett Browning's Life	Literary and cultural events	Events in social, political and economic history
1820–1	EBB writes 'Glimpses into My Own Life and Literary Character', another autobiographical prose piece.	Keats, *Lamia, Isabella, Hyperion*. Scott, *The Abbot, Ivanhoe*. Robert Southey, *A Vision of Judgement*. Wordsworth, *The River Duddon; Memorials of a Tour on the Continent. London Magazine* and *John Bull* founded.	Ferdinand VII of Spain forced to reinstate 1812 constitution (March). Tories win general election (March). The Queen Caroline affair: Caroline tried for adultery (June). Revolts in Naples against the rule of Ferdinand I (July). Revolution in Portugal (August).
1821	EBB writes private essay 'My Character and Bro's Compared'. April: EBB and sisters unwell. Sisters recover but EBB continues to be ill. In July sent to Spa Hotel, Gloucester, to recuperate but doctors unable to reach a diagnosis. May: 'Stanzas, excited by some reflections on the present state of Greece' published in *The New Monthly Magazine*. July: 'Thoughts awakened by contemplating a piece of palm which grows on the summit of the Acropolis at Athens' published in *The New Monthly Magazine*.	Keats dies. Gustav Flaubert born. Thomas Beddoes, *The Improvisatrice*. Byron, *Cain; Don Juan* Cantos 5–8; *The Two Foscari*. Clare, *The Village Minstrel*. Goethe, *Wilhelm Meister's Travels*. Letitia Landon, *The Fate of Adelaide*. Scott, *Kenilworth*. P.B. Shelley, *Adonais; Epispsychidion*. Southey, *A Vision of Judgement*. Royal Pavilion built at Brighton.	Napoleon dies (March). Outbreak of Greek War of Independence (June). George IV's divorce plans defeated. Queen Caroline barred from attending coronation (July). Caroline dies in August.

Year	Events in Elizabeth Barrett Browning's Life	Literary and cultural events	Events in social, political and economic history
1822	May: EBB returns to Hope End from Gloucester.	Shelley dies by drowning. Matthew Arnold born. Caroline Bowles, *The Widow's Tale and Other Poems.* Byron, *Don Juan* Cantos 9–12; *The Vision of Judgement.* P.B. Shelley, *Hellas.* Wordsworth, *Memorials of a Tour of the Continent; Ecclesiastical Sketches.*	Turks invade mainland Greece (July). Congress of Verona meets to discuss problems in Europe (October). Orangemen riot in Dublin (December).
1823	June: EBB travels with other members of family to Boulogne to improve her French. Stays until January 1824.	Coventry Patmore born. Byron, *The Age of Bronze; The Island.* James Fenimore Cooper, *The Pioneers.* Mary and William Howitt, *The Forest Minstrel and Other Poems.* Scott, *Quentin Durward.* Mary Shelley, *Balperga.* P.B. Shelley, *Posthumous Poems,* ed. Mary Shelley. Southey, *The History of the Peninsular War.*	French troops invade Spain to crush the rebellion (April). Rebels are defeated in August. The restored Ferdinand VII of Spain begins a reign of tyranny (October). Daniel O'Connell founds the Catholic Association to campaign for Roman Catholic emancipation.
1824	June: 'Stanzas on the Death of Lord Byron' published in *The Globe and Traveller.*	Death of Byron on 19 April. Wilkie Collins born. James Hogg, *The Private Memoirs and Confessions of a Justified Sinner.*	First Anglo-Burmese War begins over seizure of Assam by Burma (February). Lisbon rebels against John VI of Portugal (April).

Year	Events in Elizabeth Barrett Browning's Life	Literary and cultural events	Events in social, political and economic history
		Letitia Landon, *The Improvisatrice*. Mary Russell Mitford, *Our Village*. Scott, *Redgauntlet*. *Westminster Review* founded. Opening of the National Gallery.	Louis XVIII of France dies and is succeeded by Charles X (September).
1825	EBB and Henrietta stay with their grandmother Moulton in Hastings July 1825–June 1826.	Anna Laetitia Barbauld, *Works*. Thomas Carlyle, *The Life of Schiller*. Hazlitt, *The Spirit of the Age*. Hemans, *The Forest Sanctuary*; *Lays of Many Lands*.	Egyptian troops land in Greece to help Turks crush the Greek rebellion (February). The Decembrist Rising by the Russian army demanding constitutional reform is defeated. Nicolas I becomes Czar following death of Alexander I. Hobshouse Act to protect child labour in cotton factories. Catholic Relief Bill defeated by the House of Lords.
1826	March: *An Essay on Mind, and Other Poems* published, paid for by Mary Trepsack, the companion of EBB's grandmother Moulton. June: Uvedale Price, classics scholar, contacts EBB to praise her for *Essay* and begins a long-standing correspondence.	Joanna Baillie, *The Martyr and the Bride*. Thomas Hood, *Whims and Oddities*. Amelia Opie, 'The Black Man's Lament or How to Make Sugar'. Mary Shelley, *The Last Man*.	First Anglo-Burmese war ends (February). The St Petersburg Protocol: Britain and Russia agree to mediate between the Turks and Greeks for Greek autonomy under Turkish suzerainty (April). Tories win general election (June).

Year	Events in Elizabeth Barrett Browning's Life	Literary and cultural events	Events in social, political and economic history
1827	March: Hugh Stuart Boyd, an internationally renowned classical scholar, contacts EBB to praise *An Essay on Mind*, initiating one of the most important relationships for EBB's intellectual development. November: Arabella Graham-Clarke, EBB's maternal grandmother, dies.	Clare, *The Shepherd's Calendar*. Hemans, *Hymns on the Works of Nature*. Leigh Hunt, *Lord Byron and Some of His Contemporaries*. John Keble, *The Christian Year*. Landon, *The Golden Violet*. Tennyson, *Poems by Two Brothers*.	Liverpool resigns as Prime Minister (February). Canning takes over but dies in August. Goderich becomes Prime Minister. Turkey refuses to recognise Greek autonomy under Turkish suzerainty. Anglo-French fleet defeat Turkish-Egyptian fleet at the Battle of Navarino. Peel's criminal law reform.
1828	April: EBB's first meeting with Hugh Stuart Boyd. 7 July: Mary Barrett, EBB's mother, dies.	Dante Gabriel Rossetti and George Meredith born. Hemans, *Records of Women*. Landon, *The Venetian Bracelet*.	Goderich resigns as Prime Minister (January). Wellington takes over. In Britain, Roman Catholics and non-conformists are allowed to hold public office after the repeal of the Test and Corporation Acts (May). Daniel O'Connell elected MP for Clare but is barred from taking his seat because he is Catholic (July).
1829	September: Uvedale Price dies. December: EBB's paternal grandmother, Elizabeth Moulton, dies, leaving EBB £4000.	Maria Jane Jewsbury, *Lays of Leisure Hours*. John Stuart Mill, *Analysis of the Phenomena of the Human Mind*.	Catholic Emancipation Act allows Catholics to sit in Parliament (April). Treaty of Adrianople ends Russo-Turkish war.

Year	Events in Elizabeth Barrett Browning's Life	Literary and cultural events	Events in social, political and economic history
		John Henry Newman, *Poetry with Reference to Aristotle's Poetics.* Scott, *Anne of Greierstein.*	Turkey recognises Greek autonomy (September). Start of cholera outbreak across Europe.
1830		William Hazlitt dies. Emily Dickinson and Christina Rossetti born. Carlyle, 'On History'. Cobbett, *Rural Rides.* Augustus Comte, *Cours de Philosophie Positive.* John Galt, *The Life of Lord Byron.* Hemans, *Songs of the Affections.* Charles Lyell, *Principles of Geology.* Thomas Moore (ed), *Letters and Journals of Lord Byron.* Scott, *Tales of a Grandfather.* Tennyson, *Poems, Chiefly Lyrical.* *Fraser's Magazine for Town and Country* founded.	Greece is formally declared independent (February). The First Reform Bill is rejected (March). 'Captain Swing' riots against new threshing machines and rural unemployment (June). George IV dies, succeeded by his brother William IV (June). Revolutions in Paris against Charles X (July), who abdicates in August. Louis Phillippe is elected king and a new liberal constitution is adopted. Duke of Wellington resigns as Prime Minister (November) and is succeeded by Lord Grey who forms a Whig administration. Belgium becomes independent (December).
1831	1831–2 EBB keeps her diary, recording her feelings about her family and Hugh Stuart Boyd.	Carlyle, *Characteristics.* Ebenezer Elliott, *Corn-Law Rhymes.* Hegel, *Lectures on the Philosophy of History.*	Italian states of Modena, Parma and Papal States revolt (February). Mazzini founds the Young Italy society in Marseilles, dedicated

Year	Events in Elizabeth Barrett Browning's Life	Literary and cultural events	Events in social, political and economic history
		Victor Hugo, *Notre Dame de Paris*. Letitia Landon, *Romance and Reality*. Thomas Love Peacock, *Crotchet Castle*. Mary Shelley, *Frankenstein* (revised).	to bringing about Italian unification. In Britain, First Reform Bill defeated (April). Reintroduced in June. Defeated by the Lords in October. Reintroduced in the Commons in December. Belgians elect Leopold of Saxe-Coburg as King (June). Dutch invade Belgium (August) but are driven out by the French.
1832	February: EBB translates Aeschylus' *Prometheus Bound*. June: Hope End sold. August: Barretts leave Hope End and move to Sidmouth, Devon.	Scott, Goethe and George Crabbe die. Lewis Carroll born. Carlyle, 'Biography'. Goethe, *Faust, Part II*. Anna Jameson, *Characteristics of Women*. Harriett Martineau, *Illustrations of Political Economy*. P.B. Shelley, *The Mask of Anarchy*. Tennyson, *Poems*. Wordsworth, *Poetic Works*.	Austrian troops halt riots in Italy's Papal States (January). Reform Bill passed by the Commons (March) but delayed in the Lords. Grey resigns, but when Wellington fails to form a government, Grey resumes office and the Reform Act is passed by the Lords. Greece elects Prince Otto of Bavaria as King (August).
1833	May: EBB publishes *Prometheus Bound, Translated from the Greek of Aeschylus, and Miscellaneous Poems*. RB publishes *Pauline* (March).	Caroline Bowles, *Tales of the Factories*. Thomas Carlyle, *Sartor Resartus*. Harriet Martineau, *Poor Laws and Paupers Illustrated*.	British Emancipation Bill prohibits slavery in British colonies (July). Factory Act forbids children under nine working in textile factories (August). Oxford Movement begins.

Year	Events in Elizabeth Barrett Browning's Life	Literary and cultural events	Events in social, political and economic history
1834		Death of Samuel Taylor Coleridge. William Morris born. Edward Bulwer-Lytton, *The Last Days of Pompeii*. Maria Edgeworth, *Helen*. Felicia Hemans, *National Lyrics and Songs for Music*. Harriet Martineau, *Illustrations of Taxation*. Richard Monckton Milnes, *Memoirs of a Tour in Some Parts of Greece*.	The Tolpuddle Martyrs are sentenced to transportation for trade union activity (March). Lord Grey resigns as Prime Minister (July) and is succeeded by Lord Melbourne. Melbourne resigns in November and Robert Peel takes over. Don Carlos, brother of the late Ferdinand VII of Spain, claims the Spanish throne (July) and begins a civil war which lasts until 1839. New Poor Law makes changes to the relief offered.
1835	September: EBB's 'Stanzas Addressed to Miss Landon' published in *The New Monthly Magazine*. December: Barretts move to 74 Gloucester Place, London. RB publishes *Paracelsus*.	Felicia Hemans dies. John Clare, *The Rural Muse*. Felicia Hemans, *Songs of the Affection*. David Strauss, *Das Leben Jesu*.	Whigs and the Irish leader Daniel O'Connell plot to bring about the fall of Peel's government (March). Peel is defeated in April and resigns. Lord Melbourne (Whig) forms a new ministry.
1836	27 May: John Kenyon introduces EBB to Mary Russell Mitford, who subsequently becomes a very close friend. May 28: EBB meets Wordsworth, one of her great heroes, at a dinner at Kenyon's house.	Death of William Godwin. Dickens, *Sketches by Boz*. Felicia Hemans, *Collected Works*. Pugin, *Contrasts*.	Thiers becomes French Prime Minister (February) but is forced to resign in September after his plans to invade Spain are opposed. Chartist movement begins in Britain (June).

Year	Events in Elizabeth Barrett Browning's Life	Literary and cultural events	Events in social, political and economic history
	October: 'The Poet's Vow' published in *The New Monthly Magazine*.		
1837	July: 'The Young Queen' and 'Victoria's Tears' published in *The Athenaeum*. October: 'A Romance of the Ganges' published in *Findens' Tableaux*, edited by Mary Russell Mitford. December: EBB's uncle, Samuel Moulton-Barrett, dies in Jamaica, leaving her money and shares in the ship *David Lyon*. RB publishes *Strafford: A Tragedy* (May).	Algernon Swinburne born. Carlyle, *The French Revolution*. Dickens, *Pickwick Papers*. Nathaniel Hawthorne, *Twice-Told Tales*. J.G. Lockhard, *Life of Scott*.	'People's Charter' published (May). William IV dies (June) and is succeeded by Victoria.
1838	April: Barretts move to 50 Wimpole Street. June: *The Seraphim, and Other Poems* published under Elizabeth B. Barrett (the first volume to appear under her own name). August: EBB moves to Torquay for health reasons, where she remains until September 1841. October: 'The Romaunt of the Page' published in *Findens' Tableaux*.	Letitia Landon (L.E.L.) dies. Dickens, *Oliver Twist*. Lyell, *Elements of Geology*. Completion of the National Galley.	Poor Law for Ireland sets up workhouse schemes (July). Richard Cobden establishes the Anti-Corn Law League (September) Development of Chartist movements; petition ignored by government.

Year	Events in Elizabeth Barrett Browning's Life	Literary and cultural events	Events in social, political and economic history
1839	January: 'LEL's Last Question' published in *The Athenaeum*. October: 'A Dream' and 'The Legend of the Browne Rosarie' published in *Findens' Tableaux*.	Thomas Carlyle, *Chartism*. Eliza Cook, *Poems*. Harriet Martineau, *Deerbrook*. George Sand, *Spiridion*. P.B. Shelley, *Poetical Works*, ed. Mary Shelley.	Chartist convention meets in London (February). Issue of first Factory Inspectors' Reports. The Offences Against the Person Act makes abortion illegal in Britain and the Empire. Start of First Anglo-Afghan War (October). Start of Opium War between Britain and China (November).
1840	February: EBB publishes 'The Crowned and Wedded Queen' in *The Athenaeum*, five days after Victoria marries Albert. July: EBB publishes 'Napoleon's Return' (later 'Crowned and Buried) in *The Athenaeum*. 11 July: Bro is drowned while sailing with friends in Tor Bay. His body is missing until early August. EBB is distraught and ill for several months. December: *The Poems of Geoffrey Chaucer, Modernized* published, ed. R.H. Horne, including EBB's 'Queen Annelida and False Arcite' and 'The Complaint of Annelida to False Arcite'.	Carlyle, *On Heroes, Hero Worship, and the Heroic in History*. Eliza Cook, *Melaia and Other Poems*. Charles Darwin, *Voyages of the H.M.S. Beagle*. Dickens, *Barnaby Rudge*; *The Old Curiosity Shop*. R.H. Horne, *History of Napoleon*. Edgar Allen Poe, *Tales of the Grotesque and Arabesque*. *Punch* is founded.	Queen Victoria marries her cousin, Prince Albert of Saxe-Coburg-Gotha (January). Thiers forms his second government (January). Prince Louis-Napoleon Bonaparte, nephew of Napoleon, fails in a coup to overthrow the French government (August). Thiers resigns as French Prime Minister (October). Houses of Parliament finished by Barry and Pugin (October).

Year	Events in Elizabeth Barrett Browning's Life	Literary and cultural events	Events in social, political and economic history
	RB publishes *Sordello* (March).		
1841	January: Mary Russell Mitford sends EBB the gift of a spaniel, Flush. September: EBB returns to London from Torquay. RB publishes *Pippa Passes*, the first of the *Bells and Pomegranates* series (April).	James Fenimore Cooper, *The Deerslayer*. Tennyson, *Poems*.	Melbourne resigns as Prime Minister (August). Peel (Tory) forms new government. Queen Victoria gives birth to a son, Edward (November). Afghans massacre 16,000 Britons during Afghan War (November). Government report on *The Health of Towns* published.
1842	February–March: *Some Account of the Greek Christian Poets* published in *The Athenaeum*. June: *The Book of the Poets*, a study of British literature from Chaucer to the present, is published in *The Athenaeum*. RB publishes *King Victor and King Charles* (March).	Dickens, *American Notes*. Thomas Macaulay, *Lays of Ancient Rome*. John Henry Newman, *Essay on Miracles*. Tennyson, *Poems*.	Second National Convention of Chartists in London (April). Treaty of Nanking between Britain and China gives Hong Kong to Britain (August). End of Anglo-Afghan War (October). Child Labour Laws outlawing women and children from working in mines. Government report on *The Sanitary Conditions of the Labouring Population*.
1843	August: 'The Cry of the Children' published in *Blackwood's Magazine*. September: Flush stolen and ransomed. RB publishes *The Return of the Druses* (January) and *A Blot in the 'Scutcheon* (February).	Henry James born. Carlyle, *Past and Present*. Dickens, *A Christmas Carol*; *Martin Chuzzlewit*. Ruskin, *Modern Painters* (1843–60).	Britain proclaims Natal a colony (May).

Year	Events in Elizabeth Barrett Browning's Life	Literary and cultural events	Events in social, political and economic history
1844	March: *A New Spirit of the Age* published, ed. R.W. Horne. EBB has submitted essays on Carlyle, Leigh Hunt, Monckton Milnes and Wordsworth. She is unhappy about her own representation by Horne. April: Elizabeth Crow leaves her post as EBB's maid after becoming pregnant by the butler William Treherne. May: Elizabeth Wilson becomes EBB's new maid. August: *Poems* published by Moxon. October: *A Drama of Exile, and Other Poems*, the American version of *Poems*, published. RB publishes *Colombe's Birthday* (April).	Robert Chambers, *Vestiges of the Natural History of Creation.* Dickens, *The Chimes.* Benjamin Disraeli, *Coningsby.*	The Factory Act limits the working day to 12 hours for women and $6\frac{1}{2}$ hours for children between eight and thirteen (June). Franco-Moroccan War (August–September).
1845	January: RB starts correspondence with EBB which will eventually lead to marriage. EBB turns down the opportunity to write a poem for the Leeds Anti-Corn Law League Bazaar under the influence of both her father and Kenyon. 20 May: RB's first visit to EBB at Wimpole Street. On 22nd RB writes declaring his	Margaret Fuller, *Women in the Nineteenth Century.*	Famine in Ireland following potato blight. Crop failure, famine and evictions when tenants fail to pay rents. Peel resigns as Prime Minister (December) but is recalled a fortnight later. Anglo-Sikh war breaks out with India (December). Oxford Movement breaks as Newman converts to Catholicism.

Year	Events in Elizabeth Barrett Browning's Life	Literary and cultural events	Events in social, political and economic history
	love but apologises after EBB reacts badly. August: EBB starts writing *Sonnets from the Portuguese*. September: RB and EBB declare their love.		
1846	EBB starts reading more about Italy and planning her future life there with RB. September: Flush is stolen again. This time EBB herself goes to Shoreditch to ransom him. Mr Barrett announces the family are to move out of Wimpole Street while it is redecorated, causing EBB & RB to finalise their wedding plan. 12 September: EBB & RB married at 11am at St Marylebone Church, witnessed by Elizabeth Wilson and James Silverthorne, RB's cousin. 19 September: EBB, RB, Wilson and Flush meet at Hodgson's bookshop, Great Marylebone Street, travel to Southampton and then to France. 21 September: Reach Paris where they stay for a week. 29 September: EBB receives letter	Charlotte, Emily and Anne Brontë, *Poems by Currer, Ellis and Acton Bell.* Dickens, *Dombey and Son.* George Eliot, translation of Strauss' *Das Leben Jesu.* Friederich Engels, *The Condition of the Working Class in England.*	Anglo-Sikh war ends (March). Napoleon, imprisoned for treason in France, escapes to England (May). Corn Laws repealed (May). Chadwick's study of the Poor Law commissions' work in the slums of Liverpool, London and Lancashire published. 'Railway Mania' begins.

Year	Events in Elizabeth Barrett Browning's Life	Literary and cultural events	Events in social, political and economic history
	from Mr Barrett disowning her. 2–14 October: travel to Pisa with Anna Jameson. December: Finishes 'The Runaway Slave at Pilgrim's Point'.		
1847	March: EBB's first miscarriage at five months. April: EBB & RB move to Florence. July: rent rooms in Casa Guidi. 12 September: First anniversary. From their apartment windows, they watch the procession to celebrate Grand Duke Leopold granting the Florentines a civic guard. EBB will use this as the basis for Part One of *Casa Guidi Windows*. October: They move to Via Maggio as they cannot renew the lease on Casa Guidi. Unhappy with this accommodation, however, they move to rooms in the Piazza Pitti, opposite the palace.	Anne Brontë, *Agnes Grey*. Charlotte Brontë, *Jane Eyre*. Emily Brontë, *Wuthering Heights*. Tennyson, *The Princess*. Thackeray, *Vanity Fair*.	Ten Hours Factory Act passed, limiting work hours for women and 13- to 18-year-olds (June). Austrian troops occupy Ferrara in Italy (July).
1848	'The Runaway Slave at Pilgrim's Point' appears in the Boston anti-slavery publication *The Liberty Bell*.	Emily Brontë dies. Elizabeth Gaskell, *Mary Barton*. Karl Marx and Frederick Engels,	Revolutions across Europe. Revolt in Sicily against the tyrannical King Ferdinand II (January).

Year	Events in Elizabeth Barrett Browning's Life	Literary and cultural events	Events in social, political and economic history
	March: EBB suffers a second miscarriage at two months. May: Brownings move back to their previous rooms in Casa Guidi. Hugh Stuart Boyd dies. July–August: Brownings travel around Italy for the summer. October: *Casa Guidi Windows* Part One rejected by *Blackwood's*.	*The Communist Manifesto.* Thackeray, *Pendennis.* Pre-Raphaelite Brotherhood founded.	Grand Duke Leopold grants a constitution to the people of Tuscany. Celebrations in Florence (February). After a revolt in Paris, Louis-Philippe abdicates and France is declared a republic (February). Revolts break out in Vienna; Metternich resigns; revolts in Venice against Austrian rule; revolt in Milan; revolution in Berlin leads to Wilhelm IV granting concessions (March). Czechs revolt against Austria but are suppressed; Pope Pius IX declares the papacy neutral in the Italian troubles; revolts in Rome (April). Battle of Custozza where the Austrians defeat the Italians from Piedmont and Lombardy (July). Pope Pius IX flees from Rome (November). Emperor Ferdinand of Austria abdicates and is succeeded by Franz Josef I; Louis-Napoleon is elected president of France (December).
1849	9 March: Robert Wiedemann Browning (Penini) born.	Anne Brontë and Maria Edgeworth die.	British troops defeat the Sikhs in India (February).

Year	Events in Elizabeth Barrett Browning's Life	Literary and cultural events	Events in social, political and economic history
	18 March: RB's mother dies. July: EBB gives RB *Sonnets from the Portuguese*. RB publishes *Poems* (January).	Matthew Arnold, *The Strayed Reveller and Other Poems*. Charlotte Brontë, *Shirley*. Dickens, *David Copperfield* (also founds *Household Words*). Ruskin, *The Seven Lamps of Architecture*.	Disraeli becomes Conservative leader (February). Leopold II of Tuscany leaves for Siena and sails from there to Gaeta to join Pius IX. Rome declared a republic. Mazzini arrives in Florence (February). Austria adopts a new constitution. Piedmont defeated by Austrians at Novara. Charles Albert of Sardinia abdicates and Victor Emmanuel II succeeds (March). Francesco Guerrazzi, Tuscan dictator, is overthrown (April). Austrian troops occupy Florence aiming to restore Leopold (May). French troops enter Rome to crush the republic (July). Austrians capture Venice (August). Mayhew publishes *London Labour and the London Poor* in *The Morning Chronicle* (1849–50).
1850	April: Henrietta, EBB's sister, marries William Surtees Cook and is disowned by her father. June: a piece in *The Athenaeum* suggests EBB should be considered for the	Death of Wordsworth. Tennyson succeeds to the Laureateship, although EBB proposed in *The Athenaeum*.	Pope Pius IX is restored to the Vatican by the French (April). France abolishes universal suffrage (May). US Congress passes Fugitive Slave Law

Year	Events in Elizabeth Barrett Browning's Life	Literary and cultural events	Events in social, political and economic history
	Laureateship following Wordsworth's death. July: EBB suffers miscarriage at three months. August: Brownings travel to Siena, where they stay until October. October: 'Hiram Powers' "Greek Slave"' published in *Household Words*. November: EBB's expanded and revised *Poems* published. RB publishes *Christmas-Eve and Easter-Day* (April).	Robert Louis Stevenson born. Hawthorne, *The Scarlet Letter*. Kingsley, *Alton Locke*. Tennyson, *In Memoriam*. Wordsworth, *The Prelude* (posthumous). The Pre-Raphaelites found *The Germ*.	whereby runaway slaves must be returned to their owners (September). Count Camillo Cavour becomes a minister in Piedmont (October).
1851	May: *Casa Guidi Windows* published. Brownings travel with the Ogilvys to Venice. June: Brownings travel through Italy, Switzerland and France to Paris. July: Travel to London, renting rooms near Wimpole Street. EBB's father refuses to see them and returns all EBB's letters unopened. Meet with RB's parents, EBB's brothers, Carlyle, Anna Jameson, Kenyon, Mitford, Dante Gabriel Rossetti. Attend the Great Exhibition. September: Travel to Paris with Carlyle. October: Move into lodgings in the Champs-Elysées.	Mary Shelley, Joanna Baillie and J.M.W. Turner die. Hawthorne, *The House of Seven Gables*. Herman Melville, *Moby Dick*. Meredith, *Poems*. John Ruskin, *The Stones of Venice*. The Great Exhibition.	Louis Napoleon changes the French constitution with a *coup d'état* (December). Palmerston, Britain's foreign secretary, supports the new constitution and Victoria subsequently forces him to resign. Austria abolishes its constitution (December).

Year	Events in Elizabeth Barrett Browning's Life	Literary and cultural events	Events in social, political and economic history
1852	February: EBB meets George Sand twice in Paris. July–October: Brownings visit London where they see Henrietta, Anna Jameson and Ruskin, and meet Mazzini and Charles Kingsley. October: On return to Paris, the Brownings watch Louis Napoleon's entry into Paris. November: Arrive back in Florence. RB publishes 'Essay on Shelley' (February).	Dickens, *Bleak House*. Harriet Beecher Stowe, *Uncle Tom's Cabin*. Thackeray, *Henry Esmond*.	Second Anglo-Burmese War starts (April). Carvour becomes Piedmont's Prime Minister (November). The French Second Empire is founded. Louis Napoleon becomes Emperor Napoleon III (December). Lord Derby resigns as Prime Minister (December). Lord Aberdeen forms a coalition government.
1853	EBB working on *Aurora Leigh*. July–mid-October: Brownings stay at Bagni di Lucca. November: Travel to Rome where they stay until the end of June 1854.	Arnold, *Poems: A New Edition*. Charlotte Brontë, *Villette*. Elizabeth Gaskell, *Cranford*; *Ruth*. Hawthorne, *Tanglewood Tales*.	Russia claims protectorate over Turkish Christians (May). Russia invades the Danubian Principalities (July). Turkey declares war on Russia (October). Anglo-Burmese War ends (June).
1854	March: EBB writes 'A Plea for the Ragged Schools of London' to be sold at a bazaar organised by her sister Arabella in April. June: Return to Florence. Flush dies.	Dickens, *Hard Times*. Charles Kingsley, *Westward Ho!* Tennyson, 'Charge of the Light Brigade'. Thoreau, *Walden*.	Crimean War: Britain and France declare war on Russia (March). Russian troops quit the Danubian Principalities (August). Austrian troops take over. Allied British and French troops land in the Crimea. Battle of the Alma (September). Siege of Sevastopol. Battle of Balaclava (October).

Year	Events in Elizabeth Barrett Browning's Life	Literary and cultural events	Events in social, political and economic history
			Florence Nightingale arrives in Crimea (November).
1855	June: Elizabeth Wilson marries the Brownings' other employee, Ferdinando Romagnoli. She is already four months pregnant but doesn't tell the Brownings. Brownings travel to Paris and then on to London in July to visit friends. August: Alfred, EBB's brother, marries his cousin Lizzie Barrett and is also disowned by his father. October: Brownings travel to Paris where they stay until June 1856. RB publishes *Men and Women* (November).	Charlotte Brontë dies. Dickens, *Little Dorrit*. Elizabeth Gaskell, *North and South*. Herbert Spenser, *Principles of Psychology*. Tennyson, *Maud*. Trollope, *The Warden*. Whitman, *Leaves of Grass*.	Piedmont joins the Allies against Russia (January). Palmerston becomes Prime Minister (February). Czar Nicholas I of Russia dies and is succeeded by his son Alexander II (March). Allies enter Sevastopol (August). Sweden joins Allies against Russia (November).
1856	EBB's 'A Curse for a Nation' appears in *The Liberty Bell*. June: EBB finishes *Aurora Leigh*. The Brownings travel to London. August: They move to the Isle of Wight to work on proofs of *Aurora Leigh*. September: Return to London. October: Return to Italy.	G.B. Shaw and Oscar Wilde born. Flaubert, *Madame Bovary*. Caroline Norton, *A Review of the Divorce Bill*.	The British annex Oudh in India (February). Treaty of Paris ends the Crimean War (March). Anglo-Chinese War starts (October).

Year	Events in Elizabeth Barrett Browning's Life	Literary and cultural events	Events in social, political and economic history
	November: *Aurora Leigh* published. December: John Kenyon dies, leaving the Brownings enough money for them to be financially secure.		
1857	January: 2nd impression of *Aurora Leigh* published. March: 3rd impression of *Aurora Leigh* published. 17 April: EBB's father dies. July: Brownings travel to Bagni di Lucca where they stay until October. August: Wilson, pregnant again, leaves the Brownings' employment.	Baudelaire, *Les Fleurs du Mal.* Charlotte Brontë, *The Professor* (posthumous). Hughes, *Tom Brown's Schooldays.* Trollope, *Barchester Towers.*	Dred Scott case in the US states that no blacks, free or slave, can be a US citizen (March). Indian Mutiny (May–September).
1858	July: Brownings travel to Paris where they stay until October. November: Travel to Rome for EBB's health, where they stay until May 1859.	George Eliot, *Scenes from Clerical Life.* *Englishwoman's Journal* founded.	Italian revolutionary Felice Orsini tries to assassinate Napoleon III in Paris but fails (January). Napoleon III and Count Cavour plan unification of Italy. Lord Palmerston resigns as Prime Minister and is succeeded by Derby (Tory) (February). Anglo-Chinese War ends (June). British proclaim peace in India (July). British government takes over the ruling of India from the East India Company (August).

Year	Events in Elizabeth Barrett Browning's Life	Literary and cultural events	Events in social, political and economic history
1859	May: Brownings return to Florence. Summer: EBB's health deteriorates, seemingly in part as a reaction to political affairs in Italy. July: Travel to Siena where they stay until October. September: EBB's 'A Tale of Villafranca' is published in *The Athenaeum*. October: Brownings return to Florence. November: Leave for Rome for the winter.	Darwin, *Origin of Species*. Dickens, *A Tale of Two Cities*. George Eliot, *Adam Bede*. John Stuart Mill, *On Liberty*. Tennyson, *Idylls of the King*.	Treaty of Turin: Napoleon III forms an alliance with Sardinia-Piedmont (January). Austria attacks Sardinia-Piedmont (April). France declares war on Austria (May). France and Piedmont defeat Austria at Battle of Magenta (June). French and Sardinians defeat the Austrians at Solferino (June). Palmerston forms Liberal administration (June). France and Austria sign the Treaty of Villafranca, declaring peace (July). Lombardy to be united with Piedmont. Other sections of northern Italy to remain with Austria.
1860	March: EBB's *Poems Before Congress* published. June: Brownings return to Florence. 'First News from Villafranca' published in *The Independent*. July: Brownings travel to Siena, where they stay until November. August: 'King Victor Emmanuel Entering Florence, April, 1860' published in *The Independent*. November: Brownings travel to Rome.	Wilkie Collins, *The Woman in White*. George Eliot, *The Mill on the Floss*.	Garibaldi enters Palermo (January), captures Palermo and Sicily and sets up a provisional government. Cavour made Prime Minister of Sardinia (January). Garibaldi and Thousand Red Shirts sail from Genoa to Sicily where they set up a provisional government. Garibaldi subsequently lands in mainland Italy (August) and captures Naples

Year	Events in Elizabeth Barrett Browning's Life	Literary and cultural events	Events in social, political and economic history
	December: EBB's sister, Henrietta, dies from cancer of the uterus.		(September). Victor Emmanuel II invades the Papal States. Naples and Sicily vote to join Sardinia (October). Garibaldi elects Victor Emmanuel as King of Italy.
1861	April: Thackeray rejects 'Lord Walter's Wife' for the *Cornhill*. May: 'Mother and Poet' published in *The Independent*. June: Brownings return to Florence. EBB's health deteriorates with worsening cough and lung congestion. By 29 June she has declined and dies in Robert's arms early next morning. 1 July: EBB buried in Florence's Protestant Cemetery. Aug: Robert and Pen Browning leave Florence for London. Robert never returns.	Mrs Beeton, *The Book of Household Management*. Dickens, *Great Expectations*. George Eliot, *Silas Marner*.	An Italian parliament proclaims Victor Emmanuel King of Italy (March). American Civil War begins (April). Cavour dies (June). Prince Albert dies (December).
1862	March: EBB's *Last Poems* published. October: The Florence government erects a plaque on Casa Guidi to celebrate EBB's contribution to Italian unification.	Hugo, *Les Misérables*. George Meredith, *Modern Love*. Christina Rossetti, *Goblin Market and Other Poems*.	Italian troops capture Garibaldi but soon release him (August). Bismarck becomes Prussian Prime Minister (September). Greeks depose their King, Othon (Otto of Bismarck) (October).

ABBREVIATIONS

The following abbreviations are used throughout the text

AL   *Aurora Leigh*, ed. Margaret Reynolds, New York and London: Norton, 1996

BC   *The Brownings' Correspondence*, ed. Philip Kelley, Ronald Hudson and Scott Lewis, 14 vols, Winfield, Kan.: Wedgestone Press, 1984–1998

CW   *The Complete Works of Elizabeth Barrett Browning*, ed. Charlotte Porter and Helen A. Clarke, 6 vols, New York: Thomas Y. Cromwell, 1900, rept. 1973

D   *Diary by E.B.B.: The Unpublished Diary of Elizabeth Barrett Browning, 1831–1832*, ed. Philip Kelley and Ronald Hudson, Athens, Ohio: Ohio University Press, 1969

HSB   *Elizabeth Barrett to Mr Boyd: Unpublished Letters of Elizabeth Barrett Browning to Hugh Stuart Boyd*, ed. Barbara P. McCarthy, London: John Murray, 1955

HUP   *Hitherto Unpublished Poems and Stories of Elizabeth Barrett Browning*, ed. H. Buxton Forman, 2 vols, Boston: Bibliophile Society, 1914

MDO   *Elizabeth Barrett Browning's Letters to Mrs David Ogilvy, 1849–1861*, ed. Peter N. Heydon and Philip Kelley, London: John Murray, 1974

MRM   *The Letters of Elizabeth Barrett Browning to Mary Russell Mitford, 1836–1854*, ed. Meredith B. Raymond and Mary Rose Sullivan, 3 vols, Winfield, Kan.: Armstrong Browning Library, Browning Institute, Wedgestone Press and Wellesley College, 1983

BIBLIOGRAPHY

Armstrong, Isobel (ed) (1972), *Victorian Scrutinies: Reviews of Poetry, 1830–1870*, London: Athlone Press

Armstrong, Isobel (1993), *Victorian Poetry: Poetry, Poetics, Politics*, London: Routledge

Armstrong, Isobel and Joseph Bristow with Cath Sharrock (eds) (1996), *Nineteenth-Century Women Poets*, Oxford: Clarendon Press

Atterbury, Paul and Suzanne Fagence Cooper (2001), *Victorians at Home and Abroad*, London: V&A Publications

Avery, Simon (2000), 'Tantalising Glimpses: The Intersecting Lives of Eleanor Marx and Mathilde Blind', in *Eleanor Marx: Life, Work, Contacts*, Aldershot: Ashgate, 173–87

Blain, Virginia (ed) (2001), *Victorian Women Poets: A New Annotated Anthology*, Harlow: Longman

Bloom, Harold (1973), *The Anxiety of Influence*, New York: Oxford University Press

Bodichon, Barbara (1854), *A Brief Summary, In Plain Language, Of The Most Important Laws Concerning Women; Together With A Few Observations Thereon*, London: John Chapman

Bold, Alan (1979), *The Ballad*, London: Methuen

Bolton, John Robert Glorney and Julia Bolton Holloway (eds) (1995), *Aurora Leigh and Other Poems*, London: Penguin

Bristow, Joseph (ed) (1987), *The Victorian Poet: Poetics and Persona*, London and New York: Croom Helm

Bristow, Joseph (ed) (1995), *Victorian Women Poets: Emily Brontë, Elizabeth Barrett Browning, Christina Rossetti*, Basingstoke: Macmillan

Carleton, Marjorie (1940), *The Barretts: A Play in Three Acts*, Boston and Los Angeles: Walter H. Baker Company

Carlyle, Thomas (1850), *The Latter-Day Pamphlets*, London: Chapman and Hall

Carlyle, Thomas (1986), *Selected Writings*, ed. Alan Shelston, London: Penguin

Carlyle, Thomas (1989), *The French Revolution: A History* [1837], Oxford: Oxford World's Classics

Carlyle, Thomas (1993), *On Heroes, Hero-Worship, and the Heroic in History*, ed. Michael K. Goldber, Joel J. Brattin and Mark Engel, Berkeley and Los Angeles, California: University of California

Carter, Angela (1997), 'Notes from the Front Line,' in *Shaking a Leg*, London: Chatto and Windus, 36–43

Cartland, Barbara (1970), 'The Perfect Romance of Elizabeth and Robert Browning', *Famous Loves* 23 July 1970:7–14

Case, Alison (1991), 'Gender and Narration in *Aurora Leigh*', *Victorian Poetry* 29(1): 25–32

Chandler, James K. (1998), *England in 1819: The Politics of Literary Culture and the Case of Romantic Historicism*, Chicago and London: University of Chicago Press

Clarke, Norma (1990), *Ambitious Heights: Writing, Friendship, Love – the Jewsbury Sisters, Felicia Hemans and Jane Carlyle*, London: Routledge

Clogg, Richard (1992), *A Concise History of Greece*, Cambridge: Cambridge University Press

Cooper, Helen (1988), *Elizabeth Barrett Browning: Woman and Artist*, Chapel Hill and London: University of North Carolina Press

Cosslett, Tess (ed) (1996), *Victorian Women Poets*, London: Longman

Cox, Philip (1996), *Gender, Genre and the Romantic Poets*, Manchester: Manchester University Press

David, Deirdre (1987), *Intellectual Women and Victorian Patriarchy: Harriet Martineau, Elizabeth Barrett Browning, George Eliot*, London: Macmillan

Dennis, Barbara (1996), *Elizabeth Barrett Browning: The Hope End Years*, Bridgend: Seren

Derrida, Jacques (1992), 'Le Loi de Genre,' translated by Avital Ronnell in Jacques Derrida, *Acts of Literature*, ed. Derek Attridge, New York and London: Routledge, 221–52

Dickinson, Emily (1975), *The Complete Poems of Emily Dickinson*, ed. Thomas H. Johnson, London: Faber and Faber

Doggett, Maeve E. (1993), *Marriage, Wife-Beating and the Law in Victorian England*, Columbia SC.: University of South Carolina Press

Donaldson, Sandra (1980), ' "Motherhood's Advent in Power": Elizabeth Barrett Browning's Poems About Motherhood', *Victorian Poetry* 18(1):51–60

Donaldson, Sandra (1993), *Elizabeth Barrett Browning: An Annotated Bibliography of the Commentary and Criticism, 1826–1990*, New York: G.K. Hall and Co

Douglas, Ann (1981), Introduction to Harriet Beecher Stowe's *Uncle Tom's Cabin*, London: Penguin

DuPlessis, Rachel Blau (1985), *Writing Beyond the Ending: Narrative Strategies of Twentieth-Century Women Writers*, Bloomington: Indiana University Press

Eagleton, Mary (ed) (1986), *Feminist Literary Theory: A Reader*, Oxford: Basil Blackwell

Eliot, George (1985), *Adam Bede* [1859], Harmondsworth: Penguin

Erkkila, Betsy (1992), *The Wicked Sisters: Women Poets, Literary History, and Discord*, New York and Oxford: Oxford University Press

Forster, Margaret (1988), *Elizabeth Barrett Browning*, London: Chatto and Windus

Fuller, Peter (1972), *The Sonnet*, London: Methuen

Garrett, Martin (2001), *Elizabeth Barrett Browning and Robert Browning*, London: The British Library

Gaskell, Elizabeth (1857), *The Life of Charlotte Brontë*, London: Smith, Elder and Co

Gilbert, Sandra M. and Susan Gubar (1979), *The Madwoman in the Attic: Women Writers and the Nineteenth-Century Literary Imagination*, New Haven and London: Yale University Press

Gilbert, Sandra M. (1984), 'From *Patria* to *Matria*: Elizabeth Barrett Browning's Risorgimento', in *Victorian Women Poets: Emily Brontë, Elizabeth Barrett Browning, Christina Rossetti*, ed. Joseph Bristow, Basingstoke: Macmillan, 132–66

Graham, Colin (ed) (1996), *Selected Poems of Elizabeth Barrett Browning*, London: Everyman

Greer, Germaine (1995), *Slip-Shod Sibyls: Recognition, Rejection and the Woman Poet*, London: Viking

Gridley, Roy E. (1982), *The Brownings and France: A Chronicle with Commentary*, London: Athlone Press

Griffiths, Eric (1989), *The Printed Voice of Victorian Poetry*, Oxford: Clarendon Press

Hall, Alfred (1950), *James Martineau: Selections*, London: Lindsey Press

Hansen, Emmanuel (1977), *Franz Fanon: Social and Political Thought*, Athens, Ohio: Ohio State University Press

Hardy, Thomas (1982), *Tess of the D'Urbervilles* [1891], ed. A. Alvarez, Harmondsworth: Penguin

Hardy, Thomas (1984), *The Life and Work of Thomas Hardy*, ed. Michael Millgates, London: Macmillan

Harrison, Antony H. (1990), *Victorian Poets and Romantic Poems: Intertextuality and Ideology*, Charlottesville and London: University Press of Virginia

Harrison, J.E.C. (1971), *The Early Victorians, 1832–1851*, London: Weidenfeld and Nicolson

Hayter, Althea (1962), *Mrs Browning: A Poet's Work and Its Setting*, London: Faber and Faber

Hewlett, Dorothy (1953), *Elizabeth Barrett Browning*, London: Cassell & Co.

Hicks, Malcolm (ed) (1983), *Selected Poems of Elizabeth Barrett Browning*, Manchester: Carcanet

Hill, Karen (ed) (1984), *The Works of Elizabeth Barrett Browning*, Ware: Wordsworth

Hirsch, Pam (1995), 'Gender Negotiations in Nineteenth-Century Women's Autobiographical Writing', in *The Uses of Autobiography*, ed. Julia Swindells, London: Taylor and Francis, 120–27

Hoag, Eleanor (1984), 'Fragment of "An Essay on Woman"', *Studies in Browning and His Circle* 12:7–12

Horne, R.H. (1844), 'Miss E.B. Barrett and Mrs Norton', in *A New Spirit of the Age*, ed. R.H. Horne, London: Smith, Elder and Co, volume 2:129–40

Ingram, John H. (1888), *Elizabeth Barrett Browning*, London: W.H. Allen

Kamboureli, Smaro (1991), *On the Edge of Genre: The Contemporary Canadian Long Poem*, Toronto: University of Toronto Press

Kaplan, Cora (1978), Introduction to *Aurora Leigh and Other Poems*, London: Women's Press

Kenyon, John (ed) (1897), *The Letters of Elizabeth Barrett Browning*, 2 vols, London: Smith, Elder

Korg, Jacob (1983), *Browning and Italy*, Athens, Ohio and London: Ohio University Press

Landon, Letitia Elizabeth (1997), *Selected Writings*, ed. Jerome McGann and Daniel Riess, Ontario: Broadview

Langbaum, Robert (1957), *The Poetry of Experience: The Dramatic Monologue in the Modern Literary Tradition*, Chicago: University of Chicago Press

Leavis, F.R. (1948), *The Great Tradition*, London: Chatto and Windus

Leighton, Angela (1986), *Elizabeth Barrett Browning*, Brighton: Harvester Press

Leighton, Angela (1992), *Victorian Women Poets: Writing Against the Heart*, Hemel Hempstead: Harvester Wheatsheaf

Leighton, Angela and Margaret Reynolds (eds) (1995), *Victorian Women Poets: An Anthology*, Oxford: Blackwell

Levine, Richard A. (1982), *The Victorian Experience: The Poets*, Athens, Ohio: Ohio University Press

Levinson, Marjorie, Marilyn Butler, Jerome McGann and Paul Hamilton (1989), *Rethinking Historicism: Critical Readings in Romantic History*, Oxford: Basil Blackwell

Lewis, Linda M. (1998), *Elizabeth Barrett Browning's Spiritual Progress: Face to Face with God*, Columbia and London: University of Missouri Press

Lootens, Tricia (1996*a*), *Lost Saints: Silence, Gender and Victorian Literary Canonization*, Charlottesville, VA. and London: University Press of Virginia

Lootens, Tricia (1996*b*), 'Hemans and Home: Victorianism, Feminine "Internal Enemies", and the Domestication of National Identity', in *Victorian Women Poets: A Critical Reader*, ed. Angela Leighton, Oxford: Blackwell, 1–23

Markus, Julia (ed) (1977), *Casa Guidi Windows*, Barre, Massachusetts: Imprint Society

Markus, Julia (1995), *Dared and Done: The Marriage of Elizabeth Barrett and Robert Browning*, London: Bloomsbury

Marsh, Jan (1994), *Christina Rossetti: A Literary Biography*, London: Jonathan Cape

Martineau, Harriet (1848), *Eastern Life: Present and Past*, 3 vols, London: Edward Moxon

McGhee, Richard D. (1980), *Marriage, Duty and Desire in Victorian Poetry and Drama*, Lawrence: Kansas University Press

Mellor, Anne K. (1993), *Romanticism and Gender*, New York and London: Routledge

Mellor, Anne K. (1999), 'The Female Poet and the Poetess: Two Traditions of British Women's Poetry, 1780–1830', in *Women's Poetry in the Enlightenment: The Making of a Canon, 1730–1820*, ed. Isobel Armstrong and Virginia Blain, Basingstoke: Macmillan, 81–98

Mermin, Dorothy (1981), 'The Female Poet and the Embarrassed Reader: Elizabeth Barrett Browning's *Sonnets from the Portuguese*', *English Literary History* 48:351–67

Mermin, Dorothy (1986), 'The Damsel, the Knight, and the Victorian Woman Poet', *Critical Inquiry* 13:64–80

Mermin, Dorothy (1989), *Elizabeth Barrett Browning: The Origins of a New Poetry*, Chicago: University of Chicago Press

Milbank, Alison (1998), *Dante and the Victorians*, Manchester: Manchester University Press

Miller, Betty (ed) (1954), *Elizabeth Barrett to Miss Mitford*, London: John Murray

Moers, Ellen (1977), *Literary Women*, London: W.H. Allen

Moi, Toril (1985), *Sexual/Textual Politics*, London and New York: Methuen

Montefiore, Jan (1994), *Feminism and Poetry: Language, Experience, Identity in Women's Writing*, London: Pandora

Norton, Caroline (1855), *A Letter to the Queen on Lord Chancellor Cranford's Marriage and Divorce Bill*, London: Longman, Brown, Green

Pearsall, Cornelia D.J. (2000), 'The Dramatic Monologue,' in *The Cambridge Companion to Victorian Poetry*, ed. Joseph Bristow, Cambridge: Cambridge University Press, 64–88

Phelps, Deborah (1990), '"At the Roadside of Humanity": Elizabeth Barrett Browning Abroad', in *English Literature and the Wider World, Volume 3: Creditable Warriors, 1830–1876*, ed. Michael Cotsell, London: Ashfield

Pinch, Adela (1998), 'Thinking about the Other in Romantic Love', in Romantic Circle Praxis Series, http:www.rc.umd.edu/praxis/passions/pcts.html

Pollock, Mary S. (1996), 'The Anti-Canonical Realism of Elizabeth Barrett Browning's "Lord Walter's Wife"', *Studies in the Literary Imagination* 29(1), spring 1996, 43–54

Quin, Betty (1958), *Romantic Journey: A Play About Elizabeth Barrett Browning*, London: Kenyon House Press

Radley, Virginia (1972), *Elizabeth Barrett Browning*, Boston, Mass.: Twayne

Reynolds, Margaret (ed) (1996) *Aurora Leigh*, New York and London: Norton

Reynolds, Matthew (2001), *The Realms of Verse 1830–1870: English Poetry in a Time of Nation-Building*, Oxford: Oxford University Press

Richards, Bernard (1988), *English Poetry of the Victorian Period: 1830–1890*, London and New York: Longman

Riede, David (1994), 'Elizabeth Barrett: The Poet as Angel', *Victorian Poetry* 32:121–39

Rollin, Charles (1738–40), *The Ancient History of the Egyptians, Carthaginians, Assyrians, Babylonians, Medes and Persians, Macedonians and Grecians, translated from the French*, 2nd edition, 10 vols, London

Rossetti, Christina (1904), *The Poetical Works of Christina Rossetti*, edited with memoir and notes by William Michael Rossetti, London: Macmillan and Co

Rossetti, Christina (1997), *The Letters of Christina Rossetti, Volume One: 1843–1873*, ed. Antony H. Harrison, Charlottesville and London: University Press of Virginia

Rundle, Vivienne (1996), '"The Inscription of These Volumes": The Prefatory Writings of Elizabeth Barrett Browning', *Victorian Poetry* 34(2), 247–78

Rushdie, Salman (1990), *Is Nothing Sacred? The Herbert Read Memorial Lecture*, rept. in Salman Rushdie (1991), *Imaginary Homelands: Essays in Criticism 1981–1991*, London: Granta, 415–29

Selden, Raman, Peter Widdowson and Peter Brooker (eds) (1997), *A Reader's Guide to Contemporary Literary Theory*, 4th ed., London: Prentice Hall/ Harvester Wheatsheaf

Shanley, Mary Lydon (1989), *Feminism, Marriage and the Law in Victorian England, 1850–1895*, Princeton, N.J.: Princeton University Press

Shaw, W. David (1985), 'Philosophy and Genre in Victorian Poetics: The Idealist Legacy', *English Literature and History* 52:471–501

Showalter, Elaine (1977), *A Literature of Their Own: British Women Writers from Charlotte Brontë to Doris Lessing*, Princeton, N.J.: Princeton University Press

Showalter, Elaine (1982), 'Feminist Criticism in the Wilderness', in *Writing and Sexual Difference*, ed. Elizabeth Abel, Brighton: Harvester Press, 9–35

Sinfield, Alan (1986), *Tennyson*, Oxford: Basil Blackwell

Slinn, Warwick E. (2000), 'Experimental Form in Victorian Poetry', in *The Cambridge Companion to Victorian Poetry*, ed. Joseph Bristow, Cambridge: Cambridge University Press, 46–66

Stephenson, Glennis (1989), *Elizabeth Barrett Browning and the Poetry of Love*, Ann Arbor, Mich. and London: U.M.I. Research

Stephenson, Glennis (1995), *Letitia Landon: The Woman Behind L.E.L.*, Manchester and New York: Manchester University Press

Stiles, Andrina (1989), *The Unification of Italy, 1815–70*, London: Hodder and Stoughton

Stone, Marjorie (1995), *Elizabeth Barrett Browning*, Basingstoke: Macmillan

Stott, Rebecca (1999), 'Thomas Carlyle and the Crowd: Revolution, Geology and the Convulsive "Nature" of Time', in *Journal of Victorian Culture* 4(1):1–24

Sullivan, Mary Rose (1987), ' "Some Interchange of Grace": "Saul" and *Sonnets from the Portuguese*', *Browning Institute Studies* 15:55–68

Sussman, Herbert (1995), *Victorian Masculinities: Manhood and Masculine Poetics in Early Victorian England*, Cambridge: Cambridge University Press

Swedenborg, Emmanuel (1971), *Apocalypse Revealed*, trans. F.F. Coulson, London: Swedenborg Society

Swedenborg, Emmanuel (1995), *Conjugal Love*, trans. N. Bruce Rogers, New York: Church of the New Jerusalem

Talmon, J.L. (1967), *Romanticism and Revolution: Europe 1815–48*, London: Thames and Hudson

Todd, Janet (2000), *Mary Wollstonecraft: A Revolutionary Life*, London: Weidenfeld and Nicolson

Trevelyan, George Macaulay (1911), *English Songs of Italian Freedom*, London: Longmans, Green & Co.

Trilling, Lionel and Harold Bloom (eds) (1973), *Victorian Prose and Poetry*, Oxford: Oxford University Press

Walker, Cheryl (1999), 'The Whip Signature: Violence, Feminism and Women Poets', in *Women's Poetry, Late Romantic to Late Victorian: Gender and Genre, 1830–1900*, ed. Isobel Armstrong and Virginia Blain, Basingstoke: Macmillan, 33–49

Wallace, Jennifer (1997), *Shelley and Greece: Rethinking Romantic Hellenism*, Basingstoke: Macmillan

Wilde, Oscar (1908), 'English Poetesses', in *The First Collected Edition of the Works of Oscar Wilde*, ed. Robert Ross, 15 vols, volume 15: *Miscellanies*, London: Methuen and Co, 110–20

Wollstonecraft, Mary (1983), *A Vindication of the Rights of Woman* [1792], ed. Miriam Brody, Harmondsworth: Penguin

Woolf, Virginia (1950), 'Mr Bennett and Mrs Brown', in *The Captain's Death and Other Essays*, New York: Harcourt Brace, 90–111

Woolf, Virginia (1979), *Women and Writing*, ed. Michèle Barrett, London: Women's Press

Woolford, John and Daniel Karlin (1996), *Robert Browning*, London: Longman

INDEX

The index includes chapters 1 to 8 but not the Chronology and the Bibliography. Titles of books, magazines and longer poems (usually published on their own) are shown in italic, while titles of individual poems and articles are shown in quotation marks. Page references shown in italic indicate a definition or explanation of a term or concept. The following abbreviations are used: *CGW* = *Casa Guidi Windows*; EBB = Elizabeth Barrett Browning; *PBC* = *Poems Before Congress*; RB = Robert Browning; C19th = Nineteenth Century.

Aitken, Lucy 6
Albert, Prince Consort 86
Andersen, Hans Christian, *The Improvisatrice* 157
Anglican Church 37
Armstrong, Isobel
  Victorian Scrutinies 73
  Victorian Poetry 123
Armstrong, I. & Bristow, J., *Nineteenth Century Women Poets* 18
Arnold, Matthew 100
The Athenaeum 5, 7, 63, 95, 97, 117, 204
Austen, Jane 41
  Mansfield Park 107
Aytoun, W.E., on *Aurora Leigh* 8, 204–5

Bakhtin, Mikhael 165
ballad 127–8 *see also* poetics – EBB; Romantic/Victorian poetics
Balzac, Honore 135
Barbauld, Anna Letitia 6
Barrett, Arabella (EBB's sister) 28
Barrett, Edward (EBB's father) 35, 38, 39, 25–6
  marriage of his children 40, 107
  political & religious convictions 34, 37, 77
  relationship with EBB 26, 30
Barrett, Edward 'Bro' (EBB's brother) 30, 41
  relationship with EBB 31
  death 88

Barrett, 'Edward of Cinnamon Hill' (EBB's grandfather) 3, 39
Barrett, Elizabeth *see also* poetics – EBB; socio-political engagement – EBB
  biographers 23–5
  contemporary reputation 2, 89 *see also* under individual titles, critical reception
  critical recovery 13–14, 96–7
  early years 25
  education/intellectual development 30, 31, 41, 69
  on emotion 76–7
  fascination with Napoleon 97–8
  and George Sand 93–4
  heroes 49–50, 58, 59, 60, 94
  illness 40–1, 88, in Italy 158; Torquay 41
  literary development 21, 26 *see also* literary/intellectual influences
  political involvement 108, 111
  Prefaces/Advertisements 66–7 *see also* under individual titles
  protofeminism 90
  received ideas 24–5
  religious engagement 37, 38, 42, 206, Spiritualism 38
  as role model 8–10, 16
  self-image 3, 76
  women, models of behaviour 6, 20, 24–5, 27–8; gender roles/stereotypes 50–1, 59, 60

Barrett, Elizabeth *Continued*
Works: *see also* literary/intellectual influences
Aeschylus, *Prometheus Bound* (trans) 61–2
critical reception 63
influences 20
reappraisal 62
retranslation 111–12, 131
'An August Voice', Italy betrayed 178
Aurora Leigh 6, 16, 20, 21, 112, 135, 161, 179
Bildungsroman 182, 200
Condition-of-England 200 *see also* main entry
on contemporary poets 84
critical reception/reaction 8, 116–17, 186, 201, 204–5
crowds 193–4
dialogue 118; didactic 121; intertextual 120; with fellow writers 120
didacticism 119, 130
dissent 207; duty 208–9
dramatic monologue 119, 132–3
education of women 29–30
epic 48, 117–18, 201, 203–4
England/Italy compared 157–8
female creativity 202–3
gender roles 118, 208
generic indeterminacy 116
grotesqueness, moral/physical 190–2
heroes 204
hopefulness 163
influences, Carlyle (imagery) 192–5; Pope 207; Swedenborg 135, 136, 137–8, 139, 141, 189, 196, 201
innovations 113–14
intertextuality 14, 182
Italy 176
Kunstlerroman 182, 183, 200
London 195
love 139–41; thinking/unthinking 140–1, 149
marriage 152–3
metaphor 42, 117
oppression, complicity 186–7, 191
planning/writing 81, 83, 181, 184–5, 188
poetry, manifesto 66; social theory 189; shifting vision 83–4
power of words 199–200
prototype 107
rape 109, 187–8
reappraisal/recovery 13, 15, 66, 120, 139–40, 187, 190–1
redemption 196–7
rhetorical technique 119
sage discourse 19, 205–6; nonconformist 206–7
social/political issues 34, 188, 192, 206–7
structure 181–4
tenderness 199
violence 197–9, 200
women's grief 90
Battle of Marathon 2, 45–6
binary oppositions 6, 48–9
critical reception 46
gender roles 50–1, 52
Greece, glory 47; War of Independence 46–7
heroes 49–50
historical/political text 53–4, 69
Homeric epic 48, 90
influences 20; Classical 68–9; Wollstonecraft 70
Preface 47, 66, 78
publication 26
reappraisal 46, 51, 59
'Bertha in the Lane' 99; betrayal in love 149
Book of the Poets 170
'Bro's Character and Mine Compared' 31
Casa Guidi Windows 20, 21, 55, 60, 112, 159, 179
Advertisement 160, 173
Carlyle's influence 167–9
commerce/imperialism triumphant 174
critical reception 161, 176
despair 171–2
emotionalism, EBB 172–3
heroic Able-man 166–9
hopefulness 175, 164–6
liberty 6, 59; and violence 170
new Italy, new voice 162–3
reappraisal/recovery 66, 161
structure 159–60
'A Child Asleep' 103
'Cowper's Grave' 91
'Crowned and Buried' 94, 97–8
'Crowned and Wedded' 94, 95–6, 98
'The Cruelty of Forcement to Man' 43–4

Barrett, Elizabeth *Continued*
  'The Cry of the Children' 99–100, 108,
    159
    critical reception 101
    received religion 110
    recovery/reappraisal 101–2
    unconventionality 102
  'The Cry of the Human' 99, 103–4, 159
  A Drama of Exile 20, 131
    angels 72–3
    gender roles 90, 92
    influence 90
    Preface 72–3
    use of voice 72, 90
  A Drama of Exile, and Other poems (US
    title) *see Poems* (1844)
  'The Dream: A Fragment' 61
  An Essay on Mind 42
    Carlyle anticipated 79–80
    critical reception 7
    on education 70
    on emotion/feeling 76
    influences 20, 31
    New Historicism anticipated 24
    politics/power of knowledge 6,
      57–9
    Preface 69–70
    reappraisal/recovery 59, 69
  An Essay on Mind and Other Poems
    45
  'Essay on Woman' 42, 43
  'The Exile's Return' 91
  'First News from Villafranca' 178
  'Glimpses into My Own Life and
    Literary Character' 27, 36, 37,
    43
    themes 29
  'Hiram Powers' "Greek Slave" ' 111,
    164
  'Italy and the World' 178–9
  'Lady Geraldine's Courtship' 20, 159
    critical reception 105
    and the modern world 105, 106–7
  Last Poems 6, 16
  'L.E.L.'s Last Question' 5
  'Lord Walter's Wife' 128–9
    critical reception 130
  'Memory' 61
  'A Musical Instrument' 13
  'My Own Character' 27
  'Napoleon III in Italy', heroic Able-
    man 177
  'On a Picture of Riego's Widow' 60
  'The Past' 61

Poems (1844) 2, 107, 159, 161
    Carlyle's influence 81–2
    critical reception 7, 83
    discursive practices 90
    experimentation 89
    gender roles 90, 92
    Preface 3, 81–2, 90
    recovery/reappraisal 45, 89, 90
    socio-political issues 6, 88, 98–9
Poems (1850) 63, 159
    additions/revisions to *Poems*
      [1844] 111
    socio-political issues 88
Poems Before Congress 6, 21, 159, 177
    critical reception 179
    Preface 174
*Prometheus Bound, with Miscellaneous
    Poems* 45, 60, 61
  'Riga's Last Song' 60, 97
    voice to the oppressed 99
  'A Romance of the Ganges' 128
    betrayal in love 150
  'The Romance of the Swan's Nest'
    149–50
  'The Romaunt of Magret' 128
  'The Romaunt of the Page' 128
    exile figure 90–1
    gender roles 91–2
    recovery/reappraisal 92
  'The Runaway Slave at Pilgrim's Point'
    20, 40, 152
    anti-slavery 108–9
    feminism and slavery 107
    reappraisal/recovery 110–11
    received religion 110
    voice to the oppressed 99
The Seraphim 16, 62, 111, 131
    angels 71, 81
    critical reception 7
    exile figure 91
    Preface 71
    theme 6
    use of voice 72
Sonnets from the Portuguese 2, 20,
    111
    conversations 122–3
    gender roles 125–6
    love 142–4; courtly 145–6;
      Swedenborgian 141–2; and
      thinking 143–4
    metaphors 144
    paradox of language 145, 147–8
    publishing history 13
    reappraisal 142, 143–4

Barrett, Elizabeth *Continued*
  rhetoric 121
  speech and silence 146–7
  'Stanzas on the Death of Lord Byron'
    56, 60
  'Stanzas occasioned by . . . Mr
    Emerson's Journal' 60
  'A Tale of Villafranca' 178
  'Thoughts awakened by . . . the
    Athenian Acropolis' 55
  'To a Poet's Child' 77
  'To George Sand: A Desire' 93–4,
    126–7
  'To George Sand: A Recognition' 94,
    126–7
  'To My Father' 61
  'Verses to My Brother' 61
  'Victoria's Tears' 95
  'The Vision of Fame', exile figure 91
  'A Vision of Poets'
    angels 83
    suffering 82–3
  'A Year's Spinning', betrayal in love
    149
  'The Young Queen' 95
Barrett, E. and Browning, R. *see also*
    Brownings, correspondence
  London visit (1851) 86–7
  marriage 33, 107, 134, 156
  personal/professional relationship 24
  settle in Italy 156–7
  wedding anniversary 164–5
Barrett, E. and Horne, R.H., on Carlyle
    79–80
Barrett, George (EBB's brother) 36
Barrett, Henrietta (EBB's sister) 28, 107
Barrett, Mary (EBB's mother) 36, 40–1
  relationship with EBB 26–7,
    correspondence 47
Barrett, Samuel (EBB's uncle) 34, 38
Barrett family
  plantations/slavery 38–9
  religious convictions 36–7
Barrett Town (Jamaica) 38
Baudelaire, Charles 135
Beethoven, Ludwig van 61
Behn, Aphra 3
Bessier, Rudolph, *The Barretts of Wimpole
    Street* 11–12, 26
Berkeley, George 69
Blackwood's Edinburgh Magazine 8, 204
Blackwood's Magazine 89, 99
  Casa Guidi Windows 170
Blagden, Isabella 23

Blake, William 135
  Songs of Innocence and Experience 99
Blind, Mathilde, *The Ascent of Man* 48
Bloom, Harold, *The Anxiety of Influence* 46
Bodechon, Barbara, *A Brief Summary . . .
    Of . . . Laws Concerning Women* 153
Bowles, Caroline, *A Birthday* 48
Boston Anti-Slavery Bazaar 108
Boyd, Hugh Stuart 31, 89
  relationship with EBB 32–3,
    correspondence 38, 41, 54, 105, 108
Bristow, Joseph, *The Victorian Poet* 73
Brontë, Charlotte, *Jane Eyre* 14, 200
Brontë, Emily 13, 14
Brontë sisters 6, 41
Browning, Penini (son of EBB & RB) 175,
    178
Browning, Robert
  'Andrea del Sarto' 11
  'A Bishop Orders his Tomb at Saint
    Praxed's Church' 169
  'Fra Lippo Lippi' 11
  Madhouse Cells, poetic voice 75
  Men and Women 130
  modernist perception 11
  My Last Duchess 11, 147–8
  Pippa Passes 157
  poetics 72–3
  The Ring and the Book 11, 115, 155
  Sordello 157
Brownings' correspondence 134, 148
    see also Barrett, E. and Browning, R.
  courtship 11
  dramatic monologue 121–2
  experimental poetry 81
  on marriage 151–2
  poetics 75–6
The Brownings Correspondence 25
Buffon, Comte de 69
Byron, Lord 6, 28, 56, 59, 62, 68, 69
  Childe Harold's Pilgrimage 47, 56, 162
  Don Juan 120

Carleton, Marjorie, *The Barretts: A Comedy
    in Three Acts* 12
Carlyle, Thomas 80, 86, 100, 192–3, 206,
    207
  heroes/hero-worship 49–50, 78, 79, 94,
    Able-man 167–9
  History of the French Revolution 193–4
  on *Poems* (1844) 83
  'Present Day' 197
Carter, Angela, 'Notes from the Front Line'
    115

Cartland, Barbara, 'The Perfect Romance of Elizabeth and Robert Browning' 12
Case, Alison, 'Gender and Narration in *Aurora Leigh*' 182, 183
Cavour, Camillo Benso 176–7
Chandler, James, *England in 1819* 53
Charterhouse (school) 31
Chorley, Henry 9, 117, 204
Clarke, Norma 4
Clough, Arthur Hugh
 Amours de Voyage 115
 The Bothie of Tober-Na-Vuolich 115, 120, 182
Cobbe, Frances, on *Aurora Leigh* 8
Cocks, Lady Margaret 38, 39
Coleridge, Samuel Taylor 77, 135
 poet's role 65
Commena, Anna 42
Condillac, Etienne Bonnot de 69
Condition-of-England genre 104, 165, 192
 see also poetics – EBB; Romantic/ Victorian poetics
 and Industrial Revolution 102–3, 192–3
Congregationalists 37
Cook, Eliza, 'The Old Arm Chair' 4
Cooper, Helen, *EBB: Woman and Artist* 16, 59, 66, 110, 161, 169, 182, 183–4
Corn Laws (1815)
 consequences 103, 104
 repeal 87
Cosslett, Tess 14
Craik, Dinah Mulock 9
Crystal Palace Exhibition *see* Great Exhibition

Dacier, Anne 42
David, Deirdre, *Intellectual Women and Victorian Patrarchy* 17, 46, 102, 110–11, 174, 197, 200–1
Dennis, Barbara, *EBB: The Hope End Years* 23–4, 25, 41
Derrida, Jacques 113
Descartes, Rene 69
Dickens, Charles, *Hard Times* 103
Dickinson, Emily 16
 on EBB 10
Donaldson, Sandra
 EBB: An Annotated Bibliography 161, 179
 'Motherhood's Advent in Power' 102
dramatic monologue 73, 110, 130 *see also* poetics – EBB; Romantic/Victorian poetics
Dublin University Review 8

Duplessis, Rachel Blau, *Writing Beyond the Ending* 182

Eclectic Review (magazine) 7
Edward of Cinnamon Hill *see* Barrett, 'Edward of Cinnamon Hill'
Eliot, George 116, 207
 aesthetic manifesto (Adam Bede) 84–5
 on *Aurora Leigh* 8
Emancipation Bill (1833) 39
Emerson, Ralph Waldo 135
epics 48 *see also* poetics – EBB; Romantic/ Victorian
Erkkila, Betsy, *Wicked Sisters* 10
Euripides, *Medea* 100
Evangelical Revivals 37

Fanon, Franz 170
Field, Michael *pseud* 17
Findens' Tableaux (magazine) 91
Flush (EBB's spaniel) 12, 89
Forman, H. Buxton, *Hitherto Unpublished . . . EBB* 43
Forster, Margaret 130
 Elizabeth Barrett Browning 23, 25, 40
Foucault, Michel, discursive practices 90, 111
Fourier, Charles 188
Fox, William Johnson 73, 74
Fraser's Magazine 176
Friedman, Susan Stanford 117, 118
Fuller, Margaret 135, 153, 207
 Woman in the Nineteenth Century 209

Garibaldi's wife 175
Gaskell, Elizabeth 192, 209
 The Life of Charlotte Brontë 23
 Mary Barton 101, 102–3
 Ruth 14, 120, 186
genres 3, 113 *see also* under individual type; poetics – EBB; Romantic/Victorian poetics
 and aesthetic/social norms 115–16
George III, King of England 35
George IV, King of England, divorce crisis 35–6
Gilbert, Sandra, 'From *Patria* to *Matria*' 161
Gilbert, S. and Gubar, S.M., *The Madwoman in the Attic* 14, 15, 139–40
Gilberto, Vincenzo, *Of the Moral and Civil Primacy of the Italians* 168
Graham-Clarkes (EBB's maternal forebears) 39
Gramsci, Antonio 17

Great Exhibition (1851) 8, 111, 174
Great Tradition (Leavis) 11
Greek War of Independence 46–7, 54, 55
  EBB's first published poems 55–6
Greenwell, Dora 9
Greer, Germaine, *Slip-Shod Sybils* 18
Griffiths, Eric, *The Printed Voice of Victorian
  Poetry* 122
Guardian 176
Guerazzi, Francesco 176

Hallam, Arthur 8, 130
Hardy, Thomas, *Tess of the D'Urbervilles*
  185–6
Hawthorne, Nathaniel, *The Scarlet Letter*
  110, 186
Hayter, Alethea, *Mrs Browning: A Poet's
  Work* 13, 96, 127
H.D. *Helen in England* 118
Hemans, Felicia 3, 17, 130
  poems 4–5
  Modern Greece 47
Hewlett, Dorothy, *EBB* 59
Hirsh, Pam, 'Gender Negotiations' 4
Homer 68–9, 83
  Greek democracy 67–8
Hood, Thomas, 'Song of the Shirt' 99
Hope End (EBB's childhood home) 25,
  39
Horne, Richard Hengist 99
  correspondence with EBB 6, 46
  role in mythologisation 88
Hunt, Henry 'Orator' 53

Ingelow, Jean 6
Ingram, John, *EBB* 46
Italy 158–9
  revolutions 171
  Risorgimento 11, 158, 165, 176

James, William 135
Jameson, Anna 86, 156
  The Communion of Labour 209
John Bull 179

Kamboureli, Smaro, *On the Edge of Genre*
  115
Kaplan, Cora, *Introduction to Aurora Leigh*
  102, 120, 181, 182, 187, 209
Keats, John 156
Kenyon, John, *The Letters of EBB* 177, 186
Kingsley, Charles 176, 192
  Alton Locke 14, 120
Korg, Jacob, *Browning and Italy* 156

Landon, Letitia Elizabeth 5, 17
  The Improvisatrice 4
Langbaum, Robert, *The Poetry of Experience*
  110
The League 102
Lear, Edward 13
Leavis, F.R. 11
Leibnitz, Gottfried Wilhelm 69
Leighton, Angela
  EBB 15–16, 17–18, 59, 127, 142, 186
  *Victorian Women Poets: Writing Against
    the Heart* 4, 92, 148–9, 155
Leighton, A. and Reynolds, M., *Victorian
  Women Poets: An Anthology* 18
Leopold II, Duke 164, 165, 168, 171, 173
Levine, Richard A., *The Victorian Experience:
  The Poets* 13
Levinson, M. et al., *Rethinking Historicism*
  24
Lewis, Linda M., *EBB's Spiritual Progress*
  19
literary criticism 19 *see also* under
  individual titles
  contemporary 6–10
  fashions 2
  feminist 13–14, 17
  and gender 18
  Great Tradition (Leavis) 11
  Marxist-feminist 14, 17
  modernist (c1880–1930) 10–11
  New Criticism 13, 14
  New Historicism 17–19, 24
  Structuralism 13
literary/intellectual influences – EBB *see also*
  Barrett, literary development; Works
  Bible narratives 90
  Carlyle, T. *see* main entry
  Classical 46, 67–8, 69, 100; *Iliad* 45–6
  Eliot, G. *see* main entry
  Locke, *An Essay Concerning Human
    Understanding* 58, 69
  Milton 69, 71 *see also* main entry
  Pope, 'Essays' 42, 57, 69 *see also* main
    entry
  Rollins, *Ancient History* 46
  Sand, George 92 *see also* main entry
  Swedenborg, E. *see* main entry
  Tennyson, A. *see* main entry
  Wollstonecraft, *A Vindication of the Rights
    of Woman* 28–9, 35, 41, 59, 70
    see also main entry
Literary World 161
London Quarterly Review 179
Lootens, Tricia, 'Hemans and Home' 4

March, Frederic 12
Markus, Julia
    Casa Guidi Windows 160, 162, 164, 165
    Dared and Done 24, 39, 40, 158, 171, 173
Martin, Julia 39
Martineau, Harriet 83, 206
    Eastern Life 207
Martineau, James, *The Rationale of Religious
    Enquiry* 206
Marx, Karl 100
Matrimonial Causes Act 154, 155
Mazzini, Giuseppe 158, 173, 176
McSwiney, Daniel (Barretts' Classics tutor)
    30, 31, 47
Mellor, Anne K.
    'The Female Poet and the Poetess' 6
    Romanticism and Gender 18
Mermin, Dorothy, *EBB: The Origins of a
    New Poetry* 16–17, 26, 51, 59, 60, 62,
    89, 90, 92, 117, 142, 161, 187–8, 196
Merry, William 38
Meynell, Alice 17
Mew, Charlotte 17
Milbank, Alison, *Dante and the Victorians*
    159, 164, 166
Mill, John Stuart 75
Milton, John 83 *see also* literary influences
    Paradise Lost 90, 120
Mitford, Mary Russell 38, 86, 89, 91
    Aurora Leigh 113
    correspondence with EBB 5, 28, 30, 76,
        80–1, 98, 104–5, 108, 136, 150, 156,
        157, 162, 164–5, 168–9, 176, 180
Moers, Ellen, *Literary Women* 4, 14–15
Montefiore, Jan, *Feminism and Poetry* 18, 20
The Monthly Review 7
Moore, Thomas, *Lalla Rookh* 68
More, Hannah 6, 42
Morris, 'Haystack in the Floods' 92
Morrison, Toni, *Beloved* 107
Moulton-Barrett, Samuel *see* Barrett, Samuel
mythologisation of EBB 150
    as anti-feminist 17
    deconstruction 23
    as invalid/neurotic 13–14, 40; beginning
        88
    as romantic heroine 11–13, 21, 134

Napoleon 94, 97–8
National Anti-Corn Law League (1839)
    103, 104–5
The National Review 8
New Monthly Magazine 55
A New Spirit of the Age 88

non-conformism *37*
    duty of dissent 206–7
The North American Review 7
Norton, Caroline
    *A Letter . . . On . . . Cranworth's Marriage
        and Divorce Bill* 154–5
    'A Voice from the Factories' 99

Ogilvy, Mrs 86–7

Parkes, Bessie Rayner 9
Patmore, Coventry, *The Angel in the House*
    95, 187, 197
Peterloo Massacre 53
Phelps, Deborah, 'At the Roadside of
    Humanity' 160
philhellenism, European 47
Pinch, Adela, 'Thinking About the Other in
    Romantic Love' 143–4
Pius IX, Pope 168, 169, 173
Poet Laureate 89
    EBB proposed 7
poetic voice, impersonation 74
poetics – EBB *see also* Barrett, Works;
        genres; Romantic/Victorian poetics;
        socio-political engagement
    aesthetics 60, 61, 64, 69, 84–5, 105;
        experimentation 67; reorientation
        80–1
    angels/angel-eye view 71–2, 74–5, 80
    and Carlyle 79–80, 81–2
    ballad 149–50
    changing 80–1, 89, 105
    debates/dialogues 66–7
    dramatic lyric 72
    dramatic monologue 130
    emotion and reason 76–7
    exile figure 90–1
    form 113–14
    fully realised 84
    gender 77–8
    genres, reconfiguration 90, 91, 115
    innovation 5, 18
    love 134–5; and betrayal 149–50;
        contextualised 148–9
    perspective 81
    poetry/poets, function/role 20–1, 66–8,
        75, 89; political understanding
        163–4; primacy 58, 67
    Romantic tradition 18–19
    social/political agenda 10, 35, 55, 89,
        99–100
    sonnet 121, 122, 123, 124–7, 145
    subjects 6, 76

poetics *Continued*
    suffering 82–3, 105
    transcendence 70–1
    voice 66
Poor Laws 87
Pope, Alexander, *The Iliad* (trans) 45–6
    see also literary influences
Price, Robert 34
Price, Uvedale 31, 34
Princess Charlotte 35

Queen Caroline, divorce crisis 35–6
Quin, Betty, *Romantic Journey: A Play About*
    EBB 12

Radcliffe, Ann, *The Mysteries of Udolpho* 156
Radley, Virginia, *Elizabeth Barrett Browning*
    59
Reform Act (1832) 34, 63, 74–5
Report . . . on the Employment of Children
    (1843) 99
Reynolds, Matthew, *The Realms of Verse* 171
Romantic/Victorian poetics 75 *see also*
    under individual genres; poetics –
    EBB
    ballad revival 127
    celebration of Italy 156–7
    dramatic monologue 130, 131–2
    feminisation of feelings 76
    gender 65, 73, 74, 80, 96–7
    innovations 115
    medievalism 92
    models 76–7
    poet, prophet/sage/'vates' 76, 77, 78–9,
        of the margins 76
    Tennyson's influence 73–5
    voice 72–4
Rossetti, Christina 12, 13, 15, 17, 90
    Goblin Market 6, 14, 103
Rossetti, Dante Gabriel 12
Rundle, Vivienne, 'The Inscription of these
    Volumes' 67
Ruskin, John 100, 197
    on *Aurora Leigh* 8
    'Of Queen's Gardens' 95
    Stones of Venice 166

Sallust, Gaius 68
Sand, George 153 *see also* literary influences
    feminist-socialist novels 92–3
Scott, Walter 68, 127
Shakespeare, *Sonnet 130* 146
Shaw, W. David, 'Philosophy and Genre in
    Victorian Poetics' 116

Shearer, Norma 12
Shelley, Mary 61
    Rambles in Germany and Italy 157
Shelley, Percy Bysshe 6, 61, 156
    political poems 53, 68
Showalter, Elaine
    A Literature of Their Own 14, 30
    'Feminist Criticism in the Wilderness'
        19
Six Acts 53, 63
Slinn, E. Warwick, 'Experimental Form in
    Victorian Poetry' 115–16, 120–1
Smith, Charlotte 6
socio-political issues – EBB 6, 33–5, 45,
    87–8 *see also* Barrett, Works; poetics
    – EBB
    alienation/exclusion 91
    gender roles 29, 44, 45, 128–9
    ideological hypocrisy 86–7
    independence/liberty 44, 45, 46–7, 56,
        159, 180
    marriage and divorce 35–6, 150–1
    religion 19, 38; and the marginalised 110
    slavery 6, 21, 39, 40, 109, 111
    social hardships 6, 21, 63
    violence 48–9
sonnets *see also* poetics – EBB; Romantic/
    Victorian poetics
    pre-C19th 125
    types 122
The Spectator 179
The Spirit of the Age 79, 81
Staël, Madame de 4, 42
    Corinne 4, 120, 157
Stephenson, Glennis, *EBB and the Poetry of*
    Love 4, 16
Stodart, Mary, *Female Writers* 80, 201–2
Stone, Marjorie, *EBB* 12, 18–19, 59, 62,
    66, 90, 117, 128, 150, 189, 205–6
Stowe, Harriet Beecher, *Uncle Tom's*
    Cabin 102, 107, 109, 110–11, 209
Strindberg, August 135
Sullivan, Mary Rose, 'Some Interchange of
    Grace' 147
Sussman, Herbert, *Victorian Masculinities*
    73
Swedenborg, Emmanuel 135 *see also* under
    Barrett, Works
    conjugal love 138–9
    influence on EBB 21
    teachings 136–7, 155

Taylor, Harriet 150
Ten Hours Factory Act 99

Tennyson, Alfred, Lord
  dramatic monologue 130
  The Idylls of the King 84, 92
  Mariana in a Moated Grange 148
  Maud 115
  In Memoriam 8, 115
  Poems 127
  poetics 72–3, 73–4
  The Princess 115, 120, 182
Trilling, L. and Bloom, H., *Victorian Prose
    and Poetry* 13
The Tuscan Athenaeum 173

US Magazine 176

Vasari, *Lives of the Painters* 157
Victoria, Queen of England 94, 98
  power and gender 95
  and Albert 88, 96
Victorian period 6
  reaction against 10–11
Virgil 68–9

Walker, Cheryl, 'The Whip Signature' 16
Walpole, Horace 29, 70

Webster, Augusta 17
Westminster Review 8
Whigs/Whig philosophy 34, 35
Wilde, Oscar
  on EBB 179–80
  'English Poetesses' 8–9
Wollestonecraft, Mary 153 *see also*
    literary/intellectual influences
  on feeling 77
women poets
  ghettoisation 18
  in public discourse 209
  recovery work 3
  stereotyping 4
  tradition of political subjects 6
Woolf, Virginia
  on *Aurora Leigh* 11
  A Room of One's Own 93, 114
Wordsworth, William 7, 163
  death 89
  poet's role 65
  The Prelude 120, 170
Wordsworth, W. and Coleridge, S.T., *Lyrical
    Ballads* 127